Primo Levi (1919–87) was the author of a rich body of work, including memoirs and reflections on the Holocaust, poetry, science-fiction, historical fiction and essays. His lucid and direct accounts of his time at Auschwitz, begun immediately after liberation in 1945 and sustained until weeks before his suicide in 1987, have made him one of the most admired of all Holocaust writer-survivors and one of the best guides we have for the interrogation of that horrific event. But there is also more to Levi than the voice of the witness. He has increasingly come to be recognized as one of the major literary voices of the twentieth century. This *Companion* brings together leading specialists on Levi and scholars in the fields of Holocaust studies, Italian literature and language, and literature and science, to offer a stimulating introduction to all aspects of the work of this extraordinary writer.

ROBERT S. C. GORDON is Reader in Modern Italian Culture at the University of Cambridge and a Fellow of Gonville and Caius College.

THE CAMBRIDGE
COMPANION TO
PRIMO LEVI

EDITED BY
ROBERT S. C. GORDON

CAMBRIDGE
UNIVERSITY PRESS

CAMBRIDGE UNIVERSITY PRESS

Cambridge, New York, Melbourne, Madrid, Cape Town, Singapore, São Paulo

Cambridge University Press
The Edinburgh Building, Cambridge CB2 8RU, UK

Published in the United States of America by Cambridge University Press, New York

www.cambridge.org
Information on this title: www.cambridge.org/9780521604611

© Cambridge University Press 2007

First published 2007

Printed in the United Kingdom at the University Press, Cambridge

A catalogue record for this publication is available from the British Library

Library of Congress Cataloging-in-Publication data
The Cambridge companion to Primo Levi / edited by Robert S. C. Gordon.
p.   cm.
Includes bibliographical references and index.
ISBN-13 978-0-521-84357-7 (hardback)
ISBN-10 0-521-84357-X (hardback)
ISBN-13 978-0-521-60461-1 (paperback)
ISBN-10 0-521-60461-3 (paperback)
1. Levi, Primo – Criticism and interpretation.   I. Gordon, Robert S. C.
(Robert Samuel Clive), 1966–   II. Title.
PQ4872.E8Z572   2007
853'.914–dc22   2007002293

ISBN 978-0-521-84357-7 hardback
ISBN 978-0-521-60461-1 paperback

CONTENTS

NOTES ON CONTRIBUTORS

ZAIA ALEXANDER holds a PhD from UCLA entitled 'Beyond Babel: Translating the Holocaust at Century's End'. Her translations include *Snowed Under* by Antje Rávic Strubel and the essay 'On Translating and Being Translated' by Primo Levi. She is currently Program Coordinator at the Villa Aurora Foundation for European–American Relations, Los Angeles.

PIERPAOLO ANTONELLO is Senior Lecturer in Italian and Fellow of St John's College, University of Cambridge. His research is focused on relations between literature and science, from futurism to postmodernity; and the epistemology of René Girard and Michel Serres. He is the author of *Il ménage a quattro. Scienza, filosofia, tecnica nella letteratura italiana del Novecento* (2005), which includes a chapter on Primo Levi.

MARCO BELPOLITI is a writer, critic and cultural commentator. He is the author of *L'occhio di Calvino* (1996), *Settanta* (2001), *Doppio zero* (2003) and *Crolli* (2005), all published by Einaudi. He is the editor of Levi's complete works in Italian (*Opere*, 1997), as well as of several volumes of Levi's writings and interviews, and he is the author/editor of two further books on Levi.

BRYAN CHEYETTE is Professor of Modern Literature at the University of Reading. He has published extensively on racial representations in nineteenth- and twentieth-century English literature, Holocaust literature and film, and British-Jewish literature. He is completing *Diasporas of the Mind: Literature and 'Race' after the Holocaust* for Yale University Press, which will include a chapter on Jean Améry and Primo Levi.

MIRNA CICIONI is an Honorary Research Fellow in the School of Languages, Cultures and Linguistics of Monash University, Melbourne. She has published several articles and a book on Primo Levi (*Primo Levi. Bridges of Knowledge*, 1995) and is working on a study of autobiography and humour in the works of Levi, Natalia Ginzburg, Aldo Zargani and Clara Sereni.

ROBERT S. C. GORDON is Reader in Modern Italian Culture and Fellow of Gonville and Caius College, University of Cambridge. His work on Levi includes: *Primo*

Levi's Ordinary Virtues. From Testimony to Ethics (2001) and (co-edited with Marco Belpoliti) *Voice of Memory. Interviews, 1961–1987* (2001).

NANCY HARROWITZ is Associate Professor of Italian at Boston University, where she also teaches Holocaust studies. Author of *The Logic of Cultural Difference: Cesare Lombroso and Matilde Serao* (1994), she has edited *Tainted Greatness: Antisemitism and Cultural Heroes* (1994) and co-edited *Jews and Gender: Responses to Otto Weininger* (1995). She has published several articles on Primo Levi, and is currently writing on post-unification Jewish cultural identity in Italy.

ANNA LAURA LEPSCHY is Visiting Research Fellow at New Hall, Cambridge, Honorary Fellow of Somerville College, Oxford, and Professor Emeritus of the University of London. Her books include *Narrativa e teatro fra due secoli* (1983) and, with G. Lepschy, *The Italian Language Today* (1991) and *L'amanuense analfabeta e altri saggi* (1999).

GIULIO LEPSCHY, FBA, is Professor Emeritus of the University of Reading, Honorary Professor at UCL and Visiting Research Fellow at Downing College, Cambridge. Recent publications include *La linguistica del Novecento* (1992); *Mother Tongues and Other Reflections on the Italian Language* (2002).

CHARLOTTE ROSS is Lecturer in Italian at the University of Birmingham. Her research interests include: the relationship between science and literature; science-fiction; depictions of gender, sexuality and the body in contemporary culture. She is the author of 'Representations of Science, Literature, Technology and Society in the Works of Primo Levi' (PhD, University of Warwick, 2004).

JONATHAN USHER is Professor of Italian at Edinburgh University. His main interest is early Italian narrative, particularly Boccaccio, and the survival of the classical tradition in Dante and Petrarch. Amongst the moderns, he has written on Bontempelli, Vittorini, Calvino and Ramondino and on Primo Levi's interaction with other authors.

DAVID WARD, author of book-length studies on Pier Paolo Pasolini and Carlo Levi and the intellectuals of the Action Party in post-war Italy, is Professor of Italian and Chair in the Department of Italian Studies at Wellesley College. He is presently working on a study of the anti-Fascist intellectual, Piero Gobetti.

JUDITH WOOLF is Senior Lecturer in English and Italian at the University of York. Her research fields are twentieth-century Italian-Jewish writing, and modernism and its predecessors. Her publications include monographs on Primo Levi (*The Memory of the Offence*, 1996) and Henry James.

ACKNOWLEDGEMENTS

The editor would like to thank the following for their help and support in the preparation of this volume: all the contributors; Linda Bree, Maartje Scheltens and others at Cambridge University Press; Zyg Baranski; Martin McLaughlin; the National Humanities Center, USA (John E. Sawyer Fellowship and Andrew W. Mellon Foundation); Gonville and Caius College and the Faculty of Modern and Medieval Languages at Cambridge University; Einaudi publishers; and the Primo Levi estate.

Levi's Works

Full publication details of all Levi's books, volumes of interviews, and their English translations, are to be found in the first section of the 'Guide to further reading' (see pp. 189–92).

Quotations

Quotations from Levi's work are given in English, except where the original Italian is necessary for the analysis. Published English translations have been used wherever possible and unless otherwise indicated.

Sources

Quotations from Levi's works are sourced to both published English translations, by title and page number of first UK editions (where available and unless otherwise stated), and to the Italian original, as found (unless otherwise stated) in Primo Levi, *Opere*, vols. I–II, edited by Marco Belpoliti, Turin, Einaudi, 1997, abbreviated as OI and OII (e.g. *If This is a Man*, p. 3; OI, 7). References to book-length interviews or collections of interviews with Levi are made to English editions only (where available), using the title and page number (e.g. *Voice of Memory*, p. 71).

Titles

Titles of Levi's books are given in both English and Italian at their first appearance in each chapter, with year of first Italian publication, and then in English only thereafter. Published English titles are used wherever available (in italics; e.g. *If This is a Man*). On occasion, where a book has been only partially translated or translated with a different title, a literal translation of the title is used instead or also (in inverted commas; e.g. 'Formal Defect'). UK titles have been preferred to US titles (i.e. *If This is a Man*, not *Survival in Auschwitz*, for *Se questo è un uomo*; *The Truce*, not *The Reawakening*, for *La tregua*; *The Wrench*, not *The Monkey Wrench*, for *La chiave a stella*).

Titles of shorter pieces (chapters, poems, stories, essays), both within Levi's books and uncollected, are also given in English and Italian at first appearance in each chapter, where appropriate, and then in English only thereafter (in inverted commas; e.g. 'The Canto of Ulysses'). Page numbers are not included for titles of short pieces, but the volume they appear in is included wherever this may not otherwise be clear from the context. Again, published English titles are used wherever available. There are, however, a relatively large number of untranslated pieces and omissions from translations of Levi's collections, creating no little trouble for anyone trying to read Levi across the two languages (see 'Guide to further reading', pp. 192–4 below): in these cases, literal translations of titles are provided.

Additional note

As this book was going to press, the publication in English of a new collection of seventeen previously untranslated stories by Levi was announced for April 2007: Primo Levi, *A Tranquil Star*, translated by Ann Goldstein and Alessandra Bastagli, London, Penguin, 2007. Several of the stories labelled as untranslated in this book will be found in this new collection.

CHRONOLOGY

For those interested in investigating Levi's life in detail, there are two fascinating (and strikingly different) biographies in English, both of which are worth consulting: Carole Angier, *The Double Bond. Primo Levi, A Biography*, London, Viking, 2002, and Ian Thomson, *Primo Levi. A Life*, London, Hutchinson, 2002.

1919   Primo Levi was born in Turin on 31 July 1919, into a family that was part of the city's small, educated and largely integrated Jewish community.

1934–7   Levi attended the Liceo Massimo d'Azeglio, a school once (but by the mid-1930s no longer) renowned as a seedbed of liberal anti-Fascist views. Following the tastes of his father Cesare – an electrical engineer who had been close to the dominant positivist circles of the city's intelligentsia – Primo developed a voracious, eclectic appetite for reading but rejected the classical humanist education on offer in the *liceo*.

1937–41   He opted to read chemistry at Turin University. Despite the obstacles set in his path by Mussolini's draconian 1938 anti-semitic Race Laws, and the subsequent outbreak of war, he managed to graduate in 1941.

1942–3   Following a period of work in Milan, where he lived through the fall of Fascism and Italy's Armistice with the Allies in the second half of 1943, Levi joined the armed partisan Resistance against the rump Fascists and Nazi occupiers of northern Italy; but he was betrayed and captured almost immediately. Preferring to declare himself a Jew rather than risk execution as a partisan, he was imprisoned at the concentration camp at Fossoli in central Italy.

1944–5   In February 1944, he was deported from Fossoli to Auschwitz on a cattle-train with 650 others. Only a handful would ever return. On arrival in Auschwitz, he was assigned to the industrial slave labour camp at Auschwitz-III (Monowitz), which was run by the Nazis in collaboration with the IG Farben corporation. He remained a prisoner there until liberation by the Red Army in January 1945. He reached Turin again in October 1945 after a long, halting journey home described in *The Truce* (*La tregua*, 1963).

1945–7   On his return, he told and wrote down stories and poems about his time in Auschwitz, and also wrote, with doctor and fellow deportee Leonardo De Benedetti, a medical report on camp conditions for a general medical journal. He also met Lucia Morpurgo, whom he would marry in 1947 (*Auschwitz Report*). His stories came together in book form as *If This is a Man* (*Se questo è un uomo*) in 1947, published by a small and short-lived house called De Silva, having been rejected by Natalia Ginzburg and Cesare Pavese at the most vibrant and important of Turin's publishers, Einaudi. The book was praised by a small number of reviewers (including the young Italo Calvino) and noticed within the higher cultural milieux of Turin, but had little wider impact.

1948–55   Levi started a career as an industrial chemist and manager, which would last for thirty years. He stopped publishing with regularity, although he continued to think up and sketch out stories and poems throughout these years of apparent silence. He also did some work as a scientific translator.

1955–8   In 1955, with interest in the Holocaust growing, Einaudi agreed to republish *If This is a Man* in a slightly revised edition, although the book only appeared in 1958 after several delays and difficulties within Einaudi. The book was a success, and Levi was encouraged to write more.

1963–71   Levi published his second book, *The Truce*, in 1963, which won a literary prize and launched Levi into the role of writer *per se* perhaps for the first time. His public profile began to grow in the early 1960s also, as he was interviewed, appeared on television, began to visit schools (where his works, starting with *The Truce*, were beginning to be adopted as classroom texts) and give lectures, as well as write occasional newpaper pieces. His first book was adapted as a radio drama in Canada and staged in Italy, in a another version, in 1966. In 1966 and 1971 respectively, he published two collections of science-fantasy stories, *Storie naturali* ('Natural Histories'; selections in *The Sixth Day*) (initially under a thinly veiled pseudonym, Damiano Malabaila, to avoid causing offence to readers of his Holocaust memoirs) and *Vizio di forma* ('Formal Defect'; selections in *The Sixth Day*). Both contained stories written largely for amusement over a period of years, some dating back to those same months in 1946 when he was writing his first deportation stories. Their witty but often dark inventions have grown in stature over the years as both their subterranean links with the Holocaust work and their own literary qualities have become more evident. In particular, they are a focal point for Levi's important role as a bridge between 'the two cultures' of science and literature in Italy.

1975–8   In 1975, he published another work combining literature with science: *The Periodic Table* (*Il sistema periodico*), an autobiography loosely structured according to chemical elements. Each chapter centres on a real, fictional or metaphorical encounter with an element at a certain time of Levi's life. The book was a marked success. His next book, *The Wrench* (*La chiave a stella*, 1978), was, by contrast, very local in its style and theme, although it shared a common aim with *The Periodic Table* as a book of work stories: it consists of tales of a Piedmontese industrial rigger, Libertino Faussone, who, in his odd mixture of local brogue and technical jargon, tells of his epic and intimate struggles with bridges, dams and the other mechanical structures he encounters as he travels the world.

Set in the Soviet city of Togliattigrad, which Levi had visited for work in the early 1970s, *The Wrench* also stands as a farewell meditation on his career as a working, applied scientist: as he was writing it, he was also going into retirement to become a full-time writer.

1981–5   Levi's only fully fledged novel, *If Not Now, When?* (*Se non ora, quando?*), the story of a Jewish partisan band in World War II, followed in 1982, winning two prestigious prizes, but also some criticism for its 'over-researched' reconstruction of the Ashkenazi Jewish culture and Yiddish language of Eastern Europe. The 1980s saw a rapid crescendo in interviews and international acclaim, and Levi also began publishing several volumes of collected and new essays, stories, poems and articles. 1981 saw *Lilít e altri racconti* ('Lilith and Other Stories'; selections in *Moments of Reprieve*), containing essays, camp stories and science-fiction stories, and *The Search for Roots* (*La ricerca delle radici*), a fascinating commented anthology of his favourite or most formative books. In 1983 came his translation of Kafka's *The Trial*, an occasion for an extraordinary and traumatic clash of temperaments. His collected poems appeared in 1984 under the Coleridgean title *Ad ora incerta* ('At an Uncertain Hour'; *Collected Poems*), as did a short book recording a conversation with physicist Tullio Regge. And the following year saw his most characteristically eclectic, 'encyclopedic' (as Calvino put it) and curious volume of essays, *Other People's Trades* (*L'altrui mestiere*). In this same period, his international reputation rocketed, especially after the publication in America of *The Periodic Table* in 1984, hailed by Saul Bellow as 'a necessary book'. He undertook a book tour of America in 1985.

1986–7   In the year before his death, more of his articles for *La Stampa* were collected for the 1986 volume *Racconti e saggi* ('Stories and Essays'; selections in *The Mirror Maker*); but, far more significantly, Levi drew together his reflections on Auschwitz in possibly his most striking, profound and also darkest book, *The Drowned and the Saved* (*I sommersi e i salvati*, 1986). The essays – on memory, communication, the shame of the survivor, Nazi violence, stereotyping, the role of the intellectual and, most tellingly of all, on the 'grey zone' of moral ambiguity between victim and oppressor – revisit many of the moral and historical questions thrown up by the Holocaust itself and by Levi's own first book, *If This is a Man*, and are models in humane, ethical meditation. At the same time, *The Drowned and the Saved* also contains moments of genuine anguish, anger and ambivalence. Indeed, this acceleration in publishing and public profile in the 1980s was by no means without its pressures and anxieties for Levi, who had always been prone to bouts of depression. He was vexed by periods of writer's block, frustrated by the distortions in his reception abroad (especially in America, where he felt he was being lionized, but also absorbed into a model of the European Jewish writer which he knew he did not fit, only then to be criticized for not fitting it), and deeply concerned by pernicious negationist and 'revisionist' accounts of the Holocaust appearing in France and Germany. He was also, increasingly, disillusioned with speaking to the young: he felt they no longer understood him nor had any notion of why what he had to say was important, let alone of the detailed complexity of what he was trying to describe. Nevertheless, he remained active, talking, writing and planning future writing throughout his final years. He completed several chapters of a book on organic chemistry entitled *Il doppio legame* ('The Double Bond') or *Chimica per signore* ('Chemistry for Ladies').

1987   Levi died by suicide on 11 April 1987, in the apartment block where he had been born and, with the exception of his youthful peregrinations in the mid-1940s between Milan, Auschwitz and back across central Europe, he had lived all his life.

INTRODUCTION

Primo Levi's works of testimony, his narrative, poetry and essays about his time in Auschwitz are among the most widely read and most widely lauded of all writings on the Holocaust. For many, he has become *the* witness-writer *par excellence*. Perhaps no other survivor chronicled and considered these unbearable events with such accessible economy, elegant wit and humane power, for such a sustained period of time, stretching from his first published work in 1946 to his death in 1987. If he started out as one of many survivors who turned to some form of writing in the immediate aftermath of the outrage they had endured – only to be ignored by most around them – Levi's work came to be recognized in due course as exceptional not only for its power as witness, but also for its potential to go beyond the limits of first-hand chronicle.

Even within the pages of his first book *If This is a Man* (*Se questo è un uomo*, 1947), Levi demonstrated an extraordinary capacity to move from chronicle to wider reflection on his experiences and back again. In this way, he confronted, with directness and persistence, the array of complexities in human cruelty and human suffering which he had learned first-hand in Auschwitz. His readers consistently found in him a sane, if troubled, voice to guide them through the quagmire of moral and historical dilemmas thrown up by the Final Solution. They also found in him a bridge-builder, between the unbearable horrors of the camps and the fragile values of the liberal, modern, secular world which had formed him and which had been pushed so close to annihilation by Fascism and National Socialism. Through him, many readers – Jewish and non-Jewish alike – could see themselves living through and thinking through the events that he described; and they felt a strong personal bond with him as a result.

Furthermore, just as his work moved outwards from testimony or chronicle to embrace large issues thrown up by the Holocaust, so over the course of his *œuvre*, his interests navigated outwards from the Holocaust towards other literary and intellectual spheres, whilst never losing sight of the history that had defined him and his age. As his writing branched out in this way, often propelled by 'mere' curiosity, serendipity and the pleasures of experimentation, his work developed into one of the most distinctive literary achievements of his time and into a multi-faceted body of reflections on, and storytelling about, some of the most challenging questions facing twentieth-century modernity. These included the risks and rewards of science, the nature of historical responsibility, the limits of the human, the workings of language and the ethics of everyday life. For all of these, the Holocaust loomed as a – often *the* – key test case, but Levi knew that the Holocaust was as much the starting-point as the endpoint to his probing. The different foci and scales of Levi's concerns and the racking movements between them, both centripetal and centrifugal, are crucial to understanding the energy behind his work; and if the essays in this volume could be said to have a single, collective aim in mind, it is to follow the varied courses of these subtle movements.

Like all the *Cambridge Companions* devoted to a single writer, this volume starts out with a dual task: to introduce the student or general reader to the core components of the author's work and the principal reasons for their importance in the literature of their time, both locally and on a broader stage; and also to give a sense of what new directions and perspectives research on the author has taken in recent years, challenging or refining commonplace judgements and, on occasion, opening up strikingly original insights into their work. In Levi's case, a distinction perhaps needs to be drawn between approaches within Italy and in the wider world. Levi was lionized in the English-speaking world from the mid-1980s onwards and remains a constant reference-point not only for experts in the field of Holocaust studies but also for essayists, philosophers, journalists and writers in many other generalist contexts. Bryan Cheyette, in chapter 5 below, examines some of the problems and distortions that have come with these 'appropriations'. More fruitful in shaping this book, perhaps, were new approaches to Levi emerging in Italy from a cluster of innovative critical analyses produced by a new generation of critics in the mid-1990s,[1] which turned to Levi and to the Holocaust in general as a fixed point in an increasingly disorderly post-Cold-War, post-ideological and, some would even say, post-literary world. Their analyses tended to stretch our sense of him as 'only' a writer of testimony, to challenge assumptions that Levi was a writer of calm, rational and astonishingly untroubled sobriety, and to integrate fully into the core of his *œuvre* his many other eclectic intellectual and literary interests, genres, tones and writing styles. This volume seeks to continue that work of integration, not in order to create a second (or third or fourth) 'Levi' to set alongside 'Levi the witness', but rather to show how all these strands coalesce into a complex, cross-fertilizing and highly articulate voice and body of work.

With these aims in mind, it was decided not to structure this *Companion* in a systematic and sequential 'book by book' format. Considerations of space aside, a more important factor in making this decision was the fact that, for Levi, it was not the 'book' that constituted the core unit in which he thought, wrote and conceived of his work as a writer. Rather, the essential source of the intellectual flexibility and articulation of his work, branching into and across different modes of writing and ways of understanding the world, was his investment in short forms of writing. His core units were the short-story, the anecdote, the reflection, the short essay, review or article, the poem. When examined attentively, all his books – with perhaps the sole exception of *If Not Now, When?* (*Se non ora, quando?*, 1982) – turn out to be collations of such short-form primary material. Furthermore, the collations are often contingent; pieces from one book seem easily transferable to other books, as these shift in shape between one edition and the next or in the various posthumous collations of his work, making his *œuvre* feel strangely mobile and not defined by single published volumes. There has also been considerable and sometimes confusing movement, addition and subtraction between Italian editions and English and other foreign-language editions of his work (see 'Guide to further reading', section 1C, pp. 192–4 below). More than for many other writers, then, it makes sense to come at Levi through themes, issues and motifs which cut across the boundaries and the covers of separate books and circulate within his intellectual and, occasionally, personal biography.

This volume is divided into four main sections, each covering one over-arching area of Levi's work and formative interests. The first section is entitled 'Cultures' and looks at the two principal cultural contexts which shaped Levi and which remained as persistent substrata beneath all his life and work. His roots in the culture and history of Turin and Piedmont are explored by David Ward in chapter 1, tracing the city's modern cultural history back to its brief time as the centre and capital of the newly unified Italy in the 1860s and forward to the generations before Levi's, with its fervent philosophical, political and literary activism. Then Nancy Harrowitz in chapter 2 takes on Levi's identity and upbringing as a secular, but not quite assimilated, Jew, with all the baggage of ambivalence and historical irony this brought with it, before, during and long after his time as a victim of first Fascist and then Nazi antisemitism.

The second section, 'The Holocaust', turns to the defining event of Levi's life, the experience which propelled him into the darkest heart of twentieth-century history and also compelled him to become a writer: his deportation to Auschwitz. Three chapters tackle Levi's encounter with and responses to the Holocaust. Judith Woolf in chapter 3 follows a path through the network of different texts – the stories, poems, novels and essays, from *If This is a Man* to *The Drowned and the Saved* (*I sommersi e i salvati*, 1986) – through which, for over forty years, Levi developed his voice as a survivor-writer. In chapter 4, Marco Belpoliti and Robert Gordon show how Levi was able to articulate the Holocaust in original ways by using metaphors and maps of understanding from eclectic areas of intellectual enquiry, such as ethology, molecular science and ethics. And Bryan Cheyette in chapter 5 looks at how Levi has been appropriated, distorted and, at times, reduced as a 'Holocaust writer', in Europe, in North America and in the burgeoning academic field of Holocaust studies. In doing so, he makes a powerful case for seeing a more complex, multi-faceted and uncertain Levi in his response to the Holocaust.

The third section, 'Science', is made up of two complementary chapters, by Pierpaolo Antonello and Charlotte Ross (chapters 6 and 7), which together paint a wide-ranging picture of Levi's professional, literary and intellectual engagement with science. Antonello draws principally on Levi's two works of applied, practical science – *The Periodic Table* (*Il sistema periodico*, 1975) and *The Wrench* (*La chiave a stella*, 1978) – whereas Ross concentrates on his two main collections of science-fiction or *'fantascienza'* stories, *Storie naturali* ('Natural Histories', 1966) and *Vizio di forma* ('Formal Defect', 1971). Both show Levi grappling with complex (and often very contemporary) issues of the morality and philosophy of science, its limits and its potential and its implications for our understanding of modernity.

Finally, the fourth section of the book, 'Language and Literature', is made up of four chapters which position Levi as a writer in various ways. If Levi was a non-conventional writer within the traditional terms of the literary canon of Italy and beyond, he was nevertheless one who was constantly and engagingly fascinated by the workings of language and communication, the movement between languages, the subtleties of tone and voice and the relationship of reader to book, writer to book and books to other books. Anna Laura and Giulio Lepschy in chapter 8 bring linguisticians' eyes to bear on Levi's fascination with languages, showing how Levi dipped in and out of an extraordinary range of different language systems and idioms, from regional dialects and argots to Italian and a panoply of foreign languages. They further show how this field is linked to his deepest convictions regarding the communication of a message about the Holocaust. Mirna Cicioni, in chapter 9, lays out the subtlety and variety of Levi's humour, a core feature of his speaking and writing voice, a cultural constant as well as a set of literary devices which give great energy to all his writing. In chapter 10, Zaia Alexander offers three case studies of translation – Levi as translator, Levi translated and Levi using translation in his most powerful testimonial writing – to show how both the practice and the philosophy of translation was fundamental to his work. Finally, in chapter 11, Jonathan Usher probes Levi's extensive engagement with the canon of Italian literature (among other literatures), and the many vital ways in which he practised what we might call 'intertextuality', drawing other books into his own. Usher comments also on the awkard position Levi himself has held within that canon.

The volume is completed by an extensive Guide to further reading, including a comprehesive bibliography of Levi's own writings, in both Italian and English translation, followed by the most important critical work to have appeared on Levi. Finally, for ease of navigation, there is an index of individual works by Levi cited in the book, on pp. 200–2 below, as well as a General Index. The result, it is hoped, is an accessible advertisement for the merits of returning to Levi's work in order to discover there new and vital facets which can only reinforce his status as an essential vademecum – a companion – to twentieth-century history and literature.

NOTE

1. One volume which captures nicely the variety and energy of this wave of work is Marco Belpoliti (ed.), *Primo Levi* (Riga 13), Milan, Marcos y Marcos, 1997.

PART I
Cultures

I

DAVID WARD

Primo Levi's Turin

Turin was Primo Levi's city. Born, bred and schooled there, he lived at number 75 Corso Umberto for the entirety of his life, save two forced absences, the first as a consequence of the Racial Laws when he found work in Milan, the second during his detention in the death camps.[1] Turin and the cultural climate that had grown up in and around the city in the post-Risorgimento period onwards were vital components of Levi's world. Without placing him within this context it is hard for us to understand him fully as a writer, as a witness and as an individual. If Levi can be characterized not only as a rationalist, a late Enlightenment intellectual with a sceptical, analytical mind and faith in the power and integrity of positivist science, but also as someone who held dear a progressive liberal and anti-Fascist set of values, that is in no small part due to the cultural history of Turin.

Turin as capital

The Turin of the generation of Cesare Levi (1878–1942), Primo's father, was a city on the rebound from a period of crisis and humiliation. In the light of what Turin and Piedmont represented for Italy at unification it made sense that Turin be designated Italy's first capital. The city itself, and the Piedmont region with it, were by far the most modern and enlightened of the states that made up pre-Risorgimento Italy; city and region boasted an entrepreneurial middle class and a forward-looking ruling class; the city was on a par, or almost, with the nation that was its northerly neighbour and with which it enjoyed close contact: France. It had been the Piedmont ruling class, and its leader, Count Camillo Benso di Cavour, with their close diplomatic ties to France, who had spearheaded a unification process that otherwise might well not have succeeded. Last but by no means least, Turin was the seat of the Italian royal family, the house of Savoy, headed by the new King of Italy, Vittorio Emanuele II. Yet, compared to the overriding reason for the choice of Turin, all of the above pales into relative insignificance. Italy's 'natural' capital was not Turin, nor had it ever been, but Rome. Indeed, the eternal city had for centuries been at the very centre of a long intellectual debate about Italy's always desired, seemingly endlessly deferred national liberation and unification. The problem was that in 1860 Rome, still under papal and French control, was not yet part of the Italy that had been liberated and unified, nor were there any immediate prospects of the city joining the rest of the nation. Turin, then, was crowned capital by default, a temporary and thus rather double-edged honour.

That Turin's status as capital was only temporary was no secret to the guardians of the city. Still, in the early 1860s, the day on which Rome would come to occupy its rightful place seemed relatively far off. Imagine the surprise, then, when in September 1864 the city learned of the secret deal between the French and Italian governments, which had ended with the decision to transfer the capital away from Turin. The deal stated that in return for the transfer of the capital, Italy and the Papal States would desist from attacking each other, and France would withdraw its troops from Rome within two years. The choice of new capital was left to the Italian government, and on 18 September, only three days after the secret signing of the agreement in Paris, Florence was designated capital elect, until such a time as Rome could bear the mantle.

It can easily be imagined how the people of Turin reacted to the news of their 'decapitalization'. The city felt cheated and humiliated by the nation. If Florence was only to be another temporary home, as everyone knew, what was the point of moving at all? Riots broke out, an occurrence that was comparatively rare in the city, and demonstrators were killed; a duel was fought between the editors of two rival newspapers, the *Gazzetta di Torino* and *Gazzetta del popolo*. The cost to the city in financial terms was enormous, but this was nothing when compared to the loss of prestige. The city's great fear was that it might be reduced to a monument to a now past period in Italian national life, irrelevant to the new Italy. Turin's population had risen from its 1861 figure of 204,000 to 220,000 when it became capital, but by 1868, in the immediate aftermath of what became known as the 'excruciating deprivation' (*lacerante sottrazione*), for the sheer letdown of having its capital status snatched away so soon, it had dropped back to 191,500.

Turin regained its health and came to flourish economically and intellectually over the following decades, but this did not come about by chance. Rather, it was the result of the city guardians' understanding that something needed to be done if Turin was to have a post-capital future. Seeking to etch a new image of the city, the city guardians set about from the 1870s onwards creating a public, civic consciousness and local identity that would propel Turin's economic and intellectual life forwards. They instituted a concerted symbolic campaign of planning museums, exhibitions such as the 1884 international Exposition and grand publications, such as an 1880 volume simply entitled *Torino*,[2] to celebrate the past and imagine the future of the city.

Perhaps the most important step in this work of persuasion and creation of a new public consciousness and identity was the planning of the Museo del Risorgimento, in honour of the death of Vittorio Emanuele in 1878. This was to be a museum with a powerful agenda. It would seek, on the one hand, to offer a new interpretation of the city's recent past, claiming in the strongest of terms that Turin was unified Italy's spiritual capital (if no longer its political one), and that all the good that had come of the Risorgimento – the struggle for national liberation, unity, patriotism, sacrifice – had its roots in Turin and Piedmont. On the other hand, the museum, to be housed in the then brand new, grandly domed and spired monument the Mole Antonelliana, offered a picture of a modern, industrial, forward-looking city moving into the future propelled by its illustrious past. And it is striking to note the patriotic, civic contribution to this future Turin (and Italy) by the small but vibrant Jewish community of Turin: the Mole had been begun in 1863 as a new synagogue, only for the community to donate it to the city for its projects in 1877.

Neither the museum (which in reality opened only in 1908), nor the 1884 Exposition that was held in the Mole, nor the volume *Torino* offered pictures of a Turin that existed in reality. Image came before fact, an ideal, much desired Turin identity was, as it were, performed. The volume, for example, described Turin in glowing terms, as the 'Mecca of Italy', as the modern, economically and industrially strong city, the city that 'thinks and works', with a 'poetry of industry'. Although largely a symbolic operation, the picture of Turin launched by this manifesto was not entirely without foundation. An actual local identity and prosperous economy was being built. And the idea of a city whose citizens' feet were firmly on the ground and whose academic institutions abandoned their ivory towers to descend into the practicalities of the everyday life of industry and agriculture chimed very well with a long-established self-image that the citizens of Turin had given themselves, embodied by the figure of Gianduia. Originally a puppet created in the eighteenth century, Gianduia became the mask that exemplified the Turin and Piedmont character: sensible, serious, hard-working, a family man devoted to his wife Giacometta, measured (he enjoys a glass of wine and the chocolate that was named after him, but neither eats nor drinks himself into oblivion), straightforward, not given to flights of fancy. Both this local

Turinese self-characterization and its application to the modern world would find strong resonance in Primo Levi's later presentations of his own sense of self, his values and his intellectual principles.

By the 1890s, the city had more than made up for the lost population of the 1860s; the inhabitants of Turin numbered 330,000 in 1892, a sure sign that the city had emerged from its post-capital crisis. Among the newcomers was the young Cesare Levi, who had moved with his brothers to Turin from a small town in southern Piedmont in 1888 or 1889, following the scandalous suicide of their father Michele.[3]

Positivism

In this growing modern urban setting, with its new industries and new population, the newly dominant intellectual current was positivism, epitomized by ground-breaking work in criminal anthropology by Cesare Lombroso and others. Lombroso and his circle became very much the epicentre of intellectual life in the city, his charismatic personality drawing large numbers of people to his lectures. His Sunday salon, held in his house on via Legnano, was a meeting place for the Turin intelligentsia, including towards the end of the century Cesare Levi, trained like his father before him as an engineer.[4]

Lombroso's group of positivist intellectuals were forward-looking and socially committed. Although they called themselves socialist, what they espoused was a socialism that bore heavily on the principles of Darwin's theory of evolution and on the belief that science, the positivist observation of data in the world, and education would usher in a better, fairer world where social injustice would be overcome. In marked contrast to the socialism that would emerge from Turin in the second and third decades of the twentieth century, theirs was a socialism bereft of any class antagonism and with little or no mention of Marx. Indeed, one could surmise that the (respectively) radical liberal and communist theories that Piero Gobetti and Antonio Gramsci were to elaborate a generation later, where it is the friction between classes that sparks change, were a polemical response to what became known, a little maliciously, as Lombroso and his ilk's paternalistic and elitist 'socialism of the professors'. Far from being a socialism of revolution, this was a socialism of reconciliation and compromise, in the service of a vision of a society without divisions, whether of class or region. Although the limits of such a reformist and gradualist politics are plain to see, the Turin positivists' genuine commitment to the betterment of social life did bring with it beneficial practical effects, such as high levels of public health, hygiene and safety in the workplace.

No text illustrates better the strengths and weaknesses of the positivists' socialism than De Amicis' *Cuore* ('Heart'), a book that was to become a staple on the curriculum of Italian schools for many generations, including Primo Levi's. Published in 1886, telling in diary format the story of a year in the life of a third-year elementary school class in Turin, *Cuore* was an immediate success, becoming Italy's first literary best-seller. The school and the pupils' families are painted as an ideal space where all social tensions dissolve thanks to the good will and magnanimity of individuals. If society works, says De Amicis, it is because good-hearted people make it work. The text, in fact, responds to much the same logic of wish-fulfilment as the *Torino* volume mentioned earlier, offering its readers an image of the organic society they would like to see. In *Cuore*, danger and transgression are defused by means of a handshake or a hug, as all parties involved realize that the greater good of the community and of the still-infant nation is best served by being responsible, generous, open-minded and fair. Respect for the institutions of family, monarchy and school is paramount, as is love of country and gratitude for those who created it. It is, for example, the bourgeois Sig. Nobis who gives the class its most important lesson of the year when he proudly shakes the hand of Sig. Betti, a humble coalman, whose son had been insulted by Nobis' son. Vignettes like this argue for an inclusiveness that gives to each and all a role, whether humble or mighty, in a utopian organic society where everyone knows their rightful place and whose unity transcends and obliterates any differences of class, status and region.

One boy alone challenges and undermines the harmony, causing anguish to his mother and to the community: Franti. Through the anti-heroic Franti, De Amicis hints at the unavoidable dark side to the utopia, to those one would want neither to hug nor shake hands with. It is here that we encounter the less attractive side of positivist science and especially the area of it that made Lombroso's name, criminal anthropology, with its deterministic study of delinquents, the weak and the deviant (criminals, Jews, women and so on).

Although *Cuore* does not give us any precise details about him (apart from the fact that he has a low forehead), it is no stretch of the imagination to see Franti as a member of the category of born criminals elaborated by Lombroso. These are those members of the community who have a biologic-ally determined propensity for crime and anti-social behaviour that can be predicted in advance by measuring the dimensions of the individuals' cra-niums: beyond a certain measure they were criminals; within it, upstanding members of the community. According to Lombroso, there were two types of criminal: those who are pushed by circumstance and social and economic injustice into the ways of crime; and those who are born criminals (on the basis of the size of their cranium). For the former, a soft approach is warranted that aims at reform and the recovery of the lost soul within the embrace of the community; for the latter, there is no hope of avoiding biological destiny, and they must be separated from the community lest – or before – they do it harm. Such born criminals are criminals even before they have committed a crime, as there is no escaping their biological destiny. Although Lombroso's theories have now been thoroughly discredited both on scientific and on ethical grounds, the impact he had on Turin (as well as on the still very fragile nation of Italy as a whole, not to mention abroad) in the final decades of the nineteenth century and early twentieth century was immense.[5] Cesare Levi and his son Primo would inherit much of the culture and values of the scientific positivism and socialism of Lombroso's circle; but they would both live to see also one of the lines of descent of its pseudo-scientific eugenicist, not to say racist, social engineering.

Reactions against positivism

The Turin of the turn of the century was one of Europe's most flourishing cities with a vibrant social life and growing industrial wealth. The capital of the Italian fashion and cinema industries, Turin was also home to a small car factory, Fabbrica italiana automobili Torino, or FIAT, which was founded in 1899. Yet, despite these achievements, successive generations looked back with some disdain on this period of Turin's life, for its superficialities, its compromises and its corruptions. The sense of malaise was not confined to Turin, but was perceived by a growing number of young and not so young intellectuals the nation over. What brought together a band of men and women of varying ideological persuasions was a common project of both cultural and political renewal.

Positivism came out of this reassessment of the cultural state of Italy in a particularly bad way. The slipshod manner of Lombroso's research and its nature as self-fulfilling prophecy was challenged, as was the tendency of the positivist method to belittle the powers of human agency. If our future was already pre-determined, biologically or otherwise, what role did that leave for creativity, innovation, will, novelty? Looking back on the Lombroso years, the anti-Fascist philosopher Zino Zini, a long-time resident of Turin, whose daughter Marisa was to become Primo's private tutor in the late 1920s, spoke of a city where 'nothing is spontaneous, little is modern'. This, he went on, is a city that 'leant more toward obedience than innovation, and is not curious or sociable at all'. Recalling the days he attended Lombroso's lectures, the man he now called the 'genial Lilliputian', Zini describes a performance situated half way between science and cabaret, between 'wonder and swindle' (prodigio e ciurmeria), a smoke-and-mirrors show more at home in the theatre than in the laboratory.[6]

The waning of the primacy that positivism had enjoyed in the final years of the nineteenth century was due to a number of factors, but two in particular: first, the optimistic conviction that society would gradually and inevitably develop along predictable scientific lines with a minimum of social friction was questioned by the emergence of a working-class mass with its own political voice, for whom progress through class struggle rather than gradual evolution was paramount; and second, by the growing apprehension of many Italian intellectuals that positivism had ushered in a materialistic and bourgeois culture that ran counter to the spiritual mission to which the Italian nation had been called. If positivist materialism had eclipsed spirit, now was the time for Italy to set the balance right and embrace idealism, and with it the primacy of spirit and mind over matter.

The necessity and urgency of a cultural and spiritual renewal were central to the projects of a band of intellectuals ranging from idealists like Benedetto Croce and Giovanni Gentile to Giovanni Papini and Giuseppe Prezzolini, who were behind the influential Florence journal *La voce*; to nationalists such as Enrico Corradini; to the futurists; to literary icons like Gabriele D'Annunzio. As can be well imagined, although it may have had a common basis, the means of achieving this project were various and contradictory. Some saw salvation in the emancipation of the working classes, others saw the emergence of that class as a threat; some abhorred modernity, others loved it; some saw Italy's salvation in war, others saw it in colonialism; some saw it in both. But the glue that held the whole together, despite its many internal tensions, was the way in which it was cast as the revolt of a younger generation against their staid and now discredited father figures. This, for example, is how Gobetti spoke of the effect the philosophy of Gentile, for which the name 'Actualism' was coined, had had on the young men and women of his generation. Gentile's work, he wrote, had 'brought down (or rather: lifted up) philosophy from the level of professorial disputes to the immense concreteness of life. It is in him and in him alone that individuals recognize a master of morality and an entire new generation draws inspiration from his thought to bring about renewal'.[7]

The first rush to renewal in Italy was led by the Florentine reviews *Leonardo* and *La voce* in the opening decades of the twentieth century. Turin's contribution to the movement came a little later, initially through two reviews, both of which contain the word new in their titles: *L'ordine nuovo* (in which Gramsci was involved) and *Energie nove*, which was founded by Gobetti when, remarkably, he was still at high school. Both destined to be victims of Fascism, Gramsci and Gobetti were to become the centres of much of Turin's intellectual and cultural life in the post-World-War-I and early Fascist years.[8]

More politically minded than their more literary counterparts in Florence, the Turin reviews also marked a radical departure from the kind of socialism that had been practised by the Lombroso school of professors, with its dream of painless reform and domesticated masses. Gobetti and Gramsci both realized that the working class was the new protagonist on the social scene and in no city better than Turin, with its factories, entrepreneurs and industrial base and culture, could its dynamic potential be seen.

Gramsci and Gobetti, however, came from different ideological and regional backgrounds and envisaged different roles for the emerging working classes. Gramsci, born in a backward part of a backward island – Sardinia – had come to Turin in 1911 on a scholarship to study at the university. He became a socialist and, when the party split in 1921, he was instrumental in founding the Italian Communist Party; Gobetti, on the other hand, was Turin born and bred, the son of shopkeepers and was ideologically a liberal, albeit a frustrated one, living in a period of crisis of liberalism. Both in distinct ways found inspiration in the Turin working class and, above all, in the Factory Council Movement of 1919, when for a short time the FIAT workers took over control of the car factory. For Gramsci, the movement was a dress rehearsal for the day when, as two years previously in Russia, Italian workers would gain control of the means of production and run the factories and the state itself on their own. For Gobetti, they represented an infusion of new entrepreneurial blood into the body politic, useful to regenerate a then moribund liberalism. Much of Gobetti's considerable intellectual energy was expended on attempting to convince traditional liberals that there was little to fear and everything to be gained from understanding the real dynamic that lay just below the surface not only of the workers' movement, but also of the Russian Revolution (of which he offered an identical interpretation).

Despite these differences, both Gobetti and Gramsci held ideas on social and political change that were light years away from those of the Lombroso group. For both the one and the other, social antagonism, rather than quiescence, was crucial. Progress took the form of a generational struggle between newly emerged elites – like the one at the FIAT factory – who challenged an existing status quo and sought to take its place, in turn to be challenged by a future freshly emerged elite. Change, then, came from below, rather than being managed from above, and was the fruit of the actions of individuals autonomously creating their own world. For many of the young men and women who were deeply influenced by the charismatic Gobetti, autonomy was a key concept that spilled over from the factories to personal lives and on to inform the way the state should reorganize itself on a federalist basis according to which each component has the power to make its own decisions and laws. It would also influence, not to say inspire, a generation of anti-Fascists.

Culture and anti-Fascism

Both Gobetti and Gramsci fell victim to Fascist repression: the latter dying shortly after being released for ill health from over a decade in prison; the former dying at the age of twenty-five in voluntary exile in Paris after being severely beaten on direct orders from Mussolini. Despite the fanciful nature of some of his thinking, Gobetti's influence on young Italian intellectuals of the following generations, especially in Turin (including Primo Levi), was enormous. One of the places where his influence was most concentrated was the Liceo Massimo d'Azeglio, one of Turin's most prestigious schools and later also Levi's school. It was here that anti-Fascist-leaning professors like Augusto Monti and Zini taught; and it was here that, in the mid-1920s, a remarkable group of people, many of whom were to leave an indelible mark on Italian history and culture, studied. The list makes impressive reading, including unionist and socialist Vittorio Foa, writer Cesare Pavese, intellectual and victim of Nazi torture Leone Ginzburg, philosopher Norberto Bobbio and Communist Party cadre and journalist Giancarlo Pajetta. In 1933, another of the school's 'old boys', Giulio Einaudi, was to found the publishing company named after him, which remained throughout the post-war period one of Italy's most prestigious and intellectually committed cultural institutions. Many of Einaudi's first publications had a distinctly anti-Fascist flavour and soon attracted the attention of the Fascist authorities, leading to arrests and disruptions but also necessary accommodations. Both before and after World War II, Einaudi's core group of collaborators was drawn from the Turin intelligentsia, especially from the *dazeglini* (as graduates of the d'Azeglio school were known), Pavese and Leone Ginzburg being the most prominent. In the post-war period, Levi's friend, Leone's widow Natalia Ginzburg, and Italo Calvino joined the company and worked on a daily basis in the Rome and Turin offices. Einaudi published not only the works of Gramsci, but also a wide range of the most significant Italian and non-Italian literary and intellectual writers of the era. Primo Levi would become one of the most important of those in-house Einaudi writers, but not before 1958, and long after *If This is a Man* (*Se questo è un uomo*, 1947) had been turned down by Einaudi in 1946.

In the 1930s, many of the *dazeglini* and *einaudiani* became part of the anti-Fascist movement Giustizia e libertà (Justice and Liberty, or GL), an important group that put down deep roots in Turin's intelligentsia (and included a strong Jewish element).[9] The GL militants' opposition to Fascism was not dictated so much by narrowly ideological considerations as it was by ethical ones. For them, as it had been for Gobetti, Fascism represented an insult, an immoral affront to individual rights and responsibilities, autonomy and creativity. For these young men and women, to fight against Fascism was to fight against a way of life, which they identified in a social grouping they abhorred with a passion: the amorphous, unthinking, intellectually lazy and complacent mass of the middle classes. Their revolt was that of young bourgeois intellectuals against the very bourgeois culture that had produced them and had then shown its worst face by capitulating to or supporting Fascism.[10] Indeed, for these young men and women, given the retrograde state of the Italian bourgeoisie, Fascism had been an accident waiting to happen or, to use Gobetti's often quoted phrase from a 1922 essay, 'the autobiography of the nation'.

There was more than a dose of snobbery in the intellectual anti-Fascism of GL. In fact, the bourgeoisie's relationship to Fascism was more complicated and mediated than they implied. Primo Levi's family was a case in point. Like many bourgeois families in Italy, the Levis had a non-confrontational relationship with Fascism that was dictated not so much by acquiescence to the regime as to an understandable instinct for self-protection. Cesare joined the Fascist Party, the PNF, when it became necessary to do so; Levi ran the gamut of the Fascist youth organizations when he was growing up (Balilla, Avanguardia and later voluntary militia). Yet, the family's commitment to the regime was lukewarm, passive, with neither great enthusiasm nor great stands of principled opposition either. For them, as for many others, one can imagine that the acronym PNF stood not so much for Partito nazionale fascista as for 'Per necessità famigliare' (Out of family necessity).

None of this formal acquiescence to the regime prevented Levi from eventually (in the early 1940s) embracing anti-Fascism, however, and an anti-Fascism with a strong Turinese, GL inflection, even if the itinerary that led him towards militancy in the anti-Fascist Resistance was slower and less dramatic than that of the likes of Foa and Ginzburg. As Primo himself tells us in *The Periodic Table* (*Il sistema periodico*, 1975), young men and women of his generation knew little of these traditions when at school. By the mid-1930s, the grip the regime had over civil society had become firm, reducing radically the space for anti-Fascist activity. Indeed, many of the *dazeglini* who had joined GL found themselves either in jail (Foa, Einaudi and Ginzburg) or sent into internal exile in isolated villages in southern Italy (Pavese and Carlo Levi). The d'Azeglio school had been thoroughly purged of its anti-Fascist elements, and Levi describes in damning terms his own and his friends' ignorance at this time: 'Einaudi, Ginzburg, Monti, Vittorio Foa, Zini, Carlo Levi. These names said nothing to us, we knew hardly anything about them – the Fascism around us did not have opponents ... They talked to us about unknowns: Gramsci, Salvemini, Gobetti, the Rosselli brothers – who were they?' (*The Periodic Table*, pp. 51, 130; OI, 783, 851). But, as Levi's later choices show, some residue remained, and these names proved ripe to be rediscovered.

There is probably a degree of exaggeration for effect here: the Levi family had some indirect contact, through family ties (with the Foas, for example; or Carlo Levi, who was a relative by marriage) and friendship, with GL militants. Indeed, when many of the GL militants were arrested in two police sweeps of 1934 and 1935, the Levi family was concerned, groundlessly as it turned out, that they too might somehow be in trouble with the regime. What Levi does capture in *The Periodic Table* is the sense of isolation that he and his generation felt at that time and the gap, more cultural than temporal, that separated them from the heroic generation of some years earlier. As a result, he is at pains to point out, the first impetus of a resistance strategy for his group of peers came not from other models, but from something new ('We had to begin from scratch, "invent" our anti-Fascism, create it from the germ, from the roots, from our roots' (p. 51; OI, 783)).

Other evidence exists to qualify Levi's sense of the extreme lateness of his generation's turn to anti-Fascism. In 1986, in a rather heated reply to an essay in the American journal *Commentary* by Fernanda Eberstadt, who had claimed that Levi only committed himself to anti-Fascism after the Armistice in September 1943, he dates his own anti-Fascism to a much earlier period, that of the 1938 Racial Laws (OII, 1291–3). And indeed, in the chapters 'Zinc' ('Zinco') and 'Iron' ('Ferro') of *The Periodic Table*, he gives us many details of his nascent anti-Fascist stance. Especially important at this time was his friendship with a man he admired a great deal, Sandro Delmastro, who later died fighting with the Resistance, the first member of the Piedmont Military Command of the Partito d'azione (Action Party) to be killed (OI, 780). The liberal-socialist Partito d'azione was the political heir to Gobetti and to the GL group, and it was to their brand of anti-Fascism that Levi was drawn also. As well as Delmastro, other figures were instrumental in Levi's political tutelage. First among these were the brothers Ennio and Emanuele Artom, with whom Levi had contact via the closer ties that, paradoxically, the local Jewish community developed in the wake of the Racial Laws. Ennio, a classmate of Levi at the d'Azeglio, had been arrested, still an adolescent, in the 1934 sweep of suspected members of GL. Another important figure was Ada Della Torre, a second aunt with whom he lodged in Milan, when he began work in 1943 for the Swiss Wander pharmaceutical company, and who introduced Levi into the world of active anti-Fascism. Ada was in contact with local activists in the Partito d'azione, and it was as a result of her mediation that Levi became involved in smuggling propaganda out of Milan, his first concrete act of militancy.

In the wake of the Armistice with the Allies of 8 September 1943 and the Nazi invasion of Italy, Levi took the decision to join up with an Action Party Brigade in the area of Amay in the Aosta region. Levi saw the worst side of the Resistance movement: by all accounts, his band was badly organized and ill-equipped, its members undisciplined, a far cry from the Gobettian image of principled, morally upright, intransigent anti-Fascism associated with Action Party militants. As such, the group was a ripe target for infiltration by the Nazi forces, aided and abetted by the diehard Italian Fascists who had stayed loyal to Mussolini's puppet regime, the Repubblica sociale italiana. On 13 December, Levi, having seen almost no action as a partisan, was arrested along with the other members of his group and embarked on the first stage of the odyssey that would take him to the death camps and back.

The self-image that Levi had of himself was that of a man whose roots were deeply set in the traditions, history, culture, language and identity of his city and its region. Everything he tells us about himself seems to conform to the stereotype of an identity forged in the humus of Turin and Piedmont. Levi's own local identity, in which he had great pride, was the result, he tells us, of two factors working in parallel: geography and religion. What the Piedmontese ('the least Italian of Italians') and the Jews had in common was a traditional sense of reserve. A Piedmontese Jew, like Levi, was, then, endowed with a 'dual reserve'; they were *piemontesi* multiplied by two (or Jews multiplied by two).

The occasion for these witty, wry remarks was a preface that Levi wrote to a volume entitled *Ebrei a Torino* ('Jews in Turin') (*The Black Hole of Auschwitz*, pp. 151–5; OII, 1251–5). In this short piece, Levi speaks of a building we have already encountered, one that is close to the hearts of both the people of Turin and its Jewish community: the Mole Antonelliana. Originally built as a synagogue, the Mole has come to symbolize the entire city. In reading the few paragraphs Levi dedicates to the Mole one cannot fail to be struck by the affectionate tone of his words, as if he were in the company of trusted friends, in a safe and familiar place. He holds it dear not so much for its spectacular beauty, of which it has little (he calls it 'ugly and presumptuous', 'an overgrown exclamation mark'), but for its human qualities, its flaws: the fact that it is not functional, far too big for its original purpose; that it is held together by metal bars to prevent it from collapsing; that it has lost the place it once had in *The Guinness Book of Records*.

Despite all this (or because of it), the Mole is akin to a friend whose flaws we know and love because we are familiar with them, because they are part of our landscape, part of who we are. It was for this reason that, when Levi glimpsed the Mole from the train that was transporting him from the place of his initial arrest in Aosta to a detention camp in Fossoli, near Modena, his sense of loss and isolation took on a tangible and far more acute form: 'That was the wrenching moment for me, a farewell that broke my heart' (*Voice of Memory*, p. 57).

Levi goes to great pains to offer an image of himself immersed in the local colour of the Piedmont and Piedmont-Jewish circles in which he moved. It is hardly surprising, of course, that he set such great store by affirmations of local rootedness and belonging. In a 1976 discussion in Switzerland, Levi was asked about his bond to Turin (and Piedmont):

> My bond to my 'little homeland' [*piccola patria*] is very strong. I came into the world in Turin, my forebears were all Piedmontese; I found my vocation in Turin, I studied there, I've always lived there, I've worked, had a family, written and published all my books there, with a publisher deeply rooted in the local soil, for all its international renown. I love the city, its dialect, its streets, its pavements, its avenues, the hill and the mountains that surround it, which I climbed as a boy, I like the rural and hill-dweller roots of its people, the conscientiousness of its workers, the flair of its artisans, the rigour of its technicians. ... My way of writing is influenced for certain in no small degree by my chemical profession but also in part by having been formed in a sober, concrete and symmetrical city, a technical city where I have carved out my own niche.[11]

There is, then, powerful personal affect in these bonds, but also more than that: as we have seen, Levi was a product of the cultural, intellectual and political life of the city in which he lived, an heir both to the positivistic culture of which his father was an active part and which had such a strong bearing on his own activity and values as both scientist and rational human- ist; and also to the idealist and progressive liberal culture that developed in Turin into a very particular form of anti-Fascism, and which played no small role in deciding the political and ethical choices he made as a young man.

NOTES

1. See his description of his home in *Other People's Trades* (*L'altrui mestiere*, 1985), pp. 1–5; OII, 633–6.
2. *Torino*, Turin, Roux e Favale, 1880.
3. See Ian Thomson, *Primo Levi: A Life*, London, Hutchinson, 2002, p. 10. I have drawn on Thomson's biography for much of the personal information on Primo Levi contained in the pages that follow.
4. See *Other People's Trades*, pp. 47–8; OII, 800–1.
5. See Mary Gibson, *Born to Crime. Cesare Lombroso and the Origins of Biological Criminology*, Westport, CT, Praeger, 2002.

6. Zino Zini, *Pagine di vita torinese. Note dal diario (1894–1937)*, Turin, Centro studi piemontesi, 1981, pp. 26–7, 56.
7. Piero Gobetti, 'Giovanni Gentile', *Ordine nuovo*, 10 February 1921, p. 3.
8. Norberto Bobbio, *Trent'anni di storia della cultura a Torino (1920–1950)*, Turin, Cassa di Risparmio, 1977.
9. See Stanislao Pugliese, 'Trauma/Transgression/Testimony', in Pugliese (ed.), *The Legacy of Primo Levi*, London and New York, Palgrave, 2005, pp. 3–14.
10. On Giustizia e libertà, see Joel Blatt, 'The Battle of Turin, 1933–36: Carlo Rosselli, *Giustizia e libertà*, OVRA and the Origins of Mussolini's Anti-Semitic Campaign', *Journal of Modern Italian Studies*, 1, 1 (Autumn 1995), pp. 22–57.
11. Translated from Levi's own unpublished summary of his replies to questions, extracted in Gabriella Poli and Giorgio Calcagno, *Echi di una voce perduta. Incontri, interviste e conversazioni con Primo Levi*, Milan, Mursia, 1992, p. 236.

2

NANCY HARROWITZ

Primo Levi's Jewish identity

Primo Levi's personal position on being a Jew has been enigmatic, both for himself and for his readers and critics. He himself made differing statements on his Jewish identity: in an interview with Giuseppe Grieco, he makes it clear that he had a religious upbringing and that he has a Jewish identity that he has 'no intention of discarding' (*Voice of Memory*, p. 275); but elsewhere he relegates Jewish identity to a very small element of his overall identity and plays down the strength of his religious education (e.g. *The Periodic Table* (*Il sistema periodico*, 1975), pp. 35–6; OI, 770).

The origins of some aspects of the complexity in Levi's relation to his Judaism are to be found in his embracing of so-called 'secular' or 'cultural' Judaism, most commonly defined as a bond with Jewish tradition and culture that creates a Jewish identity for which religious observation is a matter of choice rather than of spiritual conviction.[1] He is often described and perceived as an assimilated Jew, because his immediate family was not Orthodox, and because he declared often that he had little spiritual conviction; but this alone does not capture the complexity of his and his family's rapport with their Judaism and their similarities to the Jewish community around them. In fact, in the strength of their identification with Jewish culture and in their relatively regular observance of religious ritual and calendars, Levi's family was typical of many Italian Jewish families at the time. They were perhaps closer to what contemporary British or American Jews would call, respectively, Reform or Conservative Judaism. Levi had a Bar Mitzvah at the typical age of thirteen, involving two years of religious preparation for the event, which at first he took seriously and with some fervour. At the time, he even vowed to wear *tefillin*, or phylacteries, but he was partly inspired, he later said, by the promise of a reward for his piety from his family, in the form of a new bicycle.[2] His immediate family observed major holidays and had strong ties with his mother's more religious side of the family, who were still for the most part practising Jews with strong connections to the previous generations' Orthodox practice. Given these biographical facts of his early years, it is clear that Levi's family and Levi himself had a distinct Jewish identity, which was in part religious, and could not straightforwardly be labelled 'assimilated'.

In *The Periodic Table*, Levi recounts how his father loved prosciutto, and would buy it and consume it out of the house as a guilty pleasure (p. 19; OI, 755–6). This spirit of mutiny often characterizes secular Judaism: a simultaneous recognition of and rebellion against religious practice. But it is not a mark of assimilation: rather, it indicates the stalwart presence of a culture to be rebelled against and reformulated rather than abandoned.

The misnomer of 'assimilated Jew' in Levi's case has caused much confusion and shed no light on his cultural identity. The problem, however, goes beyond the individual case of Levi. The term 'assimilation' has been broadly misused to indicate the fate of a minor culture as it encounters and negotiates the exigencies of coexisting with a dominant host culture. The implication – found in the Latin root, *assimilatio*, to render similar – is of an abandonment of the original culture in favour of the new host culture: a more accurate and less loaded term would be 'integration'. During and after the eighteenth-century Enlightenment, where modern Jewish emancipation finds its roots, Jewish assimilation was a major topic of debate both for Jewish communities and for Christian cultural figures interested in Jewish intellectual ideas, as well as for political elites from Napoleon to the Italian Risorgimento.[3] The elimination of visible difference seemed to be the only viable path to achieving tolerance if not acceptance.[4] The very fact of the mislabelling points to a serious underlying concern, that Christian society often resists the notion that culturally or philosophically identified Jews could still be Jews.

This preceding history and this issue lie at the heart of any understanding of Levi's Jewish identity: if the differences between 'assimilated' and 'secular' Judaism are not understood, then Levi's Jewish identity is bound to be a mystery as well. In fact, the label 'assimilated Jew' declares the religious and cultural identity of the individual so labelled as fair game for the cultural hegemony of others. One of Levi's biographers, for example, sees no distance between perceiving him as 'assimilated' and then presuming he celebrated Christian holidays (which he in fact did not).[5]

Levi's Jewish identity was also, of course, inextricably bound up with questions of Judaism in relation to persecution. At times Levi stated, particularly in interviews, that his Jewish consciousness was not active before being persecuted as a Jew (e.g. *Voice of Memory*, p. 262). Levi's strategies for negotiating his Jewish identity in the face of both Fascist and Nazi persecution are revealing for what they say about this particular historical moment for Italian Jews, and for what they reveal about the situation of secular Jews in the Diaspora.

In order to investigate the complexities of Levi's Jewish identity between historical processes of integration and persecution, this chapter will first survey the phases of his engagement with his Judaism before looking at two key texts where he engages with Jewish genealogy and tradition.[6]

Phases of Jewish identity

Jewish connection for Levi falls into chronological phases: his early school years and Bar Mitzvah; his involvement in the Jewish community after the Racial Laws had forced segregation; his passion for Holocaust education after the war and especially from the 1960s onwards; a renewed interest in Ashkenazi Jewish culture beginning in the late 1960s and culminating in the early 1980s; and finally an engagement with Israel and the concept of the Diaspora, most publicly in the 1980s.

Levi was raised in a specifically Italian-Jewish context that to a large degree determined the construction of his Jewish identity. His family had moved to Turin from the Piedmontese countryside only a generation before, leaving the small town of Bene Vagienna, where they had encountered both overt and covert discrimination. Born in 1919, the year the Fascist Party was formed in Italy, Levi was educated under the strictures of Fascism. The two dominant institutions exemplifying and actively promoting cultural hegemony in this period of Italian history, Fascism and Catholicism, became joined at the hip after the Lateran Pact of 1929, when the Roman Church and Mussolini's Fascist state came to a mutually beneficial understanding. As the years of Fascism wore on, more and more attempts were made to achieve national homogeneity. Theories purporting common racial origins of all Christian Italians were propagated. For several years, an antisemitic campaign was launched in the form of newspaper articles, antisemitic children's books and a magazine entitled *La difesa della razza* ('Defence of the Race') that proposed theories of racial inferiority and superiority. There was a covert movement as well on the part of Mussolini quietly to exclude Jews from positions of power all over Italy beginning as early as 1929. These campaigns excluded from 'Italianness' (*italianità*) an entire generation of patriotic Italian Jews, many of whom had fought in World War I and had sworn such a strong allegiance to the King, Victor Emmanuel, that they often named their sons and daughters after the King and Queen. The culmination came in 1938–9, first with the publication of the state's 'Manifesto della razza' ('Race Manifesto') and then with the extreme antisemitism of the Racial Laws.[7]

Levi was nineteen years old in 1938. The Racial Laws prohibited Jewish students from attending public schools, but Levi managed to finish his degree at Turin University, although not without problems. Around this time he became involved in the local Jewish community in Turin. He attended a study group for two years in which he became engrossed in Jewish intellectual culture. As part of these studies, Levi gave a talk on the topic of antisemitism to the community. The talk was a traumatic event for him as he suffered from extreme shyness and found his first attempt at public speaking tortuous. Ironically, his thesis was the claim that antisemitism was at an all-time historical low.[8]

At this point a persecuted Jewish identity had been stamped upon him from the outside, a process that began with the Racial Laws and culminated in his deportation to Auschwitz, and the ramifications of this marking go very deep. Later, when he became a universally recognized Holocaust writer and survivor, these identities – again, external in origin – also became indelibly marked upon him. Levi felt that bearing witness and testifying through his work was an important mission, both for his own need to re-establish himself as an individual after being treated as less than human by the Nazis and for educational purposes. At times, this led him to foreground the specifically Jewish aspect of his experience and this history; at others he underscored universal lessons learned from suffering and injustice. He embraced the role of Holocaust educator, visiting schools, meeting children and describing his experiences to them. At the same time he tried to establish his career as a writer whose topics were not limited to the Holocaust. Tensions between different components of his identity became apparent at this time: known almost exclusively as a Holocaust writer and survivor, Levi had to struggle to get himself seen in any other light.

In the late 1960s, Levi became interested in exploring Yiddish and Ashkenazi language and literature. This Eastern European Jewish tradition is not prevalent in Italy, which is dominated by Sephardic (of Spanish origin) Jewish culture. Levi wanted to familiarize himself with the predominant Jewish culture that was largely destroyed by the Holocaust, in order to better understand the lives of Eastern Europeans Jews. These interests and research included prefaces, essays and stories[9] and culminated in the writing and publication of his Jewish partisan novel, *If Not Now, When?* (*Se non ora, quando?*) in 1982.[10]

Finally, in the 1980s, Levi became ensnarled in debates about Israel and Palestine in which he tried to make clear the distinctions between Jews and Zionists, pleasing neither the left in Italy nor supporters of Israel. This also brought with it reflections on the identity of the diasporic Jew, in relation to Israel and to Jewish identity and culture (*Voice of Memory*, p. 267). In an interview with Edith Bruck, Levi says that he is incapable of an objective judgement on Israel; that the Israel supported by the right is precisely that aspect of Israel that he likes the least (*Voice of Memory*, p. 263). After the

Israeli invasion of Lebanon in 1982, Levi, along with many others, called for Prime Minister Menachem Begin's resignation. He says in an 1983 interview with Giampaolo Pansa that 'I am certain that Israel must be defended . . . But I am equally sure that it would do the Israeli government good to deal with support from us which is never unconditional' (*Voice of Memory*, p. 292). Levi was roundly attacked for such views; accused of being anti-Israel, although this was far from the truth. As both a Jew and a well-known Holocaust survivor, Levi was expected to support Israel uncritically. His opinions on the matter, however well thought out, became a sign of a perceived lack of loyalty to his Jewish identity.

Levi's self-portrait as a Jew: the genealogy of identity

Aside from examining the cultural and religious context in which Levi was raised, it is crucial to see how he himself viewed his own Jewish experience and the Jewish experience in general. Levi writes about the history of Jewish experience in modern Italy in several chronological periods. The first treats the previous generations and is historical and genealogical, the second the years before the war, then his best-known works about the Holocaust, and finally his experiences in the post-war years. At each stage he develops the theme of Jewish identity set against forces that oppose it.

Nazi persecution of Jews is, of course, the chief topic of *If This is a Man* (*Se questo è un uomo*, 1947), and much of Levi's work thereafter. It is in *The Periodic Table*, however, that Levi is most revealing on Jewish identity. In this literary elaboration of his life as a chemist, Levi imaginatively recasts the Jewish experience of his family and himself, charting their various strategies of integration, especially in the opening chapter, 'Argon'.

'Argon' is dedicated to his Piedmontese Jewish ancestors, but not only his own: several of the characters described in this chapter are not actually related to him. Levi is, in other words, raising the general issue of Jewish immigration into Piedmont and the ancestors of the Turinese Jewish community taken as a whole.[11]

Levi uses the element argon as a metaphor in order to illustrate characteristics of these forebears and their strategies for integrating into rural Piedmontese life in earlier centuries. He begins with a discourse on the nature of inert gases, including argon:

> There are the so-called inert gases in the air we breathe . . . They are indeed, so inert, so satisfied with their condition, that they do not interfere in any chemical reaction, do not combine with any other element, and for precisely this reason have gone undetected for centuries.   (*The Periodic Table*, p. 3; OI, 741)

The rich and complex metaphor charges the tale with ambivalences regarding the cultural ramifications of integration. Looking carefully at the description of inert gases that he gives us, we are struck by the language used: 'so inert, so satisfied with their condition ... do not interfere ... do not combine ... have gone undetected for centuries'. Levi then makes a direct comparison between these gases and his ancestors:

> The little that I know about my ancestors presents many similarities to these gases. ... all the deeds attributed to them have in common a touch of the static, an attitude of dignified abstention, of voluntary (or accepted) relegation to the margins of the great river of life. Noble, inert, and rare ...   (p. 4; OI, 741–2)

Levi's comparison of his ancestors to noble gases addresses the vulnerability of the Jews in their potential visibility, not the invisibility of the gases he describes. This manifests itself as a kind of anti-assimilationist dream on Levi's part: imagine how different the history of Jewish persecution would be if Jewish communities were not perceived as presenting the threat of combining, interfering with or contaminating other cultures, and so could go undetected – and therefore unmolested – for centuries! In the post-Holocaust context in which Levi writes, this comparison between the qualities of argon and his ancestors is particularly forceful: a longed-for invisibility that is precisely the opposite of what Levi describes in his recounting of his ancestors' tense relations with the gentile community.

A certain ambivalence mixed with pride characterizes this chapter, as he begins with the history of these ancestors' immigration to Italy in around 1500, recounting their difficulties in settling into the region:

> Rejected or given less than a warm welcome in Turin, they settled in various agricultural localities in southern Piedmont, introducing there the technology of making silk ... They were never much loved or much hated; stories of unusual persecutions have not been handed down. Nevertheless, a wall of suspicion, of undefined hostility and mockery, must have kept them substantially separated from the rest of the population. ... *As is always the case, the rejection was mutual.*   (pp. 4–5; OI, 742–3; emphasis added)

Levi raises the notion of integration in provocative ways, as it is clear that any blending with the local population is not a goal for this generation of Jews; in fact, the nervous cohabitation of the two cultures is characterized by secrecy and tension. Levi's ambivalence about integration and what it means is clear in the very choice of metaphor for this episode. Argon is chosen as the element to which he compares his relatives: and argon, as he tells us, does not interfere – but it also does not combine well. How then does argon work as a metaphor for these ancestors? Levi creates a paranomastic tension in the very choice of argon from amongst the other noble gases he lists: the notion of *argon* (from the Greek for inert, idle, without work) in the case of these Jewish settlers in Piedmont is really closer to *agon* (from the Greek for struggle or contest), and perhaps is meant to suggest it, as they struggle with their environment, new culture and new neighbours, creating a linguistic shield along the way which he describes as both protective and aggressive.

In his analysis of the rapport between the two cultures in this opening chapter, Levi looks extensively at the interaction of two languages, Piedmontese dialect and Hebrew, that resulted in the development of a jargon specific to the region. He discusses this jargon as a linguistic accommodation that expresses both the richness and the difficulty of this cultural standoff:

> it contains an admirable comic force, which springs from the contrast between the texture of the discourse, which is the rugged, sober, and laconic Piedmontese dialect, never written except on a bet, and the Hebrew inlay, snatched from the language of the fathers … There exist a good number of disparaging words, used sometimes to judge persons but more typically employed, for example, between wife and husband in front of a Christian shopkeeper's counter when uncertain about the purchase.
>
> (pp. 9–10; OI, 746–7)

The culture that these ancestors bring with them is not easily subsumed or abandoned; in fact, one of the more fascinating aspects of this chapter is the description of the inventive and resistant ways in which they negotiate the new culture around them. This is particularly noteworthy in the development of jargon vocabulary to describe Christian culture:

> The original Hebraic form is corrupted much more profoundly, and this for two reasons: in the first place, secrecy was rigorously necessary here because their comprehension by Gentiles could have entailed the danger of being charged with sacrilege; in the second place, the distortion in this case acquires the precise aim of denying, obliterating the sacral content of the word, and thus divesting it of all supernatural virtue … Completely cryptic and undecipherable – and that was to be foreseen – is the term Odo, with which, when it was absolutely unavoidable, one alluded to Christ, lowering one's voice and looking around with circumspection; it is best to speak of Christ as little as possible because the myth of the God-killing people dies hard. (pp. 10–11; OI, 748)

The only example Levi gives of antisemitism during his father's childhood in the small town of Bene Vagienna is a ritualistic greeting mocking Jews wearing the prayer shawl that his schoolmates used to give his father. Levi describes this gesture as a remnant of intolerance, mocking but 'without malice'. But there were certainly other episodes of intolerance, one in particular that to a large degree shaped his immediate family's future. Levi refers to it only in an oblique manner.

Near the end of his chronological ancestral recounting, Levi arrives at the description of his paternal grandmother, of whom he has early childhood memories. He refers almost jocularly to a very painful episode in his family's life:

> In her youth she was known as 'the heartbreaker'; she was left a widow very early and the rumour spread that my grandfather had killed himself in desperation over her infidelities. She raised alone three boys in a Spartan manner and made them study; but at an advanced age she gave in and married an old Christian doctor, a majestic, taciturn, bearded man, and from then on inclined to stinginess and oddity. (p. 18; OI, 754)

The rest of the episode not mentioned in this chapter (or anywhere else in Levi's opus) is the actual context of the story of his grandmother's widowhood. Levi's paternal grandfather Michele and his great-grandfather Giuseppe had owned a family bank in Bene Vagienna in the latter part of the nineteenth century. In July of 1888, as the bank was recovering from some economic hardship along with the rest of the region, they were forced out of business by a Dominican friar. The friar spread a rumour that the bank was failing, resulting in a run on the bank that then caused the bank to fail. The friar used antisemitic rhetoric to incite mobs, expel the family from the town and eventually open his own bank. Levi's grandfather committed suicide in 1888, right after the failure of the bank, and his great-grandfather was almost lynched by an angry mob. The precise relationship of his grandfather's suicide to his wife's purported infidelities and the loss of the family business (and subsequent need to leave the town altogether) is not completely clear, but certainly the bank failure was the immediate catalyst for this tragedy and was reported in local papers. Levi conflates the idea of a rumour (infidelity) with another rumour (the bank is failing) that was at the very least an equally significant catalyst for his grandfather's suicide. What is most striking, however, about this rendition of Levi's family story is what is missing, rather than what is articulated. This clearly constitutes a case of 'unusual persecution', to use Levi's own term, yet it is omitted in favour of a more benign framing of the tale.

In Levi's story of his grandmother, more questions are raised than answered: why does she marry a non-Jew after the persecution and suicide of her Jewish husband, and why does Levi describe this as 'giving in'? Why does she become so miserly after marrying the second husband? Levi's rendition of this story indicates his desire to see these episodes as witty, idiosyncratic turns in his family's story rather than the tale of a difficult and troublesome integration into Piedmont and therefore also a story of the persecution of Jews in Italy at this time.[12]

Even though *The Periodic Table* is an autobiography of his own life as a chemist, Levi begins with these Jewish ancestors and the resistance against their integration into their life in Piedmont. This sets the tone for the chapters to follow, some of which engage his own tense negotiations with Fascist Italy, post-war adjustments, and a chapter in which he recounts an episode in Auschwitz. What is being set up here, in other words, under the cover of anecdote, is a working through of the tensions and difficulties his integrated, secular but not assimilated Jewish identity brings with it.

Levi's remarks in a later chapter of *The Periodic Table* regarding his Jewishness follow a similar pattern to the one he sets up in 'Argon', when he omits the serious persecution that his grandfather's family endured in Bene Vagienna. Another kind of benevolent blindness characterizes his representation of his early years in Fascist Italy:

> In truth, until precisely those months it had not meant much to me that I was a Jew: within myself, and in my contacts with my Christian friends, I had always considered my origin as an almost negligible but curious fact, a small amusing anomaly, like having a crooked nose or freckles; a Jew is somebody who at Christmas does not have a tree, who should not eat salami but eats it all the same, who has learned a bit of Hebrew at thirteen and then has forgotten it. (pp. 35–6; OI, 770)

In 'those months' – during 1938 – Levi's situation was changing: he was learning what it meant to be considered 'impure', according to the Fascist racialist doctrine; to be marginalized, to have problems finding a mentor at the university because of his Jewishness. But his Jewishness was already more than a 'small amusing anomaly'. As noted earlier, Levi was at this time involved in the new educational programmes implemented by the Jewish community of Turin as it reeled from racial laws preventing Jewish students from attending public schools and other restrictions severely circumscribing their rights as citizens. In fact, even earlier, in his childhood, Levi had been subject to some harassment partly because he was Jewish, although again, he never mentioned this directly in his writings, instead channelling some of that experience, much later on, into tales of science-fiction with no apparent connection to Judaism nor to his own life-story.[13]

The language that Levi employs to discuss this 'anomaly', a 'crooked nose', is also noteworthy. The representation of the purportedly 'Jewish' nose had already been used in antisemitic discourse and in propaganda for years, and was being renewed in *La difesa della razza* and elsewhere at that time.[14] Levi's decision to rewrite antisemitic discourse into his image of an unimportant crooked nose is indeed telling, as he substitutes a harmless version for a powerfully damaging image, but he nevertheless works within the stereotype. This strategy of containment and reduction is a familiar refrain in Levi's presentation of Jewish life during Fascism.

Identity misprisions

Our comprehension of Levi's Jewish identity is dependent on several factors, both internal and external: how he himself experienced this identity, how he chose to present it to the world, how the outside world viewed him, and finally the relation of his Judaism to other key components of his identity.

Inevitably, there were misunderstandings in how he was viewed as a Jew by the outside world. As we saw, before Auschwitz his Jewish identity was at least partially constituted by racialist policies in Fascist Italy; and after his return, Levi himself complained when his Jewish identity was viewed as inseparable from his identity as a Holocaust survivor. That side of his identity was, in other words, overdetermined and multi-faceted; and it also ran concurrently with other aspects of his self-image, for example, his dual identity as chemist and writer, which develops even as he writes about Auschwitz. More, he survived Auschwitz because he held onto his formation as a chemist and came through his second Polish winter as a result by obtaining work in a laboratory.

Levi was frequently interested in thematizing the interactions of those other identities – as scientist, as writer – in stories, essays and interviews, and does so in interesting and thoughtful ways, even comparing the process of writing to chemical combinations and processes. He does not, however, often engage with the subject of his Jewish identity, nor does he thematize it or relate it to those other facets, except to relegate it to the effects of persecution or to indicate his level of interest in Jewish culture. In 1982, Levi summed up his relation to Jewish culture and topics in a lecture given at a conference on Jewish literature. Entitled 'Itinerary of a Jewish Writer', it acknowledges that he is viewed as a Jewish writer by his readers and critics, but: 'I have accepted this definition cheerfully, but not right away and not without resistance. Indeed, I fully accepted it only relatively late in my life and in my itinerary as a writer'.[15] In a 1976 interview with Edith Bruck entitled 'Jewish, Up to a Point', Bruck asks Levi what it means to him to be Jewish. Levi replies, 'I was turned into a Jew by others. Before Hitler I was a middle-class Italian boy. The experience of the Race Laws helped me to recognize, amongst the many threads that made up the Jewish tradition, a number that I could accept.' He goes on to elaborate that spiritual independence and the Talmudic tradition of 'impassioned but precise argument' were part of the Jewish legacy that he has adopted. But when asked about antisemitism, Levi replied that, even during Fascism, the antisemitism was 'never more than superficial and inconsistent' (*Voice of Memory*, p. 262).

Our understanding of Levi's Jewish identity is ultimately tempered by an understanding of the strategies he employs to contain the antisemitism he himself experienced in Fascist Italy before the Holocaust. What were the stakes for Levi in the sanitized version of bigotry he gives in his works? One can only speculate that the *italianità* of his identity was deeply unsettled by rising antisemitism in Italy. Feeling himself to be foremost an Italian, he could not reconcile this self-image with the reality of exclusion and betrayal that was Fascist Italy for Italian Jews after the mid-1930s. And the late nineteenth-century genealogy of bigotry apparent in Levi's own family can only be seen as a precursor to what was to come two generations later. Rather than the 'lowest ebb' of antisemitism that Levi describes in his talk given to the Jewish community in 1939, he finds himself in the middle of a wave of antisemitism that was not by any means a historical anomaly ascribable to Hitler's influence on Mussolini, a myth now largely debunked by scholars.[16]

As his reputation grew, Levi was made to represent all things to all and was caught in webs of misprision: if he criticized a policy or action of the Israeli government, he was in turn criticized for being 'anti-Israel'; if he was understood to be Jewish, then he was expected to mould himself to certain expectations of what a Jew and a Jewish writer should be; if he was described as 'assimilated', then his Judaism was taken away from him completely. For many years his writings were pigeonholed by many as 'only' survivor testimony and therefore of interest, by and large, only to Jews; he was considered to be out of the mainstream of Italian literary culture because of his Jewishness and because of his survivor identity (as well as his scientific formation), despite his assertions of being an Italian first. His writings on other subjects were not taken as seriously as his Holocaust writings for a long time. Only when Levi's true qualities as a writer's writer finally became obvious to critics, and he was praised abroad, did talk about him as an Italian writer, a native son, ensue, only then to marginalize aspects of his work touching on secular Jewish identity.[17]

The compelling ways in which Levi himself negotiates his Jewish identity and the issue of secularization in relation to his Holocaust experience are apparent in a poem he wrote in January 1946 (later entitled 'Shemà'), which appears as an epigraph to his best known work, *If This is a Man*, and sets the tone for the testimony to follow:

> You who live safe
> In your warm houses
> You who find, returning in the evening,
> Hot food and friendly faces:
> Consider if this is a man
> Who works in the mud
> Who does not know peace
> Who fights for a scrap of bread
> Who dies because of a yes or a no.
> Consider if this is a woman,
> Without hair and without name
> With no more strength to remember,
> Her eyes empty and her womb cold
> Like a frog in winter.
> Meditate that this came about:
> I commend these words to you.
> Carve them in your hearts
> At home, in the street,
> Going to bed, rising:
> Repeat them to your children,
> Or may your house fall apart,
> May illness impede you,
> May your children turn their faces from you.[18]

The title of the poem is taken from the name of the central prayer in Judaism, taken from Deuteronomy, which is a call to monotheism and also a call to Jews to remember who they are and who their God is. *Shema*, the first word of the prayer in Hebrew, means 'listen':

> Hear, O Israel, the Lord is our God, the Lord is One.
> Blessed be the name of the glory of His kingdom forever and ever.
> You shall love the Lord your God with all your heart, with all your soul and with all your might. And these words which I command you today shall be on your heart. You shall teach them thoroughly to your children, and you shall speak of them when you sit in your house and when you walk on the road, when you lie down and when you rise up. You shall bind them as a sign upon your arm, and they shall be for a reminder between your eyes. And you shall write them upon the doorposts of your house and upon your gates.
>
> (Deuteronomy 6: 4–9)

The correlations between prayer and poem are clear: Levi echoes the command to bind the words upon the body, to inscribe them on doorposts and gates with his injunction to carve the words in the heart and to repeat them to our children. These injunctions begin, through the title itself, with the commandment to listen, and therefore to remember.

The last three verses of the poem emphasize, conversely, the dangers of forgetting and this also constitutes a rewriting, here of the end of the second passage of the *Shema*, from later in Deuteronomy:

> Be careful that your heart be not tempted and you turn away to serve other gods and bow to them. For then God will be furious with you and will block the heavens and there will be no rain and the land will not yield its produce, and you will perish quickly from the good land that God gives you.
>
> (Deuteronomy 11:16–17)

The adaptation, appropriation even, of part of the *Shema* prayer as a call for Holocaust memory and commemoration raises significant questions. Levi's self-positioning in his poem – 'I commend these words to you' – suggests more than a secular rewriting: the survivor, who invokes his readers to remember and to tell their children, is putting himself in the position of an ultimate authority.

In Levi's apparently secular 'Shema', the writing that memorializes the Holocaust must become part of Jewish memory, in order to make sure that future generations know what happened. Writing alone, however, is not sufficient to ensure this: he goes beyond the injunction of literal inscription found in the prayer commanding us to carve the words in our hearts. The role that Levi as survivor and writer takes on is to command, not just commend, intimate remembrance, through this rewriting of the most central prayer in the Jewish religion. The last lines are also indicative of this imperative – if you fail to listen and pass along the tradition of remembering, the next generation will not recognize the last. In other words, generational continuity and therefore history will be abolished, if this particular history is not remembered. This poem reveals Levi's most unveiled sentiments about Holocaust writing and remembrance.

The issue of secularization is thus subsumed within the command for Holocaust remembrance: the imperative shifts from the monotheistic enterprise of traditional Judaism to the urgency of a commemorative mode. This strategy is emblematic of Levi's subject position *vis-à-vis* Judaism as well as the persecution which so deeply marked him as a Jew. It is his knowledge and comprehension of the depth of Jewish tradition that allows him to integrate that same tradition with a secular reinscribing. Finally, the date of composition of this poem is also noteworthy. Written immediately after the war and Levi's return, as he was immersed in vivid memory and the impulse to testimony, the poem can be seen as a negotiation between what happened to Levi as a Jew during the Holocaust, his upbringing as a secular, cultural, integrated Jew, and his understanding of his Jewish identity, past and present, as it had been transformed by Fascist and Nazi persecution. To confirm the particular conjunction of forces evident in this 1946 work, it would suffice to look at any of the several declarations in Levi's later work of his instinctive distrust of (modern) prophets: as he says in the 1976 'Afterword' to *If This is a Man*, 'it is as well to regard all prophets with suspicion'.[19]

The Jewish part of Levi's overall cultural identity poses vital questions: how does being persecuted as a Jew confer Jewish identity, and what are the ramifications of such an identity formation? Levi stated in an oft-quoted interview with Ferdinando Camon that the Holocaust sewed a yellow star of David not only on his sleeve, but also within, in his heart (*Conversations with Primo Levi*, p. 68). Persecution penetrates identity much deeper than the external symbol. The use of the yellow star during the Holocaust was a perversion and degradation of the Star of David, a symbol of the Jewish people and religion: it becomes a mark not of religious belief but of racialist persecution and victimization. If this form of the star is sewn into the heart, as Levi suggests, a deep conundrum is sewn along with it, suggesting the impossibility of a Jewish identity that is not bound up with persecution and with memory. Like the carving of memory into the heart he advocates in his version of the *Shema*, persecution carves its place as well.

NOTES

1. See Yaakov Malkin, *Secular Judaism: Faith, Values and Spirituality*, London, Vallentine Mitchell, 2003.
2. See Ian Thomson, *Primo Levi. A Life*, London, Hutchinson, 2002, p. 42; Carole Angier, *The Double Bond: Primo Levi, A Biography*, London, Viking, 2002, p. 78.
3. On Jewish assimilation in Europe, see Bryan Cheyette and Nadia Valman (eds.), *The Image of the Jew in European Liberal Culture, 1789–1914*, London, Vallentine Mitchell, 2004.
4. In Italy, for example, Cesare Lombroso, the famous Italian-Jewish criminologist, expressed this view in his book *L'antisemitismo e le science moderne* (1894).
5. Thomson, *Primo Levi*, p. 408.
6. There is relatively little analysis in English of Levi's Judaism (although see several essays in Stanislao Pugliese (ed.), *The Legacy of Primo Levi*, New York, Palgrave, 2005). For a good account in Italian, see Sophie Nezri-Dufour, *Primo Levi: una memoria ebraica del Novecento*, Florence, La Giuntina, 2002; and important essays by Paola Valabrega, Alberto Cavaglion and others in Ernesto Ferrero (ed.), *Primo Levi: un'antologia della critica*, Turin, Einaudi, 1997.
7. On Fascist antisemitism, see Susan Zuccotti, *The Italians and the Holocaust*, Lincoln, NE, University of Nebraska Press, 1996.
8. Thomson, *Primo Levi*, p. 93.

9. See, for example, his 1966 preface to a translation of Yitzhak Katzenelson's *Song of the Murdered Jewish People* (OI, 1195–7) or to a conference on the 'Jews of Eastern Europe' (OII, 1284–8; *The Black Hole of Auschwitz*, pp. 171–3); or essays such as 'Ritual and Laughter' ('Il rito e il riso') in *Other People's Trades (L'altrui mestiere*, 1985).

10. See Valabrega in Ferrero (ed.), *Primo Levi.*

11. On Levi's genealogy, see Angier, *The Double Bond*, pp. 1–36.

12. It is not clear exactly what Levi did or did not know about the particulars of this episode: it appears that the older family members did not discuss it willingly. See Angier, *The Double Bond*, pp. 25–36, and Thomson, *Primo Levi*, pp. 6–10 for further detail.

13. See Thomson, *Primo Levi*, p. 41, who links the childhood episode to the story 'I sintetici' ('The Synthetics') in *Vizio di Forma* ('Formal Defect', 1971; not translated) about artifical, 'test-tube' babies.

14. See Sander Gilman, *The Jew's Body*, New York, Routledge, 1991.

15. *The Black Hole of Auschwitz*, p. 155 (translation slightly altered); 'Itinerario di uno scrittore ebreo', OII, 1213.

16. See note 7 above.

17. See chapter 5 in this volume.

18. A different translation of the same poem is to be found in *Collected Poems*, p. 9. For the original text (with slight differences in layout), see OI, 3 and OII, 525.

19. OI, 199; in English editions after 1979 (e.g. Primo Levi, *If This is a Man; The Truce*, Harmondsworth, Penguin, 1979, p. 396).

PART II

The Holocaust

3

JUDITH WOOLF

From *If This is a Man* to *The Drowned and the Saved*

The 'maelstrom' of Auschwitz

Primo Levi disclaimed the role of prophet or seer, describing himself instead as 'a normal man with a good memory who fell into a maelstrom and got out of it more by luck than by virtue, and who from that time on has preserved a certain curiosity about maelstroms large and small, metaphorical and actual' (*Racconti e saggi* ('Stories and Essays', 1986; selections in *The Mirror Maker*), pp. 3–4; OII, 859). This self-description, with its characteristically wry modesty and its equally characteristic foregrounding of curiosity about phenomena 'metaphorical and actual', recalls Canto 26 of Dante's *Inferno*, central to the famous chapter, known to English-speaking readers as 'The Canto of Ulysses' ('Il canto di Ulisse'), in his first book, *If This is a Man* (*Se questo è un uomo*, 1947), implicitly equating the 'maelstrom' (*vortice*) of the *Lager* with the 'whirlwind' (*turbo*; *Inferno* 26, l. 137) which sweeps Ulysses' ship to destruction, while the 'virtue' (*virtù*) to which Levi refuses to attribute his own survival is compared to the 'virtue and knowledge' (*virtute e canoscenza*, l. 120) the pursuit of which Ulysses enjoins on his crew as the activity which distinguishes men from beasts. Tellingly, both words derive from the Latin *virtus*: the courage and worth which is fitting for a man, and which the Nazi death camps were designed to strip from their victims.

As he tells us at the start of *If This is a Man*, the maelstrom engulfed Levi in January 1944 when, along with his fellow internees in the detention camp at Fossoli, near Modena, he received what was in effect a coded death sentence: 'on the morning of the 21st we learned that on the following day the Jews would be leaving. All the Jews, without exception. Even the children, even the old, even the ill. Our destination? Nobody knew' (p. 5; OI, 8). So terrifying was this ignorance that it was actually 'with relief' that the prisoners herded into the closed cattle trucks discovered where they were bound: 'Auschwitz: a name without significance for us at that time, but it at least implied some place on this earth' (p. 8; OI, 11–12). Of the 650 men, women and children on that train, only those judged suitable for slave labour would enter the *Lager*. The old, the sick, and the children, along with the mothers from whom they could not be parted, would be gassed on arrival. Only sixteen men and eight women would eventually return.

Considerable work has been done on establishing the number and identities of Italian deportees. Liliana Picciotto Fargion's *Il libro della memoria* ('The Book of Memory') names 6,806, of whom only 837 survived, though these figures do not include the 900 to 1000 victims it has so far been impossible to identify.[1] In all, about 15 per cent of Italy's Jewish population perished, including several hundred Jews murdered on Italian soil. In the escalating arithmetic of genocide, it is estimated that some 1.1 million people died at Auschwitz, almost a million of them Jews, though it is important to remember that among those exterminated because their captors regarded them as sub-human were Romanies, Russians and Poles. The SS destroyed the records when they evacuated the camp, making it impossible to establish the precise number of their victims, and the names of many who died will never be recorded because their killers also obliterated everyone who had known them.

The historian Michael Marrus describes Auschwitz as 'that immense death factory',[2] and this is no metaphor. In *The Mirror Maker*, Levi vividly details the industrialization of mass murder: 'the gas was produced by illustrious German chemical plants; and to other German plants went the hair of the massacred women; and to German banks went the gold of the teeth extracted from the corpses' (p. 166; OII, 1323). But beyond this, the vast complex of concentration camps which made up Auschwitz was created by the SS in conjunction with IG Farbenindustrie, which made use of the endless supply of cheap slave labour in the attempted production of the synthetic rubber called Buna, after which Levi's camp, Buna-Monowitz, was named. Levi notes that the 'German chemical trust . . . paid four to eight marks a day as salary for our work. Paid, but not to us: just as you don't pay a horse or an ox, so this money was handed to our masters, that is, to the SS ruling the camp' (p. 85; OII, 923). Even the sign – 'brightly illuminated (its memory still strikes me in my dreams): *Arbeit Macht Frei*, work gives freedom' (*If This is a Man*, p. 15; OI, 16) – which greeted Levi and his companions on their arrival at the camp was provided by IG Farben; the mocking words were a company slogan. The victims of this grotesque alliance between capitalism and genocide usually died within three to four months, broken down by starvation, beatings and exhaustion. John Cornwell, in his book *Hitler's Scientists*, details the derisory sentences, 'ranging from six to eight years' for 'slavery and mass murder',[3] handed down to IG Farben executives in the Allied trials of war criminals at Nuremberg, despite the evidence 'of IG Farben's participation in selections that would mean death for those selected, of company workers witnessing the

hanging of prisoners, of Farben people being aware of the gassing and crema-
tion of inmates in other parts of Auschwitz'.[4]

The justice with which Primo Levi was concerned was not the justice of
Nuremberg. As he tells us in *The Drowned and the Saved* (*I sommersi e i
salvati*, 1986), 'it was fine with me that the very just hangings should be taken
care of by others, professionals' (p. 138; OII, 1125). Instead, with his abiding
belief 'in reason and in discussion as supreme instruments of progress',[5] he
wanted to understand his adversaries and to confront them by forcing them
to confront themselves. In the effort to achieve this he reflected on and spoke
and wrote about Auschwitz – the complex hierarchy of its many victims, its
Nazi planners and perpetrators and its industrial sponsors – in genres including testimony, autobiography, poetry, fiction, journalism and interviews, for
over forty years after his return from the 'maelstrom'. This chapter traces
some of the principal themes in this sustained and compelling body of work.

The compulsion to testify

When in 1959 Levi agreed to the publication of a German edition of *If This is
a Man*, he realized that 'its true recipients, those against whom the book was
aimed like a gun' were those who had collaborated or pretended not to know
what was happening in the camps: 'Before, they were oppressors or indifferent spectators, now they would be readers: I would corner them, tie them
before a mirror' (*The Drowned and the Saved*, p. 138; OII, 1125). In the
'Vanadium' chapter of *The Periodic Table* (*Il sistema periodico*, 1975) he
shows us the partial and problematic achievement of this aim in the fable of
Dr Müller, 'one of the not so few one-eyed men in the kingdom of the blind'
(pp. 221–2; OI, 193–4), who tries to get Levi to give him absolution for his
part in the crimes of IG Farben, a complicity which, even years after the
liberation of the Buna-Monowitz camp, Müller is unable fully to admit to
himself. The character of Müller is based on a real German industrial chemist
(significantly not called Müller) who had visited the Buna laboratory where
Levi worked as a slave labourer.[6] By fictionalizing his story, Levi extends it to
include all the petty collaborators who had tried to salve their consciences
with small propitiatory gestures while closing their eyes to the ongoing
reality of genocide. Confronted by this adversary who had also been, however self-deceivingly, a benefactor, Levi is at a loss: 'I did not feel capable of
representing the dead of Auschwitz, nor did it seem to me sensible to see in
Müller the representative of the butchers' (p. 218; OI, 928), but neither was it
possible for him to forgive a former enemy so selectively prepared to
acknowledge his guilt. When, at the end of the story, 'the announcement of
the unexpected death of Doktor Lothar Müller in his sixtieth year of life'

(p. 223; OI, 933) prevents the meeting which might indeed have tied Müller 'before a mirror', the implication is that he died rather than confront his true face. Even poetic justice is justice of a kind.

By 1976, when Levi wrote his 'Afterword to *If This is a Man*', answering the questions most often asked by a new generation of readers, the acclaim which had greeted the publication of *The Periodic Table* the previous year had confirmed his status as a major twentieth-century writer. In the 'Afterword', out of which would grow over the following decade his last great book, *The Drowned and the Saved*, he asserts the primacy of his role as witness to atrocity, and makes it clear that what he requires of his readers is something very different from the imaginative involvement which writers of great literature usually demand:

> when describing the tragic world of Auschwitz, I have deliberately assumed the calm, sober language of the witness, neither the lamenting tones of the victim nor the irate voice of someone who seeks revenge … only in this way does a witness in matters of justice perform his task, which is that of preparing the ground for the judge. (*Voice of Memory*, p. 186; OI, 175)

The passage ends not, as in Ruth Feldman's otherwise meticulous translation, 'The judges are my readers' but '*you* are the judges' ('I giudici siete voi'). However, as he tells us in *The Periodic Table*, the imperatives which originally drove Levi to write were simpler and more visceral.

> The things I had seen and suffered were burning inside of me; I felt closer to the dead than the living, and felt guilty at being a man, because men had built Auschwitz, and Auschwitz had gulped down millions of human beings, and many of my friends, and a woman who was dear to my heart. It seemed to me that I would be purified if I told its story, and I felt like Coleridge's Ancient Mariner, who waylays on the street the wedding guests going to the feast, inflicting on them the story of his misfortune.
> (*The Periodic Table*, p. 151; OI, pp. 871–2)

Levi returns repeatedly to this image of himself as the Ancient Mariner, with whom, on his return to Italy in 1945, he shared a 'narrative impulse' which he himself described as 'pathological' (*Voice of Memory*, p. 129). In 1984, he incorporated into his poem 'The Survivor' ('Il superstite') the verse in which Coleridge's Mariner describes his inescapable urge to retell the story of his nightmare voyage:

> Since then, at an uncertain hour,
> My agony returns:
> And till my ghastly tale is told,
> This heart within me burns.[7]

although with the telling alteration (missing from Feldman's translation) that it is until the survivor finds a listener ('chi lo ascolti') (OII, 576, l. 4) that his heart burns in his breast. This analogy, in which Levi the survivor is trapped into an endless pattern of narrative re-enactment, is paired, though, with an equally strong identification with the episode in Homer's *Odyssey* in which the great voyager Odysseus, 'tired as he is . . . spends the night telling the story of his adventures' (quoted in *Voice of Memory*, p. 102). In *The Drowned and the Saved*, Levi combines this passage with a reference to *Inferno* Canto 5 to gloss the Yiddish saying, 'troubles overcome are good to tell':

> Francesca tells Dante that there is 'no greater sorrow / than to recall happy times / in misery', but the contrary is also true, as all those who have returned know: it is good to sit surrounded by warmth, before food and wine, and remind oneself and others of the fatigue, the cold and hunger. In this manner, Ulysses immediately yields to the urgent need to tell his story before the table laden with food, at the court of the king of the Phaeacians. (p. 121; OII, 1109)

The mention of Dante here is significant. The tale of shipwreck related by the Greek hero is the source material for the Ulysses canto which Levi tried to reconstruct from memory in the hell of the *Lager*. Dante's Ulisse drowns, but Homer's Odysseus escapes from 'Poseidon, god of the earthquake', whose destructive fury 'churned the waves into chaos' (Levi's 'maelstrom'), and reaches the island whose 'shadowy mountains',[8] transformed by Dante into a single mountain dusky with distance (*Inferno* 26, ll. 133–4), agonizingly reminded the captive Levi of his beloved Alps, seen 'against the dusk of evening' (*If This is a Man*, p. 133; OI, 110) on his homeward journey from Milan to Turin. At the Phaeacian court, Odysseus finds everything that Levi and his fellow prisoners lacked: kindly faces, food and wine, a warm bed, and above all (unlike Coleridge's Mariner, endlessly driven to force his 'ghastly tale' into the ears of reluctant strangers) an audience receptive to the heartfelt wish of all survivors and exiles:

> But as for myself, grant me a rapid convoy home
> to my own native land. How far away I've been
> from all my loved ones – how long I have suffered!
>
> (7, ll. 79–81)

Like Levi himself, Odysseus will have to undergo a long and circuitous journey before he finally reaches his home; and there is another similarity, too painful to recall, which must surely have subliminally influenced Levi's identification with this passage. Instead of immediately yielding 'to the urgent need to tell his story', Odysseus explains to his host that hunger exerts a stronger compulsion even than grief, preventing him from describing the hardships he has suffered until he has filled his belly, which 'Always insisting, pressing ... never lets us forget' (Bk 7, l.252). At the end of *The Truce* (*La tregua*, 1963) Levi describes how, on his return home, he brought the spectre of starvation with him:

> I found my friends full of life, the warmth of secure meals, the solidity of daily work, the liberating joy of recounting my story. But only after many months did I lose the habit of walking with my glance fixed to the ground, as if searching for something to eat or to pocket hastily or to sell for bread ... (p. 221; OI, 395)

As Levi shows in *The Drowned and the Saved*, his apparently obsessive 'narrative impulse', shared with all those survivors who chose not to deal with the trauma of the *Lager* by repression or silence, was itself a manifestation of a concern for justice. Such survivors 'speak because they know they are witnesses in a trial of planetary and epochal dimensions' (p. 121; OII, 1109). Simply by telling their story they counter the Nazi intention to turn the mass murder of the European Jews into a crime without a name. Levi quotes Simon Wiesenthal (who, after his own release from Mauthausen, dedicated the rest of a long life to hunting down the perpetrators of genocide) on how the SS used to taunt their victims:

> 'There will perhaps be suspicions, discussions, research by historians, but there will be no certainties, because we will destroy the evidence together with you. And even if some proof should remain and some of you survive, people will say that the events you describe are too monstrous to be believed ... We will be the ones to dictate the history of the *Lagers*.' (p. 1; OII, 997)

Presenting the evidence

Both Levi's compulsion to unburden himself of his own painful memories and the obligation to provide the bare but essential justice of remembrance for those whose deaths – whether from starvation, slave labour, brutality, disease and despair or through summary selection for the gas chamber – he had seen evidence of with his own eyes meant that *If This is a Man* had to be written as a first-hand account. However, Levi also needed to find ways of conveying the barely imaginable scale of the crime and the individual humanity of each of the victims, as he does, for instance, when he tells us (in one of the few episodes he added to the 1958 edition of the book) about 'three-year-old Emilia', 'daughter of Aldo Levi of Milan', whose parents managed to persuade the train driver to give them some warm water to bath her on the journey towards a death which no pity would avert, since 'the historical necessity of killing the children of Jews was self-demonstrative to the

Germans' (p. 12; OI, 14). Emilia's death is not simply a heart-rending incident; Levi's telling of it encompasses the deaths of all those loved children whose mothers had washed them in the detention camp at Fossoli on the eve of deportation, and through them the deaths of all the Jewish children of whatever nationality who died for the same barbaric reason.

To read Levi's book primarily as an autobiographical account, as if it were a more harrowing version of Anne Frank's diary, is to misread it. Levi's is not in that sense a personal voice. Though he remained all his life a reserved and private person, he told an interviewer in 1981, 'I don't recall ever having felt shame, modesty, a sense of exposure when writing *If This is a Man* or *The Truce*, perhaps because they weren't only my stories, they were everyone's' (*Voice of Memory*, pp. 151–2). In neither book does he focus on his own experience because it was his, but rather because it helps to explicate a context in terms of which his own survival was not an act of Providence – an idea which, in *The Drowned and the Saved*, he dismisses as a kind of blasphemy against the dead – but an anomaly, 'the work of chance, of an accumulation of fortunate circumstances' (p. 62; OII, 1054). Indeed, rather than seeing himself as 'a person touched by Grace', spared from death because he 'had to write, and by writing bear witness', Levi insists on the limitations of his testimony: 'we, the survivors, are not the true witnesses ... we are those who by their prevarications or abilities or good luck did not touch bottom. Those who did so, those who saw the Gorgon, have not returned to tell us about it or have returned mute ... They are the rule, we are the exception.' In telling his story, Levi is also attempting to overcome those limitations and find a way of speaking 'by proxy' for the 'drowned', those who 'even if they had paper and pen ... would not have testified' because 'weeks and months before being snuffed out, they had already lost the ability to observe, remember, compare and express themselves' (pp. 63–4; OII, 1055–6).

Levi often used to ascribe his own outstanding ability to do all those things to his training as a chemist. For him, 'chemistry wasn't only a profession, it was also ... the source of certain mental habits, above all that of clarity. A chemist who cannot express himself clearly is a bad chemist' (*Voice of Memory*, p. 102). The witness, like the scientist, has the task of presenting evidence for assessment, and both need to do so accurately and objectively. Levi attached a paramount importance to this kind of clarity, insisting in his essay 'On Obscure Writing' that 'he who is not understood by anyone does not transmit anything, he cries in the desert' (*Other People's Trades*, p. 159; OII, 678). To any reader inclined to argue that, for an Auschwitz survivor, crying in the desert might seem to be an appropriate way of expressing the inexpressible, he has a carefully reasoned reply:

For those who howl, provided they have valid reasons for doing so, one must have understanding: weeping and mourning, whether restrained or theatrical, are beneficial because they alleviate pain. Jacob howls over Joseph's bloodied coat; in many civilizations the howled mourning is ritual and prescribed. But the howl is an extreme recourse, good for the individual as tears, inert and uncouth if understood as a language ...   (p. 160; OII, 678)

Hence the spare lucidity with which Levi reports the manner of Emilia Levi's death and, lest anyone should imagine that this restraint means he has forgiven her killers, hence too the controlled anger with which, in *The Drowned and the Saved*, he counters the claim of his German correspondent 'Doctor T. H. of Hamburg' that the German people had simply been the innocent dupes of Hitler, telling him, 'I myself found in Katowitz, after the liberation, innumerable packages of forms by which the heads of German families were authorised to draw clothes and shoes for adults *and for children* from the Auschwitz warehouses; did no one ask himself where so many children's shoes were coming from?' (p. 148; OII, 1134).[9] Here, the presentation of a single piece of first-hand evidence, followed by the inescapable question which it raises, adds up to a devastating indictment of collective culpability.

Commanding a hearing

In order to present the evidence it is first necessary to have an audience, and in the immediate aftermath of the genocide this was not easy, as Levi discovered in an episode he describes in *The Truce*, in which he attempts to tell his story to a Polish lawyer a few weeks after the liberation of Auschwitz. 'I had a torrent of urgent things to tell the civilized world ... things which (it seemed to me) ought to shake every conscience to its very foundations' (p. 54; OI, 244–5); but his listener, translating into Polish for the bystanders, deliberately distorts Levi's words, describing him 'not as an Italian Jew, but as an Italian political prisoner'. When Levi, 'amazed and almost offended', asks him why, he replies, '*C'est mieux pour vous. La guerre n'est pas finie*' ('It is better for you. The war is not over'). He was right. As the historian Martin Gilbert relates, 'within seven months of the end of the war in Europe, and after a year in which no German soldier was on Polish soil, 350 Jews had been murdered in Poland'.[10]

Levi's written testimony began in the transit camp at Katowice, where he collaborated with his friend and fellow survivor Dr Leonardo De Benedetti in writing a report for the Russian authorities on medical conditions in the Buna-Monowitz camp. After his return to Italy, an expanded version of this report was published in an important medical journal, *Minerva Medica*, in

1946 (*Auschwitz Report*; OII, 1339–60) but Levi still found it hard to secure a publisher, let alone an audience, for the first version of *If This is a Man*. In 1947 there were few readers anywhere prepared to engage with the experiences of death camp survivors, and Italians were preoccupied by the need to unify and rebuild their country. The German occupation had provoked what was in effect a civil war, while the slow Allied advance which eventually liberated the peninsula, though longed for and welcomed by most, had itself been a humiliating invasion by foreign powers. Understandably, in the immediate post-war years, many Italians preferred to forget that some of their fellow citizens had been guilty of betraying Jews to the Germans or helping to round them up for deportation.

Given this reluctance, Levi could not imitate the Ancient Mariner, who 'holds' the Wedding-Guest 'with his glittering eye' so that 'He cannot choose but hear' (ll. 13–18). A book full of horrors would not have found readers. In any case, horror is seen as an aberration: the mind builds barriers against it. Jon Bridgman illustrates the truth of this in his study of the liberation of the camps, when he relates how attempts by Allied military commanders to confront the local populace with the reality of what had taken place, forcing 'German civilians in the vicinity of the camps to visit them and in some cases to help bury the dead',[11] bred indifference rather than remorse or pity. For those whose own lives had brought them into closer proximity to the horror, revulsion and fear could freeze all possibility of human understanding, as Levi's German correspondent Mrs Hety S. discovered when she tried to talk about her father's experiences as a political prisoner in Dachau to her ex-husband's second wife, 'a refugee from Eastern Prussia' haunted by the memory of being 'forced to go down the route by which the Auschwitz prisoners had been evacuated'. The unforgettable images of that road which 'ran between two hedges of dead bodies' left her unable to 'bear to read or listen to' accounts of the camps (*The Drowned and the Saved*, p. 161; OII, 1144).

Many survivors, too, felt that it was impossible to communicate what they had witnessed and undergone. Speaking to Alexander Stille in 1986, Franco Schönheit explained his own forty-year silence about Buchenwald:

> This science of organized extermination was unique. And because it was unique, it is untellable and unexplainable. Carrying a ninety-year-old woman on a train in order to kill her six hundred kilometres away, even though she is going to die on the trip anyway – this belongs to a dimension of the absurd ... How can you learn something from an experience of this kind?[12]

This example of what Levi calls 'useless violence' was made even more gratuitously cruel by the deliberate decision to provide neither drinking water nor sanitary facilities on the transports. Levi himself travelled to Auschwitz in the same truck as 'quite a few old people, men and women ... For everybody, but especially for them, evacuating in public was painful or even impossible: a trauma for which civilization does not prepare us, a deep wound inflicted on human dignity ...' (p. 88; OII, 1077). It would take forty years before Levi was able to write about that particular degradation.

In *If This is a Man* he solves the problem of reader reluctance by concentrating not on how prisoners died in the *Lager* but on how they were forced to live there. Writing almost as an anthropologist (an anthropologist of himself, like those 'historians of themselves' (*The Drowned and the Saved*, p. 2; OII, 998) who left their buried records in the rubble of the Warsaw ghetto), he details a nightmare world with which, none the less, we are able to identify because it is a parodic version of the world we know, one in which the prisoners organize a market and devise ingenious trades in order to supply themselves with the basic essentials they lack – spoons, needles and thread, anything that can be bartered for extra rations to enable them to live for one more day – although their only currency is a lump of grey bread. The society he describes resembles the one imagined for the sake of argument by the seventeenth-century political philosopher Thomas Hobbes, in which 'the life of man', besieged by 'continual fear, and danger of violent death', is inevitably 'solitary, poor, nasty, brutish, and short'[13] – although Hobbes himself could hardly have imagined a form of human life so brutish and so short that '*Morgen früh*' (tomorrow morning) would ironically come to signify 'never' (*If This is a Man*, p. 156; OI, 129). In such a society, as Hobbes tells us, both community and morality are impossible since survival depends on the struggle of all against all: 'To this war of every man against every man, this also is consequent; that nothing can be unjust. The notions of right and wrong, justice and injustice have there no place.'[14]

Hobbes's thesis is perfectly illustrated by the guard who snatches away the icicle with which Levi had hoped to relieve his intolerable thirst, replying to his timid question why with the words '"*Hier ist kein Warum*" (there is no why here)' (p. 24; OI, 23). As this example shows, Levi manages to convey a vivid sense of the grotesque and absurdly legalistic barbarities of Auschwitz through examples from which the reader cannot turn away on the pretext that they are too horrifying to read. Such characters as Doktor Ingenieur Pannwitz, who looks at Levi as if through 'the glass window of an aquarium between two beings who live in different worlds' (p. 123; OI, 102) while questioning him about his training and qualifications as a chemist, and Alex, the stupid and brutal Kapo, who 'without hatred and without sneering' (p. 125; OI, 103) wipes his greasy hand on Levi's shoulder as if on a piece of rag, serve to make immediate the nature of an offence which 'our language lacks words to express ... the demolition of a man' (p. 21; OI, 20).

Those prisoners, and 'their number is endless', who were unable to resist that demolition, crowd the book, as they do Levi's memory, 'with their faceless presences'. It is against this background of the 'anonymous mass, continually renewed and always identical, of non-men who march and labour in silence' (p. 103; OI, 86) that Levi shows us the Hobbesian and yet heroic struggle of the cunning and the violent against constant brutality and almost inevitable death. Exceptional among these combatants are the few prisoners who have somehow managed to retain their humanity – Schlome, whose 'serious and gentle face of a child' welcomes Levi 'on the threshold of the house of the dead' (p. 27; OI, 25); Steinlauf, the old soldier who lectures him on the need to wash, even 'without soap in dirty water', because preserving 'at least the skeleton ... of civilization' strengthens the will to resist (p. 39; OI, 35); Jean, the Pikolo, who listens to his urgent attempt to translate the Ulysses canto; Levi's friend Alberto, who lives 'unscathed and uncorrupted' in the *Lager* although 'he understood before any of us that this life is war' (p. 60; OI, 51); and, lest we should be tempted to believe in a Providence which spares the innocent even in Auschwitz, Kraus, the honest, clumsy boy on whom Levi takes pity, though out of an empty heart, and who will all too soon be reduced to the state of poor Null Achtzehn, known simply as Zero Eighteen, the final digits of his camp number, because 'only a man is worthy of a name, and ... Null Achtzehn is no longer a man' (p. 42; OI, 36). It is Levi's Dantean ability to invest these concisely drawn figures with paradigmatic meaning while maintaining our sense of their individual humanity which helps to give *If This is a Man* its tragic power. When he revised the book for publication by Einaudi in 1958, Levi built on this Dantean quality, introducing the passages portraying Emilia, Schlome and Steinlauf and adding to the description of Alberto, although significantly Kraus's story remained unchanged.

In his second book, *The Truce* (published in 1963, when he already had an international audience), Levi feels able to subject his readers to sudden glimpses of horror, all the more shocking for being set in the context of a picaresque narrative in which the hell of the *Lager* is succeeded by the limbo of a chaotic Russian 'Displaced Persons' camp. As we have seen, some of Levi's most searing testimony involves children; at the start of *The Truce* he shows us the end product of the Nazis' attempt to reduce their victims to the condition of animals in the depiction of a dying child so deprived that his very name is a meaningless sound, yet who nonetheless struggles indomitably to acquire human speech:

Hurbinek, who was three years old and perhaps had been born in Auschwitz and had never seen a tree; Hurbinek, who had fought like a man, to the last breath, to gain his entry into the world of men, from which a bestial power had

excluded him; Hurbinek, the nameless, whose tiny forearm – even his – bore the
tattoo of Auschwitz . . .   (*The Truce*, p. 23; OI, 216)

Later, in a flashback to the final days of the camp, Levi returns to the story
of the two Italian prisoners in the dysentery ward to whom, too exhausted
to feel the compassion he was enacting, he had taken water and soup. It
is only now, though, that he describes that 'kingdom of horror' in which
only 'the infectious breath of the fifty living patients' heats 'an enormous
cavern' full of 'corpses stiffened by the cold' (p. 71; OI, 261). And on the final
page of the book, Levi checks our instinctive response to what we assume
will be a happy ending of homecoming, leaving us instead with the description of a recurrent 'dream full of horror' in which the homecoming has itself
turned out to be a dream and the sleeper awaits with anguish 'the dawn
command of Auschwitz, a foreign word, feared and expected: get up,
"*Wstawać*"' (p. 222, emended; OI, 395). We are still inside Levi's nightmare
when the book ends.

'Our war is never over'

After the publication of *The Truce*, Levi claimed to have finished with the
subject of Auschwitz. 'I've said everything I had to say. It's all over' (*Voice of
Memory*, p. 81). He had temporarily forgotten the words of the wily Greek
merchant, Mordo Nahum: 'There is always war' ('guerra è sempre') (*The
Truce*, p. 51; OI, 242). Levi would return to Nahum's warning in his poem
'Partisan' ('Partigia'), written in 1981, in which he calls the old resistance
fighters of the German occupation to take part in a new struggle against age
and their divided selves:

> On your feet, old men, enemies of yourselves:
> Our war is never over.   (*Collected Poems*, p. 48; OII, 561)

Although he was not to publish his third great book about the Nazi genocide
until 1986, Levi never ceased to engage both halves of his own divided self in
the lifelong struggle to bear witness, refusing to cordon off the subject of
Auschwitz from his other concerns as a writer and scientist and repeatedly
returning to it in poems, essays, short stories, novels and his brilliant account
of his life as a chemist, *The Periodic Table*, as well as in public talks, school
visits and the many interviews which make him the best commentator on his
own writing.[15] The book known to English readers as *Moments of Reprieve*
is an example of this cross-fertilization. The Italian text from which it is
excerpted, *Lilít e altri racconti* ('Lilith and Other Stories', 1981), places
dystopic science-fiction and fables about the dangers of technology alongside

vivid memories of Levi's fellow prisoners, including the tragic story 'Lorenzo's Return', which demonstrates how insidiously the recollection of Auschwitz could colour the later lives of those who had experienced, or even witnessed, its horrors. Lorenzo, the 'civilian worker' whose gifts of food saved Levi and other Italian prisoners from starvation, did not undergo the suffering of the true survivors but he returned home a broken man and 'died from the survivors' disease' (*Moments of Reprieve*, p. 160; OII, 66).

By the 1980s, the subject of Auschwitz had taken on a new urgency as the rise of 'Holocaust denial' and 'revisionism', combined with the misleading stereotypes of films and popular fiction, led a new generation of young people to question the reality and relevance of the story Levi had to tell, or at best to see it in absurdly optimistic terms, like the little boy who solemnly offered him an escape plan to use 'if it should happen to you again' (*The Drowned and the Saved*, p. 128; OII, 1115). In *The Drowned and the Saved*, Levi attempts to combat the 'simple model' of history 'which we atavistically carry within us', and which made even 'newcomers to the *Lagers*' expect to find 'a terrible but decipherable world' (p. 23; OII, 1018), by concentrating on the 'grey zone'[16] of culpability which stretches from Muhsfeld, the sadistic SS man who briefly contemplated sparing a young girl taken alive from the gas chamber, to all the petty functionaries among the prisoners themselves who made use of their positions to survive a little longer than their fellows. In this most wide-ranging, and in some ways most despairing, of all his books, Levi also writes about the *Sonderkommandos* whose job it was

> to maintain order among the new arrivals (often completely unaware of the destiny awaiting them) who must be sent into the gas chambers; to extract the corpses from the chambers, pull gold teeth from jaws, cut the women's hair, sort and classify clothes, shoes, and the contents of the luggage; transport the bodies to the crematoria and oversee the operation of the ovens; extract and eliminate the ashes. (p. 34; OII, 1028)

The medical report Levi wrote in 1945–6 with Leonardo De Benedetti had judged these 'crematorium ravens' very harshly, although its authors can have had no contact with members of this 'carefully segregated' work squad: 'Their clothes gave off a sickening stench, they were always filthy and they had an utterly savage appearance, just like wild animals. They were picked from amongst the worst criminals, convicted of serious and bloody crimes' (*Auschwitz Report*, p. 45; OI, 1358). Levi now knew that, on the contrary, 'the Special Squads were largely made up of Jews', deliberately chosen by the SS for their horrific task because 'it must be the Jews who put the Jews into the ovens' (p. 35; OII, 1030), and he warns us that 'no one is authorized to judge' these 'miserable manual labourers of the slaughter' (p. 42; OII, 1035), quoting one of the very few among them who survived as saying, 'You mustn't think that we are monsters; we are the same as you, only much more unhappy' (p. 36; OII, 1031).

It is in this context that we can understand the shame felt even by those survivors who 'haven't dispossessed anyone, / Haven't usurped anyone's bread' ('The Survivor'; *Collected Poems*, p. 64; OII, 576). Levi unsparingly analyses the many forms this can take: the shame of being powerless and humiliated and unable to resist the oppressor; the shame of having adapted to the demands of a Hobbesian universe, losing all concern for any 'companion who is weaker, or less cunning, or older, or too young' (*The Drowned and the Saved*, p. 59; OII, 1051); the shame caused, after liberation, by 'the reacquired consciousness of having been diminished' and forced to live 'for months and years at an animal level' (p. 56; OII, 1048–9); the shame at the very fact of having lived when so many have died. However, standing out from these, and forming the fundamental motivation for all Levi's writing about Auschwitz, is a different kind of shame, which he first described in *The Truce* in a passage which he quotes at the start of *The Drowned and the Saved*: 'the shame which the just man experiences when confronted by a crime committed by another, and he feels remorse because of its existence, because of its having been irrevocably introduced into the world of existing things'.[17] This is the emotion felt by the four young Russian soldiers at their first sight of the starving prisoners in the abandoned Buna-Monowitz camp; by the prisoners themselves at the atrocities they have been forced to witness; by Cesare, the amiable trickster of *The Truce*, when he throws down his artfully plumped-up fish at the feet of the starving mother and her 'three pale children' and runs away 'like a thief' (p. 150–1; OI, 332–3). It is this shame which Levi wants to inculcate in his readers, since without it we cannot perform the crucial task he has laid on our shoulders.

NOTES

1. Liliana Picciotto Fargion, *Il libro della memoria: Gli ebrei deportati dall'Italia (1943–1945)*, Milan, Mursia, 2002.
2. Michael R. Marrus, *The Holocaust in History*, London, Penguin, 1989, p. 161.
3. John Cornwell, *Hitler's Scientists: Science, War and the Devil's Pact*, London, Penguin, 2004.
4. Ibid., pp. 374–5. I have slightly emended this passage.
5. 'Afterword to *If This is a Man*' (in all editions after 1976 and in *Voice of Memory*, p. 186; OI, 175).
6. See Carole Angier, *The Double Bond: Primo Levi, A Biography*, London, Viking, 2002, pp. 581–3.
7. Samuel Taylor Coleridge, *The Rime of the Ancient Mariner*, ll. 582–5. Levi's poem is in *Collected Poems*, p. 64; OII, 576.

8. Homer, *The Odyssey*, tr. Robert Fagles, London, Penguin, 1997, Bk 5, ll. 306–22.
9. Italicization slightly altered to conform with Levi's.
10. Martin Gilbert, *The Holocaust: The Jewish Tragedy*, Glasgow, Fontana/Collins, 1987, p. 816.
11. Jon Bridgman, *The End of the Holocaust: The Liberation of the Camps*, London, Batsford, 1990, p. 112.
12. Alexander Stille, *Benevolence and Betrayal: Five Italian Jewish Families Under Fascism* (London: Jonathan Cape, 1992), p. 347.
13. Thomas Hobbes, *Leviathan*, ed. J. C. A. Gaskin, Oxford, Oxford University Press, 1998, ch. XIII: 9, p. 84.
14. Ibid., ch. XIII: 13, p. 85.
15. Marco Belpoliti, the editor of Levi's collected works, has drawn up a table of nearly 100 different pieces of writing drawing on and developing *If This is a Man* (OI, 1414–16), as well as over 200 interviews (OI, cxvii–cxxvi).
16. This mistranslation of Levi's '*zona grigia*' (grey area) has become a key term in Holocaust studies.
17. *The Truce*, p. 12; *The Drowned and the Saved*, p. 54 (OI, 206; OII, 1047).

4

MARCO BELPOLITI AND ROBERT S. C. GORDON

Primo Levi's Holocaust vocabularies

One of the key problems of writing and thinking about what we now call the Holocaust has been that of finding apt working tools for representing and understanding, for forging a language in which to write about such a phenomenon. Back in Turin in late 1945 and 1946, only months after the liberation of Auschwitz in January 1945, as he wrote the stories that would make up *If This is a Man (Se questo è un uomo*, 1947), Primo Levi was already struck forcefully by the problems of language and representation which would so trouble generations of reflection on the Holocaust to come. There are at least three key moments in that book where Levi sets out these problems in stark relief:

> Then for the first time we became aware that our language lacks words to express this offence, the demolition of a man. (p. 21; OI, 20)

> We now invite the reader to contemplate the possible meaning in the *Lager* of the words 'good' and 'evil', 'just' and 'unjust'; let everybody judge, on the basis of the picture we have outlined and of the examples given above, how much of our ordinary moral world could survive on this side of the barbed wire. (p. 98; OI, 82)

> Just as our hunger is not the feeling of missing a meal, so our way of being cold has need of a new word. We say 'hunger', we say 'tiredness', 'fear', 'pain', we say 'winter' and they are different things. They are free words, created by free men who lived in comfort and suffering in their homes. If the *Lager*s had lasted longer, a new harsh language would have been born ... (p. 144; OI, 119–20)

These very phrases have become core entries in a commonplace (on occasion, clichéd) vocabulary for writing testimony about the Holocaust, in which the essence of the latter is expressed by its very ineffability: its 'saying the unsayable', 'writing the unwritable' and so on. As his writing about the Holocaust developed, in *If This is a Man* and beyond, Levi tackled the problem directly and indirectly in several different ways. First of all, he wrote with a keen sensitivity to the nature, breadth and limitations of all kinds of language and of 'semiosis'.[1] To give one highly pertinent example, he was well aware of the history, etymology and moral implications of using the vocabulary of testimony itself, variously noting and extending its juridical origins to position himself and us his readers in relation to the Holocaust; distancing himself from Graeco-Christian connotations of the witness as martyr; and suspending it and indeed all judgement when these are inadequate to the appalling moral complexities of the events he has to relate.[2]

Thus, far from stalling at hackneyed paradoxes of 'saying the unsayable', Levi developed in his written work (and also, from the 1960s onwards, through his extensive work as a speaker and interviewee) a series of flexible and interrelated vocabularies for probing and transmitting to others the reality and idea of genocide. The roots of these vocabularies lie, as much as in his eclectic personal interests and curiosities, or in a loosely defined worldview, in Levi's particular cultural and professional formation. They represent a mapping, conscious or otherwise, of his rationalist mindset, rooted in the values of the European Enlightenment, with its belief in the 'encyclopedic' capacity for analysing and knowing the universe, onto the dark, thorny and personally devastating subject-matter of what he saw in Auschwitz.[3] Set in the wider context of the Holocaust 'memory culture', they amount to a rich field of alternative approaches to what have since become the settled idioms for representing and commemorating what Levi simply called 'the offence' (*If This is a Man*, p. 21; OI, 20).

This chapter looks at three examples of these working vocabularies or methodologies for thinking about the Holocaust embedded in Levi's work: first, an ethological or anthropological vocabulary which allowed Levi to read the 'behavioural patterns' or 'cultures' of the camp system; secondly, an aspect of Levi's scientific vocabulary, through which he read the camps as a manifestation of a particular pattern of asymmetry found in molecular analysis; and, finally, an ethical (and, to a degree, political) vocabulary, through which he read the camps as source for a set of fundamental questions about how to live, both as an individual and as a community.

Animal sciences

Animals are one of the most interesting and all-pervading presences in Levi, often appearing at climactic or clinching moments, in his writing about Auschwitz and indeed in all his other works. They are present as metaphors, models and myths – in other words as language – but also as real presences, vivid objects of observation and interest, tools for understanding behaviour. A bald classification of the animals creatively and literally evoked by Levi would include (in no particular order): dogs, horses, spiders, butterflies, fleas, crickets, beetles, seagulls, ants, moles, mice, snails, oxen, flies, camels, crows, cats, rabbits, hens, chickens, snakes and many others besides.[4] And this would be to exclude Levi's telling curiosity for the category of fictional, mythical or invented animals, and what their 'creation' tells us about our Creation, our origins, scientific and religious: for example, in the story 'The Servant' (*The Sixth Day*; 'Il servo', *Vizio di forma*, 1971), which retells the legend of the golem, a Frankenstein-like tale of a living, man-made creature; or in one of the most engaging essays of *Other People's Trades* (*L'altrui mestiere*, 1985) called 'Inventing an Animal' ('Inventare un animale'), where he muses on how difficult it would be, in practice, to invent an animal that might actually survive. And crucially, in 'Novels Dictated by Crickets' ('Romanzi dettati dai grilli'), Levi draws on his fascination for the work of Aldous Huxley to explain how the observation of animals (cats, crickets, spiders) is a key resource for the novelist or student of human behaviour.[5] This mass of different, strange animals, this bestiary, also functions as one of Levi's primary tools for probing the Holocaust.

First (and most conventionally, perhaps), Levi, like many others, describes the dehumanizing effect of Nazi treatment of Jewish prisoners as one of 'bestialization'. This stands literally first of all; for example, in the use in Auschwitz and elsewhere of Zyklon B gas as a poisoning agent for mass murder, since Zyklon B was originally manufactured as an insecticide. But, of course, the term 'bestialization' stands for more than this grim association and ironic essence of Nazi racist ideology. It or its cognates occur in at least two framing moments of fundamental importance in *If This is a Man*. First, the Austrian prisoner Steinlauf imparts a lesson of great power (although Levi is not without his reservations):

> precisely because the *Lager* was a great machine to reduce us to beasts, we must not become beasts ... even in this place one can survive, and therefore one must want to survive, to tell the story, to bear witness   (p. 39; OI, 35)

Secondly, in January 1945, as Levi and a few sick companions are abandoned by the SS embarking on the final death marches back to German territory, the interlude before liberation by the Soviet army is of such squalor that Levi comments:

> We lay in a world of death and phantoms. The last trace of civilization had vanished around and inside us. The work of bestial degradation, begun by the victorious Germans, had been carried to its conclusion by the Germans in defeat.   (p. 204; OI, 166)

These framing moments establish the category of the 'bestial' as the prime referent for the non- or better sub-human residue envisaged by the title *If This is a Man*. Here, the animal stands in by analogy for all the terrible anti-social, inhuman indignities foisted upon the prisoners – nakedness, lack of private space, loss of name, loss of language and identity, the brutal primacy of hunger and the struggle for survival.

In a sense, however, for all its rhetorical power, this use of the category of the bestial is the most unelaborated of Levi's forays into zoology: elsewhere Levi uses animals ethologically, that is, as a means to understanding complex behavioural mechanisms which can be mapped onto both prisoners and guards (and the many 'grey' levels in between) in the extreme, altered reality of the camps.[6] To take one example, dogs appear frequently in *If This is Man*: indeed, they are the most common animals of all in Levi's work.[7] The very first sound Levi hears on arrival in Auschwitz is the 'curt, barbaric barking of Germans in command which seems to give vent to a millennial anger' (p. 10; OI, 13). Later, in a powerful passage of *The Drowned and the Saved* (*I sommersi e i salvati*, 1986), he uses the biblical image of Gideon, who chooses his soldiers – that is, the virtuous, strong and dignified – by observing them drink at the river: those who lap at the water as dogs lap are not worthy to be chosen (pp. 91; OII, 1080–1).

The full 'ethological' importance of dogs for Levi becomes clear in retrospect, however, if we look at a 1987 essay on an Italian translation, by novelist Gianni Celati, of Jack London's dog-centred novel *The Call of the Wild* (OII, 1317–20).[8] Levi reviews the work, the story of Buck's ferocious struggle for survival in the snow, as an extended reprise of his concentration-camp experience (and of that of the Gulag): Buck suffers 'deportation' in 'an interminable journey by train', he is 'tamed: he learns that a man with a cudgel is invincible', 'he learns that he must adjust (*adattarsi*), learn new and terrible things, that he must distrust everyone ... to dig himself a hole in the snow ... to endure the arctic freeze'. All is hunger, exhaustion and whippings. And if the half-hidden reprise of the experience and even the exact vocabulary of *If This is a Man* were not clear enough already, Levi first draws a comparison with Solzhenitsyn's Ivan Denisovich; and then, when Levi describes Buck's rebellion against Spitz, his fight to become the leader of the pack of dogs himself, the link becomes still more explicit: Buck, Levi writes, is now 'un capo (un Kapo?)'. As Levi says, London writes here both as survivor of his own harsh struggles in the Alaskan gold rush and as 'ethologist ahead of his time', probing canine behaviour and psychology with an extraordinary, modern intuition which echoes and illuminates the complexity of Levi's ethological descriptions of his own and his fellows' animal-like behaviour in Auschwitz.

The figure of the dog is just one example of the many animals populating Levi's writing. Through the range of his use of them, there emerges a taxonomy of contrasting animal types and behaviour in his work, a taxonomy which works within the concentration-camp setting not only by analogy but also by actual behavioural affinity. For example, there are individualistic versus social animals, throwing into relief the core question of cooperation and survival in the camps: in the 1980 poem 'Dark Band' ('Schiera bruna'; *Collected Poems*, p. 43; OII, 557), for example, ants are images both of cooperation but also of creatures blindly heading for death, recalling the *Lager*; whereas butterflies are images of freedom and beauty corrupted by imprisonment (such as in the story 'Angelic Butterfly' (*The Sixth Day*; 'Angelica farfalla', *Storie naturali*, 1966)). Then there are animals of open spaces versus animals who prefer dark, enclosed spaces; visible versus invisible (i.e. microscopic and smaller) animals; and also the more loaded contrast of positive versus negative animals. Each pattern or type offers precious knowledge about and images for how to survive and adapt in given situations, environments and communities.

Behind all this imagery and often meticulous observation lies a larger analogy, or affinity (if not identity) between animals and mankind. Man is, of course, an animal, sharing many characteristics with many other species, but also with many specificities or unique zoological attributes of its own. Levi is interested in the porous borders and exchanges between the animal and the human, thereby defining what is human ('if this is a man') and posing profound metaphysical questions as a result. He is interested, in other words, in a hybrid creature he calls the 'man-animal' ('l'animale-uomo').

The hybrid term 'man-animal' is used first by Levi in one of the key passages in *If This is a Man*, at the start of a chapter called 'The Drowned and the Saved' ('I sommersi e i salvati'), where he declares that the camps were, among other things, 'a giant biological and social experiment'. The set-up of the experiment is described as follows:

> Thousands of individuals, differing in age, condition, origin, language, culture and customs, are enclosed within barbed wire; there they live together a regular, controlled life which is identical for all and inadequate to all needs, and which is much more rigorous than any experimenter could have set up to establish what is essential and what adventitious to the conduct of the human animal [*animale-uomo*] in the struggle for life   (pp. 99–100; OI, 83)

In this overarching light, we can return to Levi's use of animal vocabulary and see it (ironically) as an extension of this perverse experiment, but using his own data and adapting it to his own behavioural study. Here, in a powerful passage echoed directly in the essay on Jack London discussed above, he uses animal vocabulary to interrogate the physiological-psychological workings of human instinct.

> Man's capacity to dig himself in, to secrete a shell, to build around himself a tenuous barrier of defence, even in apparently desperate circumstances, is astonishing and merits a serious study. It is based on an invaluable activity of adaptation, partly passive and unconscious and partly active: of hammering in a nail above his bunk from which to hang up his shoes; of concluding tacit pacts of non-aggression with neighbours; of understanding and accepting the customs and laws of a single Kommando, a single Block. By virtue of this work, one manages to gain a certain equilibrium after a few weeks, a certain degree of security in face of the unforeseen; one has made oneself a nest ... (pp. 59–60; OI, 50)

Several different vocabularies converge in a passage like this, in a way which is typical in Levi (perhaps a sign of the freedom of a relatively inexpert, non-abstract – and young – thinker): zoology, ethology and psychology coexist with a further crucial framework for interpreting Levi's 'man-animal', that of anthropology. The human and humanizing rituals of public and private spaces and communities – here, the marking of intimacy through images and objects, the alignment with the rules and regulations of the local 'culture' – are constant objects of Levi's interest. In fact, his later interests in anthropology were concrete: as well as translating major works of anthropology by leading figures in the field Mary Douglas and Claude Lévi-Strauss, Levi also developed this line of thinking in a number of important later stories set in and around tribes, isolated communities and remote geographical settings, with their tellingly distinct cultures and practices; for example 'Westwards' ('Verso Occidente') and the two 'Recuenco' stories in *Vizio di forma* (and *The Sixth Day*). *The Wrench* (*La chiave a stella*, 1978) also has a strong anthropological element in its treatment of work and Faussone's encounters with different cultural practices. Many of the defining themes of Levi's Holocaust work are replayed and reworked in this anthropological key in these later writings.

Most striking of all, perhaps, the whole passage above and much of Levi's understanding of the processes and experiences of the concentration camps is underpinned by an evolutionary or Darwinist vocabulary of adaptation.[9] Levi's entire focus in *If This is a Man* could be described as centring on survival of the fittest, *not* in the sense of the most strong, but in the correct Darwinian sense of the most fit, the best adapted to the environment. The key chapter of the book, in this respect as in many others, is 'The Drowned and the Saved', which is taken up with a (partly ironic, partly pseudo-Darwinian) typology of adaptation – those who are likely to survive and those who are not in this very strange, inverted environment of Auschwitz. The 'man-animals' that he describes there, the specimens of the 'drowned' and the 'saved', take us back to the hybridity of Levi's animals and to his interest in the inventing or creating of living creatures noted above. Who could invent such creatures as would survive or even flourish in this place, the book implicitly asks; and at another powerful moment of climax it answers in a way that recovers and inverts the mythical power of Creation by figuring the Nazi project as a sort of anti-Genesis:

> To destroy a man is difficult, almost as difficult as to create one: it has not been easy, it has not been quick, but you Germans have succeeded. Here we are, docile under your gaze; from our side you have nothing more to fear; no acts of violence, no words of defiance, not even a look of judgement. (p. 177; OI, 146)

Visual symmetries and asymmetries

Much has been written, by Levi himself and by others, about the direct impact of his chemistry, his work career as a chemist and his scientific formation in general on his testimonial work (see Part III below). The purest example we have of this is the very first piece of writing about the camps Levi ever published, a co-authored technical report written with fellow survivor (and doctor) Leonardo De Benedetti for a medical journal in 1946: 'On the Sanitary and Medical Organization of the Monowitz Concentration Camp for Jews (Auschwitz, Upper Silesia)' (*Auschwitz Report*; OI, 1339–60). In many respects, Levi's use of science constitutes a prime and highly self-conscious instance of precisely what we are investigating here, the adaptation of distinct secondary vocabularies to serve as tools for representing and interpreting the Holocaust. Instead of revisiting standard accounts of Levi's views on the language of science and his own testimony, however, this section will focus on a less declared, but nevertheless persistent, interest of Levi the scientist in a certain molecular patterning and its traces in his representations and analyses of Auschwitz.

In 1941, Levi completed his university degree with a research dissertation, as was the norm in Italian universities. Because of the Racial Laws, however, he was not able to submit an experimental piece of work in chemistry as he had hoped and had to rush to complete instead a theoretical thesis on so-called 'Walden Inversions', that is, the turning inside-out of certain molecules – or 'chirality' – in certain chemical reactions. The theme and the heuristic power of inversion, which attracted his interest as a student, would stay with Levi well beyond his university days. We see it, for example, at several points in the technical aspects of *The Wrench*, in stories concerning both engineering and chemistry. And in 1984, Levi returned to the topic in a fascinating essay for a popular science magazine, *Prometeo*, where he pushed the significance of molecular inversion well beyond the chemical into something approaching metaphysics. The essay is called 'Asymmetry and Life' ('L'asimmetria e la vita').[10] In it, Levi notes with some awe that the 'major players in the living world, such as proteins, cellulose, sugars and DNA, are all asymmetrical. Right-left asymmetry is intrinsic to life, and indeed it coincides with life. It is invariably present in all organisms from viruses to lichen to oaktrees, fish and man' (*The Black Hole of Auschwitz*, p. 143; OII, 1232). Ranging wide over the possible reasons for and implications of this remarkable pervasive bond between asymmetry and organic life, Levi ends by positing a pattern of chiral asymmetry to the entire universe; a pattern in which the universe of matter is mirrored by an identical but inverted 'realm of anti-matter' which, like our left and right hands, cannot be mapped onto each other except through rotation in higher dimensions. They are mirror images, or, as the technical term has it, 'enantiomorphic'.[11]

Looking back from the elegant exposition of 'Asymmetry and Life', we can hypothesize that significant elements of Levi's account of Auschwitz, and the implicit world-view that shapes his account of it, tap into this fascination for patterns of inversion, asymmetry and near-symmetry, mapping and mirroring. We can touch on four levels at which such patterns are operating in his testimonial work.

First and foremost, we can see them in his general conception of the world of the concentration camp – the so-called *'univers concentrationnaire'*, a phrase coined by the French writer-survivor David Rousset and used regularly by Levi – as a combination of extreme rationality – the brutal efficiency and demonic patterns of complicity in the Nazi administration of the camps – and extreme unreason, what he calls in *The Drowned and the Saved* the 'uselessness' or redundancy, even absurdity at the heart of Nazi violence (pp. 83–102; OII, 1073–90). Similarly, a pairing of closely similar but inverted human types recurs throughout Levi's testimony: from his own alter egos such as Alberto in *If This is a Man* or Cesare in *The Truce* (*La tregua*, 1963), who are both like him and opposite to him; to the general and defining categories of 'the drowned' and 'the saved', as we saw in the previous section. At the most general of levels, Auschwitz is for Levi an inverted world, a mirror of the civilized world or of human nature; both in the sense of showing the latter for what it is at its essence, and in the sense of its being turned against itself, literally inverted.

In a distinct, but closely related, metaphor, Levi famously linked his science-fiction stories about the risks of modern technological invention to his testimony, by describing both as 'vizi di forma', 'formal defects' that transform or invert the intended function or effect of a mechanism. A key story in this regard, because it addresses the physical and moral issue of pain – central both to the Holocaust and to all philosophies of happiness at least since Aristotle (and ethics; see below) – would be 'Versamina' (*The Sixth Day*; from *Storie naturali*), in which Levi imagines the dramatic and fearful effects of a chemical substance (with an asymmetrical molecular structure, of course) which converts pain into pleasure. The story ends with perhaps the most famous of literary inversions, evoking moral and political collapse and perverse disorder: 'Fair is foul and foul is fair / Hover through the fog and filthy air' (p. 54; OI, 476; from *Macbeth*, I, i, 10–11).

Resonances of patterns of asymmetry and inversion – and the necessity of both as a priori conditions for the very existence of life – are also traceable in a famous and fundamental declaration in *The Periodic Table* of Levi's faith in diversity, in impurity, in the infinitesimal difference contained within the apparently identical which is capable of transforming or inverting predicted reality, with vital results:

> In order for the wheel to turn, for life to be lived, impurities are needed, and the impurities of impurities, in the soil too, as is known, if it is to be fertile. Dissension, diversity, the grain of salt and mustard are needed: Fascism does not want them, forbids them, and that's why you're not a Fascist; it wants everybody to be the same and you are not.   (p. 34; OI, 768)

Asymmetry here is the necessary (even if unstable) element of disorder, the irregularity that allows for life, just as Darwinian evolution (another of Levi's core models for understanding the world as we saw above) works by the slight flaws in genetic reproduction which allow for adaptational selection. In *Other People's Trades*, Levi underlines this reliance of ours on chaos: 'life is rule, it is order prevailing over Chaos, but the rule has crevices, unexplored pockets of exception, license, indulgence, and disorder … perhaps they contain the germ of all our tomorrows' (p. 213; OII, 798).

In purely heuristic terms, asymmetry and near identity also resonate with Levi's interest in modelling, mapping or other visual schematizations of the world: his work makes extensive use of maps, diagrams and the like, each with their own scale and perspective, as ways of opening up new understanding of systems and human actions, in his writings on Auschwitz and elsewhere. These pick up on the visually transformative power of modelling such as the rotation of models in molecular chemistry, to show how these can both simplify, at times distort, but also clarify and explain. Thus, the closely similar maps which preface both *The Truce* and *If Not Now, When?* (*Se non ora, quando?*, 1982) represent in neat visual synthesis the chaos, confusion and fluidity of Eastern Europe in the final months of the war and the first post-war period. Levi also insisted on including a map of concentration camps in the 1973 Einaudi schools edition of *If This is a Man*, which he edited himself.[12] Geography reflects a moment of historical dissolution here, but also, for Levi, one of renewed vitality. By contrast, Levi tells the story in *The Drowned and the Saved* (pp. 127–9; OII, 1115–16) of the boy who listened carefully to his account of his camp experiences given at a school, only for the boy to get up and draw a map on the classroom blackboard of how he should have planned his getaway. Here the map represents a travesty of reality, a category error in which the camp reality has been transformed into a scene for a Hollywood-style 'Great Escape'. Mapping is a form of stereotyping, which has its uses but also its risks of over-simplification: in a similar vein, Levi broadly defended the usefulness of the 1978–9 television mini-series *Holocaust* against its detractors.[13] Finally, mapping is also a form of narrative, perhaps especially narratives of war and survival: he was fond of quoting a phrase from the Latin poet Tibullus, '*at mihi potanti possit sua dicere facta miles et in mensa pingere castra mero*' ('so that he can tell me his war exploits, as I am drinking, and draw the encampments on the table in wine') (*Voice of Memory*, p. 129).

One final example underlines how deeply embedded in Levi's mindset this attention to inversions, transformations and shifts of perspective came to be. Half way through compiling *The Search for Roots* (*La ricerca delle radici*, 1981), his anthology of favourite and formative books, Levi catches himself by surprise (as he tells us in one of the prefaces to each extract):

> I am beginning to realize that in these pages there are many examples of worlds turned upside down. I swear that this was not premeditated; it is a result I had not foreseen. Nevertheless, painters know well that in looking at a painting upside down one can see virtues and defects that were not at first observed. (p. 172, adapted to reflect the original; OII, 1491)

Levi subconsciously adapts his fascination for asymmetry into a form of optics, a way of seeing and understanding the ordinary world, especially in relation to the inverted, extraordinary world of Auschwitz.

Ethics

The dynamic (and heuristic) relationship between the ordinary world and common humanity, on the one hand, and the exceptional 'universe' of the concentration camp, on the other, also lies at the heart of the third vocabulary that we will discuss here: the vocabulary of ethics and, by extension also, political philosophy.[14] Through his encounter with Auschwitz, and through the reflections upon it embodied in his careful writing of testimony, fiction, poetry and essays, Levi tests out certain ideas, assumptions, commonsense values and practices which determine a certain way of living in the world. These are ethical, insofar as they address generalizable questions of 'how to act', in oneself and with others, or 'how to live'; they are political insofar as they address the implications of such choices and actions for a group or community or a conception of society. Without ever being a philosopher as such – indeed, his mindset as an applied scientist, as a pragmatist (and, many would add, as a Piedmontese) militated strongly against the abstractions of philosophical argumentation – Levi managed to stage in his writing a series of profoundly insightful ethical and political dilemmas thrown up by his personal history, rooted in Auschwitz; and also to move deftly between the particularity of his extreme experiences and the shared realities of everyday lives and communities. The substance of his responses, the acuity of his portraits of human action in extreme conditions and the flexible, enquiring language in which he wrote about all this allowed him to transform our understanding of Auschwitz through applying his toolbox of ethical and political values; and vice versa.

Levi's ethical interrogations of Auschwitz do not emerge in anything like the loud, moralizing, even preaching voice which often characterizes talk about 'lessons' to be learned from history or the 'duty to remember' (although Levi powerfully felt the memorial dimension of his work as means of combatting what he called in *The Drowned and the Saved* 'The Third Reich['s] ... war against memory' (p. 18; OII, 1013)). Instead, his enquiry works through meticulous undertones, and careful reasoning and distinction: much of what he writes takes the form of attempts at problem-solving, even when treating the imponderable, insoluble 'problem' of the Final Solution. His ethics are first of all to be found in the very intelligent, pragmatic flexibility and observational responsiveness of this process, a form of essayistic probing which aligns him with the exploratory enquiries found in Montaigne, or even Pascal. In this sense, his metaethics – his exploration of how we make and state ethical judgements – precede and condition his core ethics – his values as such. They make for a set of values which are as much describable through character traits – 'what we should be like' prior to 'what we should do' – as through abstract, absolute principles or morality (just as he was sceptical of the notion of 'radical evil', drawn from Kant, as a means of explaining Nazi atrocities).

To illustrate the point, we can pick up on a topic touched upon earlier, in the discussion of Levi's interest in inversion: the topic of pain (and close cognates such as suffering, cruelty, violence). Any work seriously engaged with the Holocaust must confront the question of violence and cruelty, of course; what is distinctive in Levi is the persistent and ethically alert probing and complicating of the question, going on both openly in *If This is a Man* and *The Drowned and the Saved* and other directly testimonial texts, but also in a sustained series of essays and stories of apparently quite different natures.

Pain in Levi's moral universe is a physiological reality, the product of a materialist world-view imposed by the sheer physical suffering of the camps; but it is nonetheless ethically weighted for that and nonetheless a producer of knowledge (just as it is for one of Levi's 'hidden' influences, the Italian Romantic poet Leopardi). Several of the founding moments of ethical reflection in *If This is a Man* are rooted in the new discovery of physical pain and violence, with various motivations and limitations. For example, the very first blows received from indifferent camp guards (in Italy, as they are herded into the deportation trucks) leave Levi and his fellows not just pained but also perplexed: 'how can one hit a man without anger?' (p. 7; OI, 11). This is the first in a long series of questions that pepper the opening pages of the book and mark Levi's sudden entry into a world of a new, inverted ethical order, where solidarity between fellow human beings has been excised and pain and cruelty are so normal as to be close to meaningless. This prompts a further, qualifying reflection in Levi – one of his most acute and resonant ethical reflections – that the accumulation of pain produces *not* ever more pain, but rather a new mean state; there is, in other words, no such thing as pure suffering:

> Sooner or later in life, everyone discovers that perfect happiness is unrealizable, but there are few who pause to consider the antithesis: that perfect unhappiness is equally unattainable. The obstacles preventing the realizations of both these extreme states are of the same nature: they derive from our human condition which is opposed to everything infinite. Our ever-insufficient knowledge of the future opposes it: and this is called, in the one instance, hope, and in the other, uncertainty of the following day. The certainty of death opposes it: for it places a limit on every joy, but also on every grief. The inevitable material cares oppose it: for as they poison every lasting happiness they equally assiduously distract us from our misfortunes and make our consciousness of them intermittent and hence supportable.
>
> It was the very discomfort, the blows, the cold, the thirst that kept us aloft in the void of bottomless despair, both during the journey and after. It was not the will to live, nor a conscious resignation; for few are the men capable of such resolution, and we were but a common sample of humanity.   (p. 8; OI, 11)

Later stories pick up on and develop the core ethical role played by pain. These include 'Versamina', mentioned earlier, in which pain is converted into pleasure by chemical alteration, a process which throws into crisis individual (and animal – the story is also a story of animal experimentation) identity, social interaction and all sense of value. The centrality of pain is also underlined in a strange story from *Lilít e altri racconti* (1981) called 'Un testamento' ('A Testament'; OII, 145–8; not in *Moments of Reprieve*), which is a mock will written by a dentist, in which he passes on the core of all he has learned – his philosophy – to his son and heir. He describes his profession as unique not only in alleviating pain, but also 'in penetrating its value, its vices and virtues' (OII, 145).[15] Indeed, only dentists know that pain is the most reliable, the most certain of all the data of the senses: more than Descartes's 'I think, therefore I am', he says, the philosophy of first principle should be 'I suffer, therefore I am' (OII, 147). Dentists are the ministers of pain and of the philosophy of pain they embody.

In a parallel essay in *Other People's Trades*, entitled 'Against Pain' ('Contro il dolore'), Levi reflects further on the pain mankind inflicts on others, especially animals, and the ethical reasons for not doing so. He positions himself carefully, against theological reasoning, against any hierarchy of purpose or moral value (all of which echo implicitly the racial ideology of the Nazis). Instead, respect of the other – a founding position in any ethics – is rooted in a simple imperative, 'not to create pain / suffering [*dolore*]' (unless it will alleviate an even greater pain). He quotes Leopardi – 'Arcano è tutto / fuor che il nostro dolor' ('All is mystery / apart from our pain') – and again proposes pain as the only core certainty on which to build a morality. Taking a further step, he derives from this an even balder foundational principle for his anti-solipsistic altruism, from which all the rest derives: '"other people" exist' ('gli "altri" esistono'). It is this racial principle that Nazism denied, and also this principle that the organization of the camps was designed to occlude in its victims (and its perpetrators).

This line of ethical enquiry into suffering and violence, as well as a large number of parallel lines of ethical investigation, are, finally, posited in a way that also allows them to be read also as elements of a political philosophy. Principles of community, society, the rule of law and the rights of the individual are implicitly working at or near the surface of Levi's texts, derived from and played out through similar core principles as those in the sphere of ethics. Frederic Homer has argued that Levi's works contain an 'incipient philosophy in terms that make it a comprehensive, viable alternative to other modern works of political philosophy'.[16] Homer goes on to consider Levi's understanding of power and force – a political elaboration of the ethical enquiry into violence we saw above – through a reading of the story '*Force majeure*' (*The Mirror Maker*; 'Forza maggiore', *Racconti e saggi*, 1986), in which the protagonist 'M.' is beaten without rhyme or reason in an alley. The story acts a compressed allegory of the 'useless' violence of the *Lager* and the capacity for response to humiliation and social exclusion encountered by the victims of the camps. Homer goes on to draw out the tenets of Levi's 'civilized liberalism', a form of response to the assumption – found most famously in the philosophy of Hobbes – that violence lies beneath the surface of all human society.

All the vocabularies described here – the zoological-anthropological, the 'enantiomorphic', the ethical – are developed by Levi, through the practice of writing and telling stories as ways to capture human identity, action and interaction, both in his testimonial and fictional work. Several other characteristic features of his work – his science and science-fiction, his interests in language, his use of literature and intertextual play, and so on – could be described in analogous ways, as so many vocabularies for working through a response to Auschwitz. They are all vocabularies which stretch the limits of what a narrow conception of testimony might permit. None of them is complete in itself and none is conceptually rigorous. Nevertheless, they go some way towards explaining why Levi's writing on Auschwitz contributes with such striking power, subtlety and illumination.

NOTES

1. On Levi's multi-faceted interest in language, see chapters 8–10 in this volume.
2. See Robert S. C. Gordon, *Primo Levi's Ordinary Virtues. From Testimony to Ethics*, Oxford, Oxford University Press, 2001, pp. 1–12.
3. On Levi's 'encyclopedic' qualities, which he shared with his contemporary Italo Calvino, see Marco Belpoliti, *Primo Levi*, Milan, Bruno Mondadori, 1998, p. 74.
4. See Marco Belpoliti, 'Animali' in Belpoliti (ed.), *Primo Levi* (Riga 13), Milan, Marcos y Marcos, 1997, pp. 157–209.
5. See also *Voice of Memory*, pp. 139–40.
6. Levi was fascinated by the work of one of the founders of ethology, Konrad Lorenz (despite the latter's relations with the Nazi regime). See, for example, Levi's comments in 'Racial Intolerance' (*The Black Hole of Auschwitz*, pp. 110–14; OI, 1299–1303).
7. See the fascinating lexical analysis of Levi's major works in Jane Nystedt, *Le opere di Primo Levi viste al computer. Osservazioni stilolinguistiche*, Stockholm, Acta Universitatis Stockholmiensis / Almquist and Wiskell, 1993. And cf. Belpoliti, 'Animali', pp. 166–9.
8. The piece was not included in *Other People's Trades*, but was instead added to the 'Essays' section of *The Mirror Maker*, with the title 'Jack London's Buck'. Levi had already compared Buck's Klondike to the *Lager* in *The Periodic Table* (*Il sistema periodico*, 1975; p. 140; OI, 861).
9. On Levi and Darwin, see Belpoliti, *Primo Levi*, Milan, Bruno Mondadori, 1998, pp. 64–5; Antonello, chapter 6 in this volume.
10. *The Black Hole of Auschwitz*, pp. 142–50; OII, 1231–41. On this theme in Levi see Alberto Cavaglion, 'Asimmetrie', in Belpoliti (ed.), *Primo Levi*, pp. 222–9.
11. Mirroring and doubling are recurrent motifs of Levi's science-fiction: see, for example, the title story of *The Mirror Maker*.

12. See also the mock map of 'Desolation Island' in 'Mercury' (*The Periodic Table*, p. 97; OI, 823); and, by extension, other forms of visual representations such as chemical molecular diagrams as used in 'Asymmetry and Life', *The Wrench* (p. 143; OII, 1078) and elsewhere.
13. See, for example, 'No Return to the Holocausts of the Past' and 'Images of Holocaust' in *The Black Hole of Auschwitz*, pp. 56–65; OI, 1268–80.
14. See Gordon, *Primo Levi's Ordinary Virtues*, passim.
15. Here and below, translations by Robert Gordon.
16. Frederic D. Homer, *Primo Levi and the Politics of Survival*, Columbia, University of Missouri Press, 2001, p. 5.

5

BRYAN CHEYETTE

Appropriating Primo Levi

Although Primo Levi is now firmly established as one of the essential voices of 'The Age of Camps', in Zygmunt Bauman's grim description of the twentieth century,[1] his canonization is a relatively recent occurrence. Levi did not acquire a mass readership, outside of Italy, until the mid-1980s. In early specialist studies of Holocaust literature, he was universalized as one among many who 'speaks a common truth, one known to all writers of the Holocaust'.[2] It was only after the 1984 translation of *The Periodic Table* (*Il sistema periodico*, 1975) in the United States that he was transformed into a global figure and gained a large international readership. This transformation contrasts starkly with Levi's own unease in *The Drowned and the Saved* (*I sommersi e i salvati*, 1986) about the stereotypical representations of the Holocaust which had increasingly appropriated his life and work. In fact, Levi was a particularly unenthusiastic employer of the term 'Holocaust': 'I use this term "Holocaust" reluctantly because I do not like it. But I use it to be understood. Philologically, it is a mistake.'[3] As his biographers have noted, he was also especially uncomfortable at being categorized principally as a 'Jewish writer' in the United States: ' "They put a label on me", he stated in one public lecture, "I don't like labels. Germans do." '[4]

As Marco Belpoliti has rightly argued, Levi's most consistent self-image in his interviews was as a 'hybrid' or 'centaur' which 'does not only represent the presence of opposites, but also ... an unstable union destined to break down' (*Voice of Memory*, p. xx). This creative instability can be found in Levi's complex identity as chemist and writer, witness and writer, Jew and Italian, as well as his always 'impure' narrative voice with its self-conscious 'hybrid input' (*The Search for Roots* (*La ricerca delle radici*, 1981), p. 3; OII, 1361) of differing kinds of materials: poetry, testimony, science and fiction. It is an abiding paradox concerning Levi that such a hybrid figure, who is best characterized as a sceptical humanist, has been appropriated by a range of manichaean discourses. Just as the Holocaust has become a 'central cultural icon in the West',[5] Levi, after his death in 1987, quickly became the 'emblematic survivor' of the Holocaust in Europe (with Elie Wiesel long achieving this dubious status in the United States).[6] His current iconic status, which he was particularly fearful of attaining, will be observed in a range of media including recent novels, plays, films, critical and historical works, and journalism.

That Levi, two decades after his death, has become both 'totem and text', in the felicitous phrase of Henry Louis Gates,[7] can be illustrated with reference to two recent works, a novel and a play. The novel is Martin Amis' *Time's Arrow or The Nature of the Offence* (1991), a backwards history of a Nazi doctor, which Amis tells us 'could not have been written' without the work of Levi.[8] As a number of critics have noted, Amis is most reliant on *If This is a Man* (*Se questo è un uomo*, 1947) in the 'Auschwitz' chapter of the novel where his backwards narrative finally 'makes sense' (p. 124).[9] Amis entitles the chapter 'Here there is no why' and names his character 'Odilo Unverdorben' (in the memoir a victim, in the novel a perpetrator) in homage to Levi. It is in this chapter that the Nazi doctor brings the Jewish inmates of Auschwitz-Birkenau to life in a deliberately perverse reversal of the truth. Amis has described the 'offence' of the Nazis as unique, not in its 'cruelty, nor in its cowardice, but in its style – in its combination of the atavistic and the modern' (p. 176). What I will be arguing is that the subordination of Levi's memoirs to a 'style' or aesthetic – in this instance a backwards narrative that elides victim and victimizer – is a form of appropriation.

This argument against appropriation, I should stress from the beginning, is *not* the same as the 'critical orthodoxy' in Holocaust studies which, especially influenced by Elie Wiesel, is unreasonably suspicious of those who represent the Holocaust in anything other than the documentary mode. As has been persuasively argued, only survivors, in terms of this orthodoxy, are deemed to be unswervingly faithful to the facts, and can therefore constitute the 'repository of knowledge' about the Holocaust: 'Consequently, attempts to portray, represent, explain or narrate the Holocaust in other ways, particularly through fictionalised accounts (novels, poetry, plays, films), are seen as distortions of Holocaust reality, trivialising and fundamentally negative in their effects, however well-intentioned the aims of the authors.'[10] Anthony Sher's *Primo* (2005), a stage adaptation of *If This is a Man*, conforms exactly to this critical orthodoxy, in that it merely repeats the words of Levi's memoir in dramatic form and resists any kind of naturalistic representation. But in its portrayal of Levi as a wise old sage, in stark contrast to the twenty-six-year-old who wrote his testimony out of an 'immediate and violent impulse' (*If This is a Man*, p. 15, 1979 edition; OI, 5), Sher has unwittingly reinforced the dominant stereotype of Levi as a saint-like figure who is calmness and forgiveness personified. This chapter will explore this appropriation of Primo Levi in two main contexts: Europe and the United States. It will conclude by looking at the extent to which historical and literary studies of the Holocaust have challenged or reinforced the reductive discourses which have engulfed Levi's life and work.

Appropriating Levi in Europe

Ever since *If This is a Man* was first translated into English in 1959, the life and work of Primo Levi has been appropriated by the Christianized discourses of forgiveness and redemption. By the time of *The Periodic Table*, Levi felt the need to refute explicitly the notion that he embodied the Christian message that one gains redemptive knowledge through suffering. In the 'Vanadium' chapter, Levi speaks of Dr Müller, a German chemist in Auschwitz-Monowitz, who, by coincidence, was later to be Levi's post-war supplier of chemical products. According to Levi, Müller mistakenly 'perceived in my book [*If This is a Man*] an overcoming of Judaism, a fulfilment of the Christian precept to love one's enemies' (p. 221; OI, 931). The supposed hushed voice and reasonableness of Levi's prose meant that he was to become sanctified erroneously in Europe as the most merciful and least vengeful of Holocaust survivors. This misguided reputation resulted in Jean Améry, who briefly shared a barracks with Primo Levi in Auschwitz-Monowitz, describing his fellow 'intellectual in Auschwitz' to a mutual friend as 'the forgiver' (*The Drowned and the Saved*, p. 110; OII, 1098).

Statements such as these haunted Levi for much of his life: 'to forgive is not my verb. It has been inflicted on me' (*Voice of Memory*, p. 111). He responded explicitly to Améry's charge in *The Drowned and the Saved*:

> I don't consider this either an insult or praise but an imprecision. I am not inclined to forgive, I never forgave our enemies of that time, nor do I feel I can forgive their imitators in Algeria, Vietnam, the Soviet Union, Chile, Argentina, Cambodia, and South Africa, because I know of no human act that can erase a crime. I demand justice, but I am not able, personally, to trade punches or return blows. (p. 110; OII, 1098–9)

Rather than the closed circle of violence and counter-violence ('trading punches'), Levi wished to situate the Holocaust in the context of global injustice – Algeria, Vietnam, the Soviet Union, Chile, Argentina, Cambodia, and South Africa – which displaces the desire for revenge onto the demand for justice. In the conventional discourse, vengeance and forgiveness are fundamentally opposed as forgiveness 'erases the past' whereas revenge 'preserves it' in an 'endless chain' of retribution.[11] This is why Levi, following Améry, could not be a 'forgiver' as he wished to preserve the consequences of historic genocide for the present day. To this end, he pointedly includes the detention camps and torture chambers of Algeria, which are said to imitate the Nazis, in an echo of Améry's extended dialogue with the influential anti-colonial thinker Frantz Fanon. Here the polarity between Fanon (the resister) and Levi (the forgiver) is challenged implicitly.[12]

In stark contrast with Améry, who remained trapped within the violence of the camps, Levi negotiated continually between the death camps and the values of the world at large.[13] However, this sense of responsibility to a wider community is always in danger of being appropriated by a complacent western humanism and the discourse of forgiveness. For Levi, an idealized voice of reason (never as certain as he would have liked) allows him to go beyond the particularities of 'the Holocaust'. This voice, which enables him to construct the widest possible readership, is most explicitly articulated in the Afterword ('Appendice') to the popular 1976 schools edition of *If This is a Man*. In his Afterword, written for his young readers, Levi is at his most enlightened and self-assured and uses unequivocally the received rhetoric of law, justice and reason:

> I repress hatred even within myself: I prefer justice. Precisely for this reason, when describing the tragic world of Auschwitz, I have assumed the calm, sober language of the witness, neither the lamenting tones of the victim nor the irate voice of someone who seeks revenge. I thought that my account would be all the more credible and useful the more it appeared objective and the less it sounded overly emotional; only in this way does a witness in matters of justice perform his task, which is that of preparing the ground for the judge. The judges are my readers.
> (*Voice of Memory*, p. 186)

Here the contrast with Améry is most striking. In evoking the ethics of victimhood, Améry, unlike Levi, is on the side of Shakespeare's Shylock: 'the world, which forgives and forgets, has sentenced me, not those who murdered or allowed the murder to occur. I and others like me are the Shylocks, not only morally condemnable in the eyes of the nations, but already cheated of the pound of flesh too'.[14] Levi's greatest nightmare was that 'nothing is true outside of the *Lager*' (*The Truce* (*La tregua*), 1963, p. 222; OI, 395). It is in these terms that Levi diverges completely from his interlocutor with regard to Améry's unmitigated 'devot[ion] to death': 'Perhaps because I was younger ... I almost never had the time [in Auschwitz] to devote to death ... I had many other things to keep me busy ... The aims of life are the best defence against death: and not only in the *Lager*' (*The Drowned and the Saved*, p. 120; OII, 1108).

The tension between 'life' and 'death' or the values of 'home' and the value-less 'no-place' of Auschwitz-Birkenau structures Levi's work as a whole.[15]

Levi kept faith with the values of western humanism – literature, law, science and reason – which provided an essential point of continuity between his time before and after the camps. At the same time, he recognized the extent to which Auschwitz-Birkenau completely corrupted these received values and made them suspect. His writing is a restless negotiation between these two points whereas those who appropriate him tend to stress merely one aspect of this multiple perspective.

The extent to which Levi's work is constantly moving between 'life' and 'death' can be seen when he demurs from the poetry of fellow Holocaust survivor Paul Celan, as well as Améry, for being only on the side of 'death'. His argument against Celan's 'obscure' poetry, in *Other People's Trades* (*L'altrui mestiere*, 1985) makes this position clear:

> If [Celan's poetry] is a message, it gets lost in the 'background noise': it is not a communication, it is not a language, or at most it is a dark truncated language precisely like that of a person who is about to die and is alone, as we will be at the point of death. But since we are not alone, we must not write as if we were alone. As long as we live we have a responsibility: we must answer for what we write, word for word, and make sure that every word reaches its target
>
> (pp. 161–2; OII, 680).

For Levi, Celan's modernist 'obscurity' disabled him from communicating with an expansive readership and, thus, Celan is deemed to have widened the gap between the living and the dead. As Robert Gordon has noted, a figure like Celan raises the issue for Levi of whether he adopts the 'language of fear and chaos' or, alternatively, renders his experience in as 'accessible language as possible'.[16] For Giorgio Agamben, the 'background noise' of Celan's poetry is equivalent to the 'non-language' of Auschwitz[17] which is why, perhaps, Levi included Celan's 'Death Fugue' in his *The Search for Roots*. There, Levi notes pointedly that 'Death Fugue' is the 'exception' to Celan's poetry, which he contends was written only 'for the few'. He tells the reader that he wears 'Death Fugue' 'inside me like a graft' (p. 198; OII, 1513).

Levi was particularly fearful of 'stereotypical' views of the Holocaust, which was the subject of an essay entitled 'Stereotypes' in *The Drowned and the Saved*. There, he utilized an extended etymology of the word 'stereotype', which was associated originally with the printing press and primarily concerned the fixing of words and ideas into a single (as opposed to a derogatory) meaning. For this reason, he rejected the theories on survival of psychologist (and concentration-camp inmate in the 1930s) Bruno Bettelheim, precisely because of Bettelheim's 'belief that he can explain it all', which results in a 'psychological armour which is like a gospel that brings light to all, without ever a chink of doubt' (*Voice of Memory*, p. 237). Levi's doubt or scepticism, which I have called elsewhere his 'ethical uncertainty', precisely countered such stereotypical thinking.[18] Rather than Améry's ethics of victimhood, Levi's ethical uncertainty meant that he is most concerned with 'typically grey human specimens' (*The Periodic Table*, p. 221; OI, 931). He therefore opposed consistently a manichaean view of the world: 'moral codes, all of them, are rigid by definition; they do not admit blurrings, compromises, or reciprocal contaminations. They are to be accepted or rejected *en bloc*' (*The Truce*, p. 45; OI, 237). The appropriation of Levi as a 'calm sage' (*Voice of Memory*, p. vii) meant that his multiple and uncertain voices and identities – which are always 'grey' and full of 'reciprocal contaminations' – are flattened into a single saintly representation.

The most blatant transformation of Levi into a sanctified 'forgiver' – the nadir of his iconic status as the ideal Christ-like survivor in Europe – can be seen in Francesco Rosi's 1997 cinematic version of *The Truce*.[19] Towards the end of the film, when Levi's final train home stops in Munich, a German soldier kneels before Levi after he sees his camp uniform. This entirely fictitious scene repeats the famous act of contrition when, in December 1970, West German Chancellor Willy Brandt knelt at the base of the Warsaw ghetto memorial as an act of penitence.[20] That Rosi, nearly three decades later, makes Levi the object of German repentance shows the extent to which Levi has come to represent the victims of the Holocaust *tout court*. Here Rosi makes explicit Levi's supposed power to grant atonement to the generations that followed the Nazis. To underline this point, Rosi contrasts this scene with an earlier parallel scene (which is taken from the book) when Daniele pointedly makes German soldiers, after liberation, crawl for bread. Such is the crucial difference between Levi's benevolence and Daniele's vengefulness.

Throughout the film, Daniele performs the role of Levi's rather unsympathetic alter ego, which enables Rosi to portray Levi in redemptive terms. The two figures are contrasted after their first meeting when Daniele burns his camp uniform which Levi pointedly keeps as a signifier of his soon-to-be-articulated memories (even though he was forced to sell the jacket in reality). The fictionalized opposition between Levi and Daniele reaches its climax in relation to Flora, a camp-prostitute, whom Daniele castigates for colluding with the Nazis. Flora, in the memoir, is described as 'the Italian from the Buna cellars, the woman from the *Lager*, the object of Alberto's and my dreams for over a month ... ' (p. 333; OI, 351). In the film, however, Levi's saintly demeanour reaches its apotheosis when he, echoing Christ's healing of Mary Magdalen, reminds an aggressive Daniele that the 'worse thing' about the *Lager* was that it 'crushed our soul's capacity for compassion'.

These are invented words which distort Levi's nuanced secular perspective and transform him into a symbol of sacred 'compassion'.

In the memoir Flora ends up a 'slave' (p. 335; OI, 353) to a man who regularly beats her. But in the film she is chased through a forest by Levi and they become two children of nature who eventually make love. In this way, Rosi's Flora is restored to both spiritual and physical health and Levi's overriding benevolence and renewed manhood (although in reality he was seriously ill with scarlet fever) conquers all. Not only is his supposed superior morality rewarded, but the 'passion' which defines his specifically Italian masculinity is also part of this transformation.[21]

The redemptive narrative drive in the film takes a variety of forms which includes, as we have seen, the language of Christianity, a life-giving natural world, and the restorative power of masculine sexuality and nationhood. Hollywood and American cinema also provide a range of redemptive images, such as the Soviet soldier dancing balletically to Irving Berlin on Victory Day. Rosi argues tellingly that '*The Truce* begins at the exact moment when *Schindler's List* ends' and notes also that 'at certain moments it even reaches into the comic register'.[22] If *The Truce* continues the story of *Schindler's List*, as Rosi suggests, then it is to stress the life-giving aspects of the Holocaust – that one can find a 'redemptive meaning in any event' – and that the transcendence of suffering can lead to a greater wisdom which Michael André Bernstein has called the 'sentimentalisation of victimhood'.[23] Bernstein names these characteristics, with some resonance, the '*Schindler's List* effect', predicated on the belief that 'everything in the world exists in order to end up in a popular movie or it will lose its hold on our interest altogether'.

Levi's prominent red triangle, imposed on the less visible yellow triangle, resonates eloquently with the film's Soviet iconography which, as Marcus notes, culminates with the bright red star on the engine of the Soviet locomotive which eventually returns Levi to his birthplace. This visual motif is, in fact, carried over until the last scene of the film, when a healthy-looking Levi, after returning home, places a flowering red rose in some water and takes out his pristine striped uniform to examine once again. The fact that Levi, 'swollen, bearded and in rags' (*The Truce*, p. 221; OI, 395), was forced to sell his camp jacket in order to feed himself, and had no such red rose, indicates Rosi's narrative priorities. The red star/triangle/rose brings together nature, the Soviet Union and Hollywood in a final summary of the narrative of redemption. That such narratives result in a one-dimensional version of Levi can be observed in the last scene of the film. Here the cinematic Levi, looking straight at the camera in an act of identification with his audience, recites only the first half of his poem 'Shemà' (1946), which prefaces *Se questo è un uomo*, and pointedly misses out the last seven lines. By ignoring the last half of 'Shemà', Rosi avoids

Levi's version of the Old Testament curse, taken from Deuteronomy (6: 4–7), where those who do not respond to the biblically inspired injunction to remember Auschwitz are doomed to suffer from generation to generation:

> I commend these words to you.
> Engrave them on your hearts
> When you are in your house, when you walk on your way,
> When you go to bed, when you rise.
> Repeat them to your children.
> Or may your house crumble,
> Disease render you powerless,
> Your offspring avert their faces from you.
>
> *(Collected Poems (Ad ora incerta*, 1984), p. 9; OI, 525)

But, of course, it would have been impossible to have ended the film with these lines as they would have thrown into disarray Rosi's representation of Levi as the embodiment of the Christian virtues of compassion and forgiveness. As Robert Eaglestone has rightly argued, the injunction here is to remember Levi's '*words, not the victims*'.[24] In stark contrast to the facile identification with the cinematic Levi, the unheard half of the poem reminds us that all that is left of the victims are these words of testimony. What is more, Levi's juxtaposition of his 'bloody poems' (*The Periodic Table*, p. 151; OI, 871) with his cooler prose enables his readers to question the commonly held assumption (reinforced by the film) that he had a single, unequivocal voice with which the reader could identify.[25]

Appropriating Levi in the United States

It was not until 1985 that Levi gained a significant readership in the United States. His presence in America reached a low point in 1982 when the translation of *If Not Now, When?* (*Se non ora, quando?*, 1982) was postponed after Levi signed letters in Italy protesting against the excursion into Lebanon by the Israeli army. A year before this setback, Levi was informed that an American edition of *The Periodic Table* could only be published if he was prepared to leave out (according to the envisaged publisher) any material which was not pertinent to the 'Italian Jewish experience and the Holocaust'.[26] Whereas in Europe Levi's supposed Christian characteristics made him the ideal survivor, in the United States his publishers feared that he was not 'Jewish' enough and therefore would not reach his principal audience. As his biographer notes, Levi's secularism, coupled with his liberal opposition to the Israeli government of Menachem Begin, was considered an impediment to him reaching a wide American-Jewish readership.[27]

Instead of the marginalized Levi, the iconic survivor of the Holocaust in the United States was Elie Wiesel, whose religiosity and popularism set the terms for the reception of Holocaust memoirs in America. His American publishers hoped that Levi would become a 'Mediterranean Elie Wiesel'.[28] In this context, Peter Novick has posed the question: 'What would talk of the Holocaust be like in America if a sceptical rationalist like Primo Levi, rather than a religious mystic like Wiesel, had been its principal interpreter?'[29] While this is entirely hypothetical, it does indicate, from an American perspective, the extent to which Levi's values and general outlook were opposed to those of Wiesel. What is more, federal trade regulations meant that the 1960s mistranslated American titles of *Se questo è un uomo* and *La tregua* have remained unchanged as *Survival in Auschwitz: The Nazi Assault on Humanity* and *The Reawakening: A Liberated Prisoner's Long March Home Through East Europe*. These unfortunate titles have meant that Levi, this time in American terms, has been perceived to be a singularly redemptive figure.

Unlike the living nightmare at the end of Wiesel's memoir of his time in Auschwitz, *Night* (1958), Levi, according to his Americanized titles, was a 'liberated' camp 'survivor' who, in the familiar linear narrative, eventually awoke from his nightmare and arrived safely 'home'. While this stereotypical narrative was reinforced in Rosi's *The Truce*, it was countered precisely by Levi at the end of his memoir: 'I am in the *Lager* once more . . . All the rest was a brief pause, a deception of the senses, a dream; my family, nature in flower, my home' (p. 222; OI, 395). Levi rejects the clichéd linearity of 'the survivor' passing through the camps and returning, renewed, to the bosom of his family. Instead, he ends his memoir of 'liberation' with the never-ending trauma of the camps: 'this dream of peace is over, and in the outer dream, which continues, gelid, a well-known voice resounds . . . It is the dawn command of Auschwitz, a foreign word, feared and expected: get up, "*Wstawać*"' (ibid., emended).

The jacket cover of the American edition of *The Drowned and the Saved* similarly travesties the content of the book: 'Primo Levi's luminous writings offer a wondrous celebration of life. His universally acclaimed books remain a testament to the indomitability of the human spirit and humanity's capacity to defeat death through meaningful work, morality and art.'[30] One reason why Levi's works were so crudely appropriated in the United States was that he was introduced to a mass American readership by the equivocal mediating presence of Saul Bellow. Although Bellow's endorsement of *The Periodic Table* single-handedly transformed Levi into an international figure, it was based on a profound misunderstanding of his work:

> We are always looking for the book it is necessary to read next. After a few pages I immersed myself in *The Periodic Table*. There is nothing superfluous here, everything this book contains is essential. It is wonderfully pure.[31]

After this endorsement, a large American readership began to consume Levi, and the rest of Levi's books were rapidly translated and reissued (including *If Not Now, When?*). He also began to garner a large international readership – especially in Britain, France and Germany – and a global reputation which his apparent suicide in 1987 (at the height of his growing fame) only served to enhance. In the United States, Bellow's endorsement quickly became the standard way of speaking about Levi. Irving Howe, for instance, concluded his 1988 *New York Times* review of *The Drowned and the Saved* with the following: 'Primo Levi wrote about this terrible event with a purity of spirit for which we can only feel grateful. This was a man'.[32] By the time of Cynthia Ozick's 1988 essay on *The Drowned and the Saved* in the *The New Republic*,[33] it was axiomatic that these terms were the received way of characterizing Levi. Ozick concludes stereotypically that of all the survivor memoirists Levi 'least troubles, least wounds, least implicates the reader'. His temperament is said to be like 'clear water' (pp. 40, 47).

To be sure, Ozick was well aware of the extent to which Levi was being constructed as a secular saint, not unlike Wiesel, in the United States. As a prelude to his 1985 American lecture tour, the *International Herald Tribune* had labelled Levi 'the Jewish equivalent of a saint',[34] which set the tone for his reception. In her essay, Ozick cites a number of American commentators who speak of Levi's 'magisterial equanimity', 'detachment and absence of hatred' and, above all, his 'spirit pure', a phrase which she repeats as a mantra throughout her essay (pp. 37, 46). Even more drastically than his appropriation in Europe, Levi's studied ambiguities are radically reduced in the United States so that he can be assimilated to the culture as a whole. What is particularly disturbing about this reduction is that the terms in which he was canonized in the United States (his 'purity of spirit') precisely reverse his own heartfelt beliefs. Throughout his work, Levi is quite explicit about defining Nazism as a political creed which wanted to 'purify everything' (*The Drowned and the Saved*, p. 76; OII, 1067) and, in opposition to this dogma, he defined 'the Jews' as 'impure and sowers of impurity' (p. 81; OII, 1071). What does it mean, in this context, to characterize Levi as the doyen of purity?

The purification of Levi for an American readership is not merely a distortion but precisely neutralizes what is, I believe, most interesting and challenging about his work. It is significant that Levi's least systematic work – ironically entitled in Italian *Il sistema periodico* – is, in these terms, his most explicit and thoroughgoing acknowledgement of the value of impurity. In the 'Zinc' ('Zinco') chapter, for instance, Levi is a young student performing his first experiments and is drawn into broader areas of speculation by the resistance of zinc to chemical breakdown:

> One could draw from [this experiment] two conflicting philosophical conclusions: the praise of purity, which protects from evil like a coat of mail; the praise of impurity, which gives rise to changes, in other words, to life. I discarded the first, disgustingly moralistic, and I lingered to consider the second, which I found more congenial. In order for the wheel to turn, for life to be lived, impurities are needed ... Dissension, diversity, the grain of salt and mustard are needed: Fascism does not want them, forbids them, and that's why you're not a Fascist; it wants everybody to be the same.
>
> (*The Periodic Table*, pp. 33–4; OI, 768)

Levi's distrust of moralizing, which he associates with the 'praise of purity', was, as we have seen, signalled from his earliest writings. For this reason, Levi always described himself as an unbeliever. He needed 'impurities' precisely for the 'wheel to turn, for life to be lived' so as to go beyond Fascist sameness. This fundamental link between 'impurity' and 'life' is crucial to an understanding of the power of Levi's sceptical humanism. From the very beginning of his deliberately indefinable 'chemical treatise ... autobiography ... micro-history' (p. 224; OI, 934), Levi is at pains to remain uncategorizable whether it be in relation to his Jewishness, his training as a chemist or his humanity. He states from the outset that Diaspora Jews reflect in microcosm the 'human condition' as Jews have been 'torn between their divine vocation and the daily misery of existence' (p. 9; OI, 746). This fissure is 'inherent in the human condition' because 'man is a centaur, a tangle of flesh and mind, divine inspiration and dust' (ibid.). In this impure spirit, Levi's chemistry is defined throughout as an uneasy mixture of the magic of alchemy and the exactness of physics. The gap between Levi's writing and the discourses that encircle him could not be greater.

Given Levi's impure ethic at the heart of his sceptical humanism, it is not surprising that there was a strong response against his growing influence in the United States by conservative Jewish intellectuals associated with *Commentary* magazine (Cynthia Ozick was an instance of this). In 1986, Fernanda Eberstadt attacked Levi in *Commentary* in a scurrilous essay entitled 'Reading Primo Levi'.[35] The essay had three main lines of attack. Firstly, Levi's irreligiosity is criticized as he supposedly had a 'tin ear for religion, and is incapable of representing imaginatively the life of people who practice their faith' (p. 45). Secondly, he was dismissed as a universalist (in the 'secular and humanistic tradition of Italian Jewry', p. 45) which, in the world of *Commentary*, has the implicit assertion that Levi is denying the uniqueness of the Holocaust. Finally, Levi is characterized as an opportunist for joining the anti-Fascist partisans in Italy as late as July 1943, when he was supposed to have finally found the 'will to resist' (p. 43). Such were the arguments that were deployed to discredit Levi.

Mid-way through her essay, Eberstadt makes clear the reason for her attack. She notes that Levi writes in his preface to *If This is a Man* that he does not want to 'formulate new accusations' – but rather to 'furnish documentation for a quiet study of certain aspects of the human mind' (OI, 6–7).[36] This intention, according to Eberstadt, 'separates *If This is a Man* from a book like Elie Wiesel's *Night*, with its swelling lament for the Nazis' destruction of a people and their civilization' (p. 44), as if Nazi destruction were not also a concern of Levi's memoir. The problem with Levi, clearly, is that he was not Elie Wiesel. As Eberstadt notes, Levi's secular humanism offers a completely different representation of the Holocaust to that of Wiesel and thereby endangers Wiesel's hegemony as the emblematic Auschwitz survivor in the United States.[37]

Since the publication of the first widely read editions of both *If This is a Man* and Wiesel's *Night* in 1958, there has been a long history of constructing these two figures as opposites even though, as we have noted, Levi had a marginal impact in the United States until the mid-1980s. But the extent to which Levi is perceived to be a threat to Wiesel's pre-eminence (since he gained a large American readership) can be seen from Wiesel's autobiography *All Rivers Run to the Sea* (1996), where he characterizes Levi as his polar opposite:

> [Levi] refused to understand how I, his former companion of Auschwitz III, could still call himself a believer, for he, Primo, was not and didn't want to be. He had seen too much suffering not to rebel against any religion that sought to impose meaning upon it . . . We spent many hours arguing [about religion] with little result. We were equally unwavering, for we came from different milieus, and even in Auschwitz led different lives. He was a chemist; I was nothing at all. The system needed him, but not me. He had influential friends to help and protect him; I had only my father. I needed God, Primo did not.[38]

Even for such a tendentious autobiography as *All Rivers Run to the Sea*, this is something of a low point. Levi and Wiesel were not 'companions in Auschwitz III' as they had never met there. Levi was not a 'rebel' (an odd, infantilizing word) from religion but a secular humanist who, nonetheless, uses the language of the Hebrew Bible in his poetry. It is also untrue to claim that there was a hierarchy of suffering between Levi and Wiesel. Like Wiesel, Levi was a Jew in Monowitz-Buna and, unlike non-Jewish political prisoners in Auschwitz – such as Tadeusz Borowski or Charlotte Delbo – Levi did not have access to an influential protection network to help him survive, which Wiesel implies.[39]

In the second volume of his autobiography, *And the Sea is Never Full* (1999), Wiesel goes even further in attacking Levi ('he distanced himself from my attachment to Israel')[40] while, at the same time, making extravagant claims about the extent of their friendship ('my friend Primo', p. 345). He falsely describes Levi's 'grey zone' as a theory which demeans the relative 'innocence' of the camp survivors: 'Only the criminals are guilty, I told him; to compare the victims in any way with the torturers was to dilute or even deny the killers' responsibility for their actions' (p. 347). Levi, purified for a mass American readership, was clearly not pure enough for Wiesel.

Appropriating Levi within Holocaust studies

After Levi entered the canon of global literature, he began to be assimilated as a major figure within Holocaust literary and historical studies. His work has been used to engage with the issue of ethics, humanism and perpetrator history after the Nazi genocide and has, in particular, been incorporated into theoretical readings of the Holocaust.[41] Given Levi's unease with the term 'Holocaust', as we have seen, and with being categorized unequivocally (especially in the United States) as a 'Jewish writer', this incorporation is not a straightforward matter. Critical work can be interpretative, in that it stays true to Levi's many voices and identities and his fundamental uncertainties. But such work can also be continuous with the flattening appropriating discourses that have enveloped Levi. Gillian Rose, in this latter mode, speaks of Levi's 'Olympian serenity'[42] and contrasts his memoirs, in this regard, with the work of Tadeusz Borowski (a comparison that I will return to below). Even more blatantly, Daniel Schwarz argues in a book on Holocaust literature that 'Levi's recurring theme is the therapeutic, purifying function of language' and that, through language, he 'seizes light from darkness'.[43] Such redemptive readings reinforce and echo the purification of Levi in the United States. In response to these appropriations, Lawrence Langer characterizes *If This is a Man* as a 'death story',[44] but this is to go from one extreme to the other.

Levi's 'purifying function' also has a particular salience with regard to the work of Shoshana Felman and Dori Laub, in their account of the literary deconstructionist Paul de Man's notorious post-war 'silence' about his antisemitic articles in Nazi-occupied Belgium, as revealed in the 1980s. Felman cites Levi's self-description of his memories in *The Drowned and the Saved* as a 'suspect source' that he must be 'protected against' (p. 21; OII, 1015). In so doing, she transforms this uncertainty towards his own act of bearing witness into a generalized characterization of the 'impossibility of … witnessing' which brings together both Levi and de Man.[45] As Dominick La Capra has correctly maintained, what is astonishingly missing from Felman's apologia for de Man is any sense of how the differing histories of Levi and de Man shape their subsequent scepticism towards the act of memorialization.[46] The fact that de Man, whatever the extent of his personal guilt, was on the side of those with power during the war – and that Levi was a victim of power – is crudely elided in this argument. Here, victim and victimizer, abstracted from history, are supposed to exemplify the same textual uncertainty. Millicent Marcus, following Felman and Laub, argues similarly that because Levi 'constantly' reinvents the 'text of witness', anyone who adapts Levi, in whatever form, 'fulfils the testimonial imperative of Levi's writing'.[47]

Here Levi's qualified scepticism towards the act of witnessing is universalized (in the name of theoretical complexity) and is thereby rendered meaningless. Such critical appropriations, no less than more popular appropriations, simplify Levi. Levi feared such simplifications, as he states at the beginning of 'The Grey Zone': 'Have we – we who have returned – been able to understand our experience? What we commonly mean by "understand" coincides with "simplify"' (*The Drowned and the Saved*, p. 22; OII, 1017). His anxiety is always that such simplifications, which we think of as 'knowledge' or 'understanding', will not honour the dead. For this reason, Levi makes no claims, as a survivor, to be a 'true witness' (p. 63, OII, 1055). He is also not a 'true' intellectual but rather an 'interpreter' who moves, however inadequately, from the Babel of noise and the 'phantoms', barely glimpsed on arrival at Auschwitz, to those who must now be recalled as memorable human beings. Both *If This is a Man* (p. 12; OI, 14) and *The Truce* (p. 23; OI, 216) begin by recollecting two children who died in the camps and who are now memorialized 'through these words of mine' (ibid.). Levi moves self-consciously between different realms, in this case from memory to language, as a greyish and unsure translator.

Precisely because of the ambivalences at the foundation of Levi's work, it has been easy for critics and historians of the Holocaust to stress just one dimension of his always multi-faceted (or 'impure') prose, poetry and essays. This can be seen most clearly in terms of the role that Levi has played in the debate between the historians Christopher Browning and Daniel Goldhagen with regard to the writing of perpetrator history. Both historians utilize Levi's concept of the 'grey zone' but to completely differing ends. Browning shares Levi's distrust of those who have, over the years, reduced the Holocaust to a manichaean allegory which revolves around the already known division of 'good' and 'evil', 'victims' and 'persecutors' (*The Drowned and the Saved*, p. 23; OII, 1017). Rather than moralize or sanctify the victims like Wiesel, Levi argues that the *Lager* 'degrades' those in the camps and forces its inmates to 'resemble' its 'infernal system' (p. 25; OII, 1020). While Browning embraces this moral and historical complexity in his account of the Nazi Reserve Police Battalion 101, Goldhagen draws diametrically opposed conclusions from Levi so as not to confuse the victims and perpetrators.[48] Levi's statement that he was a 'guiltless victim' and 'not a murderer' (p. 32; OII, 1027), however self-evident, is paramount for Goldhagen.[49]

To be sure, Levi's scepticism and doubt is always circumscribed by the desire for justice and his status as 'guiltless victim' which is why those who universalize his uncertainty are appropriating Levi's thought no less than those who sanctify his suffering. The limits inherent in Levi's use of the 'grey zone' have been characterized usefully as a function of his 'practical intelligence'[50] which distrusts all extremes. Here the contrast with the extremity of Borowski's *This Way for the Gas, Ladies and Gentlemen* (1951) is worth returning to in this regard. As Gillian Rose has rightly argued, Levi's notion of the 'grey zone' is an apt location for Borowski's persona, a deputy Kapo, who is both 'executioner and victim' and thereby empties the distinction of 'all greatness and pathos'. But she goes on to distinguish Levi's 'humane, temperate, restrained prose' from Borowski's prose-fiction, which makes the reader 'witness brutality in the most disturbing way'.[51] This contrast, however, underplays just how unsettling Levi's work is.

Levi's use of a conventional humanist rhetoric, as we have seen, was designed to construct the widest possible readership while Borowski, by comparison, is utterly dismissive of his readers. At the same time, Levi, in a different rhetorical mode, was quite capable of articulating a viewpoint which was identical to that of Borowski's nihilism. This can be seen at the end of 'The Grey Zone', when Levi thinks of the world as a whole as the Łódź ghetto writ large: 'willingly or not we come to terms with power, forgetting that we are all in the ghetto, that the ghetto is walled in, that outside the ghetto reign the lords of death and that close by the train is waiting' (p. 51; OII, 1044). This is an exact echo of what Borowski called the 'concentration-camp mentality', which sees the whole world through the prism of the camp experience. Citing Levi, Paul Gilroy has reconstituted this 'concentration-camp mentality' as a form of 'planetary humanism' as it means that we all have to be 'alive to the camps out there now and the camps around the corner, the camps that are being prepared'.[52] Here Gilroy's notion of a 'planetary humanism' is distinguished usefully from an uncritical western humanism which has hitherto appropriated Levi as its icon.

Instead of such easy appropriations, Levi's sceptical humanism was always agonistic and utterly aware of the dangers inherent in a categorizing science and a falsely universalizing European culture. Defining his own intellectual credentials, he argued in *The Drowned and the Saved* that his training as a chemist resulted in a habit which can be 'judged' as both 'human or inhuman' (p. 114; OII, 1102). Those around him could be considered to be 'human beings' but they were also '"samples", specimens in a sealed envelope to be identified, analysed and weighed' (ibid.). After all, in *If This is a Man* Levi did describe Auschwitz as '*pre-eminently*, a gigantic biological and social experiment' (p. 99; OI, 83; my emphasis). Levi's awareness of such simultaneous humanizing and dehumanizing systems – both within and without the law – goes to the heart of his ethical uncertainty. He understood, from the very beginning, that even he, in his memoirs, is forced to work within the very categories which decide who is, and is not, human. At one point in *The Periodic Table* he views himself again from a 'distance of thirty years':

> I find it difficult to reconstruct the sort of human being that corresponded, in November 1944, to my name or, better, to my number: 174517. I must then overcome the most terrible crisis, the crisis of having become part of the *Lager* system, and I must have developed a strange callousness if I then managed not only to survive but also to think, to register the world around me, and even to perform rather delicate work, in an environment infected by the daily presence of death. (pp. 139–40; OI, 860)

The 'strange callousness' that Levi needed to survive as part of the '*Lager* system' also enables him to write his memoirs. For this reason, he tells the story of someone who understands, only too well, his own potential to dehumanize. In this sense, Levi is in thrall to his memory – and his need to bear witness – but, at the same time, his 'delicate work' of testimony is also a betrayal of his humanity. Such is the impure scepticism of Levi which the appropriating discourses which surround him have attempted to purify.

NOTES

An earlier version of this essay was delivered as a seminar paper at Dartmouth College and the University of Michigan, Ann Arbor. I am grateful to colleagues for their helpful responses to the paper and to Robert Gordon for his many insights into Primo Levi, both written and unwritten, which have greatly enhanced this essay.

1. Zygmunt Bauman, *Life in Fragments: Essays in Postmodern Morality*, Oxford, Blackwell, 1995, p. 192.
2. Alvin Rosenfeld, *A Double Dying: Reflections on Holocaust Literature*, Bloomington, Indiana University Press, 1980, p. 28.

3. Cited in Giorgio Agamben, *Remnants of Auschwitz: The Witness and the Archive*, New York, Zone Books, 1999, p. 28.
4. Carole Angier, *The Double Bond: Primo Levi, A Biography*, London, Viking, 2002, p. 645.
5. Tim Cole, *Selling the Holocaust: From Auschwitz to Schindler*, London, Routledge, 1999, p. 6.
6. Peter Novick, *The Holocaust in American Life*, Boston and New York, Houghton Mifflin, 1999, p. 273.
7. Henry Louis Gates, 'Critical Fanonism', *Critical Inquiry*, 17 (Spring 1991), pp. 457–70, p. 457.
8. Martin Amis, *Time's Arrow or The Nature of the Offence*, London, Jonathan Cape, 1991, p. 175; the alternative title is drawn from a powerful passage at the start of *The Truce* (p. 3; OI, 206).
9. Cf. Sue Vice, *Holocaust Fiction*, London, Routledge, 2000, p. 25.
10. Anthony Lerman, 'The Art of Holocaust Remembering', *The Jewish Quarterly* (Autumn 1989), pp. 24–32, p. 24.
11. Berel Lang, *The Future of the Holocaust: Between History and Memory*, Ithaca, Cornell University Press, 1999, p. 158.
12. For a longer version of this argument, see my forthcoming *Diasporas of the Mind: Literature and 'Race' after the Holocaust*.
13. Robert S. C. Gordon, *Primo Levi's Ordinary Virtues: From Testimony to Ethics*, Oxford, Oxford University Press, 2001, pp. 1–37.
14. Jean Améry, *At the Mind's Limits*, Bloomington, Indiana University Press, 1980, p. 75.
15. Robert S. C. Gordon, '"How Much Home Does a Person Need?": Primo Levi and the Ethics of Home', *Annali d'Italianistica*, 19 (2001), pp. 215–34.
16. Gordon, *Virtues*, pp. 78–9.
17. Agamben, *Remnants*, p. 162.
18. Bryan Cheyette, 'The Ethical Uncertainy of Primo Levi', in Bryan Cheyette and Laura Marcus (eds.), *Modernity, Culture and 'the Jew'*, Cambridge, Polity 1998, pp. 268–81.
19. Much of the analysis of Rosi's film that follows is in dialogue with Millicent Marcus's highly intelligent but ovegenerous defence of the film in her *After Fellini: National Cinema in the Postmodern Age*, Baltimore, Johns Hopkins University Press, 2002, pp. 253–67.
20. See James Young, *The Texture of Memory: Holocaust Memorials and Meaning*, New Haven, Yale University Press, 1993, p. 180; and Marcus, *After Fellini*, pp. 259–60.
21. On the national dimension, see Marcus, *After Fellini*, p. 263; Carlo Testa (ed.), *Poet of Civic Courage: The Films of Francesco Rosi*, Westport, Greenwood Press, 1996, p. 151.
22. Ibid., p. 150.
23. Michael André Bernstein, 'The *Schindler's List* Effect', *The American Scholar*, 63 (Summer 1994), pp. 429–32.
24. Robert Eaglestone, *The Holocaust and the Postmodern*, Oxford, Oxford University Press, 2004, p. 40, his emphasis.
25. A more fertile and intelligent cinematic reading of *The Truce* is to be found in Davide Ferrario's *La strada di Levi* ('Primo Levi's Journey', 2006), co-written

with Marco Belpoliti, which retraces the steps of Levi's journey, using *The Truce* as a guide to the contradictory and confused landscape of contemporary, post-Soviet Eastern Europe.

26. Ian Thomson, *Primo Levi*, London, Hutchinson, 2002, p. 460.

27. Ibid., p. 444.

28. Ibid., p. 460.

29. Novick, *American*, p. 351.

30. Lawrence Langer, *Preempting the Holocaust*, New Haven, Yale University Press, 1998, p. 42.

31. Thomson, *Primo Levi*, p. 445.

32. Irving Howe, 'The Utter Sadness of the Survivor', *The New York Times*, 10 January 1988, p. 101.

33. Cynthia Ozick, 'Primo Levi's Suicide Note', reprinted in *Metaphor and Memory*, New York, Alfred A. Knopf, 1989, pp. 34–48.

34. Thomson, *Primo Levi*, p. 466.

35. Fernanda Eberstadt, 'Reading Primo Levi', *Commentary* (October 1985), pp. 41–7.

36. The Preface was not included in the first English edition of *If This is a Man*; see all later editions.

37. For Levi's letter in reply to Eberstadt, see *Commentary*, 81, 2 (February 1986), pp. 6–7 (OII, 1291–3).

38. Elie Wiesel, *All Rivers Run to the Sea: Memoirs*, New York, Alfred A. Knopf, 1996, pp. 82–3.

39. For Levi's understanding of the role of the 'protected' minority in Auschwitz-Birkenau, and his difference from them, see *The Drowned and the Saved*, p. 31–4; OII, 1025–8.

40. Elie Wiesel, *And the Sea is Never Full: Memoirs 1969–*, New York, Alfred A. Knopf, 1999, p. 347.

41. Along with the literary and historical works discussed in the essay, Levi has played a central role in Tzvetan Todorov, *Facing the Extreme: Moral Life in the Concentration Camps*, New York, Henry Holt and Co., 1996, and Agamben, *Remnants*. It is also significant that Levi is a leading presence in Neil Levi and Michael Rothberg (eds.), *The Holocaust: Theoretical Readings*, Edinburgh, Edinburgh University Press, 2003.

42. Gillian Rose, 'Beginnings of the Day: Fascism and Representation', in Cheyette and Marcus (eds.), *Modernity*, pp. 242–56, p. 248.

43. Daniel Schwarz, *Imagining the Holocaust*, New York, St Martin's Press, 1999, pp. 76–7. See also Gillian Banner, *Holocaust Literature: Schulz, Levi, Spiegelman and the Memory of the Offence*, London, Vallentine Mitchell, 2000, pp. 92–3, who argues that Levi's readers are impressed by the 'sense that there is a kind of judicious neutrality at work in Levi's indictments'.

44. Langer, *Preempting*, p. 42.

45. Shoshana Felman and Dori Laub (eds.), *Testimony: Crisis of Witnessing in Literature, Psychoanalysis, and History*, London, Routledge, 1992, pp. 139–40.

46. Dominick LaCapra, *Representing the Holocaust: History, Theory, Trauma*, Ithaca, Cornell University Press, 1994, pp. 116–25.

47. Marcus, *After Fellini*, p. 254.

48. Christopher Browning, *Ordinary Men. Reserve Police Battalion 101 and the Final Solution in Poland*, New York, Aaron Asher, 1992, and Daniel Goldhagen, *Hitler's Willing Executioners. Ordinary Germans and the Holocaust*, New York, Alfred A. Knopf, 1996.
49. For a longer discussion of the role of Primo Levi in the Browning/Goldhagen debate, to which I am indebted, see Eaglestone, *The Holocaust and the Postmodern*, chapter 7.
50. Gordon, *Virtues*, pp. 115–16.
51. Borowski, *This Way for the Gas, Ladies and Gentlemen*, Harmondsworth, Penguin, 1976, pp. 22–3; Rose, 'Beginnings', pp. 247–8.
52. Paul Gilroy, *Between Camps: Nations, Cultures and the Allure of Race*, London, Penguin, 2000, pp. 86–7.

PART III
Science

6

PIERPAOLO ANTONELLO

Primo Levi and 'man as maker'

In an interview with Gabriella Poli in 1976, Primo Levi explained that all his books had been born in pairs, as twins:[1] two books on his *Lager* experience – *If This is a Man* (*Se questo è un uomo*, 1947) and *The Truce* (*La tregua*, 1963) – were followed by two collections of science-fiction short-stories – *Storie naturali* ('Natural Histories', 1966) and *Vizio di forma* ('Formal Defect', 1971) (partly collected in a single volume in English, *The Sixth Day*). The unconventional and heterogeneous (auto)biography of an inorganic chemist, *The Periodic Table* (*Il sistema periodico*, 1975) was planned to be paired with a book on the trade of an organic chemist, with the working title of *Il doppio legame* ('The Double Bond'). Levi never completed this book;[2] instead he paired *The Periodic Table* with the fourteen stories of *The Wrench* (*La chiave a stella*, 1978), centred on a highly skilled Piedmontese master rigger, Libertino Faussone. This particular coupling might look looser than the others, but it has striking significance for our understanding of Levi's work. Its prime effect is to underscore the challenge Levi presents to abstract, systematic notions of scientific knowledge (implicit in the image and concept of the '*sistema* periodico'), in favour of the technical, applied skills common to both the (inorganic) chemist and the rigger. At the centre of Levi's concerns in these two books, in other words, is the idea of knowledge as being both a material and existential construction rather than a purely abstract or theoretical one, as well as a notion of the unity of art (as craft) and technology, at both the experimental and manual levels. Taken together, the diptych of *The Periodic Table* and *The Wrench* offers one of the most interesting of modern representations – in philosophical, epistemological, aesthetic and ethical terms – of what Levi would call the *homo faber*, man as maker or tool-maker, the fabricator and artist who works upon hard material such as stone or wood. This philosophical and anthropological concept is associated in modern critical discourse with thinkers such as Henri Bergson (*L'Evolution créatrice*, 1907) or Hannah Arendt (*The Human Condition*, 1958), for whom the human being is a maker who 'fabricates the sheer unending variety of things whose sum total constitutes human artifice'. The idea is also related to the Greek notion of *techne*, which translates as both 'art' and 'craft', and from which 'technique', 'technician' and 'technology' derive.[3] *Homo faber*'s purpose is systematically to transform the natural, via work and labour, with the help of tools and technologies, into the 'artifactual' and in the process, to manipulate and progressively extend his/her control over nature, a nature which is considered meaningless and valueless in itself.[4] This chapter attempts to show how Levi engages with, extends and also challenges and subverts such conceptions of the *homo faber*, of man as maker. It does so by briefly examining in turn certain pivotal issues or clusters of issues implicit in this category as they work their way through Levi's writing.

Philosophy and technology

Levi never showed any particular interest in philosophy *per se*, highly suspicious as he was of the abstractions of philosophical reasoning. He contested its 'inconclusive metamorphoses from Plato to Augustine, from Thomas to Hegel, from Hegel to Croce' (*The Periodic Table*, p. 23; OI, 759). Despite this scepticism, however, his work often discloses surreptitious philosophical and anthropological positions of a complex nature, and this applies perhaps above all else to questions of science and technology. As shown by Charlotte Ross in Chapter 7, in *The Sixth Day*, Levi's thematization and discussion of technology seems *prima facie* to be in tune with that strong line of modern European philosophy which has been distinctively and consistently 'technocritical'. This line of thought rejects the alienating and dehumanizing nature of technology as well as the distorted application of scientific research to warfare and other iniquities. For contemporary Italian philosophers such as Gianni Vattimo or Emanuele Severino, for instance, technology is seen as the end of metaphysics, as the nihilist, uncontrollable force which puts an end to the western philosophical tradition and potentially leads to apocalyptic violence.[5] In this they followed a long line of philosophical thinking – from Hegel in his *Science of Logic, 1812–16*, to Heidegger in the early twentieth century, to Adorno's Marxism – that identified the progressive detachment of technology from its initial design and purpose, with the effect of transforming the human being into an 'instrument' or 'slave' of technology.

Several of Levi's characters seem to fit this model: both Simpson, who appears in several stories in *The Sixth Day* experimenting with new-fangled machines, and Gilberto in 'Some Applications of the Mimer' (*The Sixth Day*; 'Alcune applicazioni del mimete', *Vizio di forma*) are semi-parodic examples or stereotypes of the amoral scientist or technician, 'ingenious and irresponsible, arrogant and foolish . . . a child of the century' (p. 39; OI, 461). The same could be said of Mr Derryck, the 'hangman for their Britannic Majesties', described in *The Wrench* as the perfect technician, 'so conscientious and so enamoured of his profession that he constantly pondered ways to perfect his instruments' (*The Wrench*, p. 31; OI, 968). The dystopian tales of Aldous Huxley praised by Levi in *L'altrui mestiere* (1985)[6] are also a reminder of the many dangers of a possible world in which 'technicians will have free rein, a world planned in all its smallest details' (OII, 639; my translation). Similarly, Levi's stories on occasion present parables of a technology functioning according to its own logic and necessity, escaping beyond human control (e.g. 'Small Red Lights' ('Lumini rossi') and 'For a Good Purpose' ('A fin di bene'), *The Sixth Day*; both in *Vizio di forma*). However, as is typical in Levi, this provisional theoretical position is qualified and balanced by its opposite.

Levi always tried to move away from the polarized positions and ideological short-cuts: 'we should reject our innate tendency towards radicalism, because it is a source of evil. Both the zero and the one leads us to inaction' (*Other People's Trades*, p. 93; OII, 855). Instead, he tended to look from simultaneously opposing angles and to correct all-encompassing generalizations with the wisdom of 'local', 'circumstantial' knowledge: as he says in a 1979 book preface, 'we need to deal with problems one by one, with honesty, intelligence and humility: this is the delicate and formidable task of today's and tomorrow's techicians' (*The Black Hole of Auschwitz*, p. 122; OI, 1314). In his science writing, Levi's preference was never for so-called *big science*, but rather for the small-scale lab science he had practised as a young man, before and after the *Lager*: 'I was more interested in the stories of the solitary chemist, unarmed and on foot, at the measure of man, which with few exceptions has been mine' (*The Periodic Table*, p. 203; OI, 915). His was a bottom-up understanding of technology and technical work, and how we relate to them. He thus privileged a pre-modern understanding of the link between human action and expression, and the manipulation of the natural world through work and craft by the *homo faber*. In his highly influential essay *The Question Concerning Technology*, Martin Heidegger illustrates this very point by contrasting craftmanship in ancient Greece and the building of a modern dam on the Rhine: while the craftsman gathers the elements – form, matter, finality – and thereby brings out the 'truth' of his materials, modern technology 'de-worlds' its materials and 'summons' nature to submit to extrinsic demands. Instead of a world of authentic things capable of gathering a rich variety of contexts and meanings, we are left, in modern times, with an '"objectless" heap of functions'.[7] Accordingly, in stories such as 'Gli stregoni' ('The Witch Doctors', in *Lilít e altri racconti*, 1981; not included in *Moments of Reprieve*) Levi emphasizes the difference between modern technological gadgetry, which totally dissociates the human being from its knowledge and control, and the pre-modern human relationship to nature and crafts. In *The Wrench*, however, Levi seems to question Heidegger's distinction by closely linking, and rooting in rich textures of meaning and context, apparently different experiences of technology and tool-making from different epochs and scales – the rigger's, the chemist's, those of Faussone's coppersmith father. In the chapter 'Offshore', Faussone watches the launching of a colossal oil rig in an Alaskan bay, which looks 'like an island, but it was an island we had made; and I can't speak for the others ... but I was thinking about the Almighty when he made the world' (*The Wrench*, p. 73; OI, 1009). In the face of this gigantic spectacle, his mind immediately goes to his father's humble trade (narrated in more detail in the chapter 'Beating copper'). The working experience of his father's hand-made copper moulding resonates in Faussone's memory with his own 'craft'; they share the emotional, affective intent and purpose of their trades, the skills and uses of technology; they share a sort of 'love' that make their crafts look alike in spite of the differences of tradition, scale, complexity and economics.

Nature/culture and ethics

One common philosophical assumption on which the definition of the *homo faber* is based is the idealistic separation between the human (or cultural) and the natural. For modern idealism, it is human rationality which creates reality, rendering it coherent and intelligible, while nature, independent of humanity, 'does not exist', so to speak. Levi implicitly rejects such philosophical idealism in relation to the understanding of nature. He sees an essential continuity between human experience and nature, between mind and body, between technology and natural forms and dispositions.

As is clear in 'Carbon', the closing chapter of *The Periodic Table*, Levi espouses a form of materialistic evolutionism, which sees a strong continuity between the natural and the human, between what we define as 'nature' and 'culture'. The boundaries between inanimate objects or the mineral world and living organisms are questioned, in fantastic form, in some of his science-fiction stories in *The Sixth Day*. In '"Cladonia rapida"' (OI, 442–6; not in *The Sixth Day*), for instance, Levi envisages the emergence of biological features and behaviours in cars; while in 'For a good purpose', he foresees the development of a global proto-nervous system, when a threshold of systemic complexity is crossed in the telephone network. In *The Wrench*, Levi also resorts to a whole spectrum of organic, biological and animal metaphors and similes to depict rigs, cranes, bridges. In the second chapter,

'Cloistered', for example, Faussone describes a tower growing like 'a baby that isn't yet born, when it is still inside its mama' (p. 15; OI, 953), and goes on to describe its 'muscles', 'bones', 'nerves' and 'guts' (p. 19; OI, 957) and its wheezing sickness. These images are not simply vividly metaphorical; they have an epistemological weight and insert Levi into a tradition going back to the arch-model of the artist-engineer Leonardo da Vinci. Leonardo saw in all organisms, including the human body, a 'monument of machines', and at the same time, he understood machines as organic structures, with their own intrinsic physiology, providing a strikingly modern, materialistic understanding of the mind/body problem.

If there is, then, no idealistic, radical separation between 'nature' and 'culture', technology itself could be seen, from a philosophical perspective, as a 'second nature' – not intrinsically human, but something intrinsically *natural*. Thus, at one point in *The Wrench* a chimpanzee playfully helps Faussone build a derrick, showing a pre-cognitive, instinctual understanding and fascination for the gigantic toy-machine (*The Wrench*, p. 32; OI, 972). One could then argue that, as with nature, technology *per se* cannot be framed through moral categories. Neither animals nor machines are themselves moral entities. Only human acts can be inscribed within an ethical framework because they are *free* acts, responsible acts. Technology is thus not good or bad in itself, but good or bad according to the social subject who uses it. With his Enlightenment attitude, Levi considers the single human being, with her weaknesses and with her virtues, with individual choice and individual responsibility, as the irreducible centre of his theoretical beliefs: as he says in another context, 'who should shoulder the blame ... the individual ... or the regime ...? ... [It] should be adjudged with great caution, and case by case. This is precisely because we are not totalitarians' (*The Black Hole of Auschwitz*, p. 81; OII, 1248).

If technology is as natural as a beehive or a nest, it is then impossible to prevent any human being from being a technician, a tool-maker, because it is an anthropological given: it is indeed the first requisite inserted in the programme of Mankind's constitution by the engineers of the first human being, in the story 'The Sixth Day' ('a particular aptitude for the creation and utilization of tools', p. 92; OI, 532). Doing away with science and technology would be giving up part of what makes us human: 'if we were to abandon it, we would betray our nature and our nobility as "thinking reeds", and the human species would no longer have any reason to exist' (*The Mirror Maker*, p. 176; OII, 993). However, as social animals, it is our moral duty not to inflict pain and therefore to try to anticipate any possible distorted use of a given technology or device. If foreknowledge is impossible, given that the complexity of the system goes beyond the intellectual reach of any single individual, we cannot simply defend ourselves by freezing scientific research and technological advancement. What are needed are ethics and moral norms relevant to all human beings in general, not only to scientists or politicians. This is the only check we can possibly impose on the growth of science and technology. Moreover, to believe that the human being is, or could be, totally subjugated to the domination of technological and/or economic rationality would be like accepting and justifying the kind of moral torpor and apathy that allowed Nazism to take control of German society with little internal struggle, opposition or individual rebellion. Nazism was for Levi, among other things, the ruthless, expert use of social and technological organization to serve a neo-pagan ideology, the perverse combination of primitive, pre-rational drives with the rationality of industrial efficency.

Daily work, money and magic

After the publication of *The Wrench*, many Italian leftist critics and intellectuals harshly criticized Levi's book for presenting such a eulogy to manual and industrial work. Faussone is indeed 'one of those men who like their job' (*The Wrench*, p. 136; OII, 1071), one who defends and proudly extols his 'taste for work' and treats the inspection of a crane 'always like a celebration' (p. 137; OII, 1071). The ideological and political climate in Italy at that time was dominated by the radical Marxist rejection of capitalism, and there was a shared 'belief that all work, particularly factory work, was oppressive and alienating, and the consequent refusal to consider it as one of the bases of human identity'.[8] In an interview, Levi remembers, for instance, the bitter articles and letters published by *Lotta continua*, an extreme leftist paper, in which he was rebuked because he dared to write about the working-class condition as an outsider (*Voice of Memory*, p. 129). He was, nonetheless, fully equipped with a pragmatic attitude to and knowledge of working conditions, through his experience of industrial work at all levels: from the enslavement of the man as toiling animal in the *Lager*, to employee and eventually executive at the paint company SIVA, starting from 1962. In *The Wrench*, he writes of the rewarding routines of '*le boulot*, the job, *il rusco* – daily work ... less known than the Antarctic, and through a sad and mysterious phenomenon it happens that the people who talk most and loudest about it are the very ones who have never travelled through it' (*The Wrench*, p. 80; OI, 1015).

In fact, there is evidence that Levi wrote with a polemical intent in mind: for example, the working title of *The Wrench* was *Vile meccanico* ('Vile Mechanic'), a phrase shot through with political irony, even sarcasm (see *Voice of Memory*, pp. 93, 123). Levi stands towards the middle of the ideological spectrum, and his polemic cuts two ways, both against those who exalt work 'in official ceremonies [where] an insidious rhetoric is displayed, based on the consideration that a eulogy or a medal costs much less than a pay rise' (p. 80; OI, 1015) and against the 'profoundly stupid' rhetoric 'which tends to denigrate [work], to depict it as base … as if, on the contrary, someone who doesn't know how to work, or knows little, or doesn't want to, were for that very reason a free man' (ibid.). To reinforce this point Levi calls the protagonist of *The Wrench* 'Libertino', literally 'free man', surely a surreptitious answer to that grotesque inscription on the gate of Auschwitz, 'Arbeit Macht Frei' – as Philip Roth remarked in his interview with Levi: 'Faussone is Man the Worker made *truly* free through his labor' (*Voice of Memory*, p. 16).

As mentioned above, Levi reads the general problem of the alienation of work in industrial society by focusing his attention on the single individual, rather than on the collectivity or on classes: 'love or, conversely, hatred of work is an inner, original heritage, which depends greatly on the story of the individual and less than is believed on the productive structure within which the work is done' (*The Wrench*, p. 80; OI, 1016). In more general terms, Levi was also keenly aware that technological issues and work are strongly linked to economics. This is evident in various of his science-fiction stories centred on Simpson, who is both salesman, keen on his commission and his profit, and magician-Prometheus, intent on transforming matter and man. Although Levi does not directly take issue with the commodification of everyday life and with the plethora of objects produced by the market society, he shows evident concern on this score; for instance, by grotesquely representing the expansion of advertising in everyday life in 'In fronte scritto' ('Written on their Foreheads'; OI, 725–32; not in *The Sixth Day*). At the same time, in 'Beating Copper' ('Batter la lastra') in *The Wrench*, he shows keen nostalgia for the kind of manual work and craft that separate the moral and aesthetic value of a given achievement from its economic and commercial aspects. Faussone's father, after he had finished his hand-made copper stoves,

> stood there and looked at his stills … When the customers came to collect them, he would sort of give them a caress, and you could see he was sorry. If they weren't too far away, every now and then he would take his bicycle and go look at them, with the excuse that he was making sure they were working all right.
> (pp. 82–3; OI, 1018)

Various social philosophers, from Georg Simmel in the late nineteenth century to contemporary Serge Latouche with his notion of the 'Megamachine', have carried this issue further, treating 'technology' and 'industrial capitalism' as overlapping concepts and equating the rationality of economic calculation which shapes and rules the global economy with technology.[9] Building on this position, the Italian philosopher Umberto Galimberti has suggested a more hierarchical relationship, with economics subject to technology, since capitalism is based on greed, a passion, while technology, by contrast, is the very manifestation of cold, calculating rationality.[10] Levi's stories subvert such a notion of hierarchy, however, by implying that technology and technical matter are always mediated by economic factors: technology does not progress unbounded, but is limited and framed by structural and material constraints and by economic profitability. What further distinguishes the rationality of economics from technology are the *gratuitous* elements of the latter. In *The Periodic Table*, Levi notes with typical irony: 'Prometheus had been foolish to bestow fire on men instead of selling it to them: he would have made money, placated Jove, and avoided all that trouble with the vulture' (*The Periodic Table*, p. 143; OI, 863). Although it is based on exact planning and mathematical calculation, technology evades these strict limits, because, as with any form of art (*techne*), it is also formed by chance, play and imagination, and is effected by unforeseeable events and *irrational* drives. In *Other People's Trades*, Levi notes: 'the history of technology demonstrates that, when it is faced by new problems, scientific education and precision are necessary but insufficient. Two other virtues are needed, and they are experience and inventive imagination', and in specific critical cases, 'imagination must prevail, which works by leaps, at a fast clip, through radical and rapid mutations' (p. 186; OII, 705).

Examples of 'technological irrationality' are explored in the chapter 'Chromium' in *The Periodic Table*, where Levi recounts the story of the unorthodox use of ammonium chloride in the composition of an anti-rust paint produced by DUCO-Avigliana, the factory where Levi worked in 1946–7. The substance is perfectly useless for the quality and stability of the end product 'and probably a bit harmful', but it was kept in the formula for decades like a superstitious, or even sacred, ingredient, because it 'had always been in it', because 'one never knows', and because 'formulas are as holy as prayers, decree-laws, and dead languages, and not an iota in them can be changed' (*The Periodic Table*, pp. 158–9; OI, 877). The first chapters of *The Wrench* also act as a sort of manifesto on the limits of technological rationality and of its intrinsic 'weakness'. In '"With Malice Aforethought"' ('"Meditato con malizia"'), the rationality of technical engineering coexists with the pre-modern 'rationality' of voodoo rituals. Although the story is set in an unspecified African country, Levi later revealed that the episode was based on a real event that occurred in Milan (*Voice of Memory*, p. 95). In 'The Bold Girl' ('La ragazza ardita'), Levi shows how, at the individual level, any skilled work can be affected and distorted by passion and personal feelings. In 'The Bridge' ('Il ponte'), Faussone keeps repeating that machines and buildings show unpredictable behaviour, 'sort of like with people. I've seen it lots of time: a tower, for example, checked and rechecked and tested, and it looks like it ought to stand for centuries, and it began to teeter after a month; and another one you wouldn't give five cents for, and it never shows a crack' (*The Wrench*, p. 118; OI, 1053). To make veritable predictions within the technological realm is, most of the time, hazardous and intellectually dishonest:

> Some engineer friends of mine have told me it's difficult even to be sure what a brick or a coil spring will do over a period of time ... It's easy to say the same causes should produce the same effects: this is an invention of people who have things done, instead of doing things themselves. Try talking about it with a farmer, or a school teacher, or a doctor, or, most of all, a politician. If they are honest and intelligent, they'll burst out laughing.   (*The Wrench*, pp. 162–3; OI, 1096)

Materialism and knowledge

Besides being useful for a discussion of the philosophy of technology, Levi's work also encapsulates a theory of knowledge. As already noted, although Levi never fully articulated and exposed a thoroughly expressed epistemology, in many of his books he extrapolates methodical, cognitive and ethical rules from his practical experience, grounding his understanding of science and technology in his practical work. On this score, Levi is quite clear:

> It's not a matter of arriving at the deepest roots of knowing, but just of going down from one level to another, understanding a little more than before. When I understand what's going on inside a retort, I'm happier. I've extended my knowledge a little bit more. I haven't understood truth or reality. I've just reconstructed a segment, a little segment of the world. (*Voice of Memory*, p. 8)

In particular, Levi's epistemology emerges from his protagonists' direct contact with material reality, and from their realist, pragmatic and anti-dogmatic attitude. Working in a lab or in a workshop or on a construction site, like Faussone, brings 'the sensation of having "learned how to do something"; which, life teaches, is different from having "learned something"' (*Other People's Trades*, p. 90; OII 814). The contrast – between 'propositional' knowledge and 'practical' or 'tacit' knowledge, between *know-what* and *know-how* – is of fundamental importance for understanding modernity, which has always tended to privilege the former, metaphysical aspect of knowledge; whereas the arts and crafts, experimental science and technology (and indeed art) have been fundamentally fostered by the latter, by knowledge built on the execution of specific tasks and the resolution of given or unexpected problems, made possible by factual familiarity with specific fields of action.[11]

In order to chart the various steps in the constitution of Levi's theory of knowledge, we can turn to the only modern philosopher to have attempted to define the epistemology of chemical research, Gaston Bachelard, and in particular his work *Le Matérialisme rationnel*.[12] For Bachelard, the cognitive dynamics of 'rational materialism' are based on the concept of 'resistance', the stubborn opposition by which the *Hyle* (matter) curbs and bends *homo faber*'s will and acts: what Levi calls the 'sly passivity' of matter, 'as solemn and subtle as the Sphinx' (*The Periodic Table*, p. 39; OI, 772). There is a constant dialectic, a silent dialogue, between the *homo faber* and material reality. Material reality, our 'Mother-Matter, our hostile mother' (p. 38; OI, 771) is for Levi 'an impartial, imperturbable, but extremely harsh judge: if one makes a mistake, one is pitilessly punished' (*Other People's Trades*, p. 175; OII 641–2); 'the judgement of men ... is arbitrary and debatable, while the judgement of things is always inexorable and just. The law is the same for all' (p. 88; OII, 812).

Although there is always a level of projectuality and planning in any technical work, for Bachelard as for Levi, the *homo faber* does not operate through abstract mental schemes, but mainly through direct, sometimes painful, contact with matter, which engenders a form of cognitive response that is channelled through the body and through the senses. For this reason, Levi's *homo faber* can never be the absolute 'master of nature', nor does he 'denaturalize nature', as Arendt claims,[13] but rather his behaviour, actions, mental images and knowledge are shaped by the structures and directions imposed by material reality onto human consciousness itself. As Francisco Varela explains, 'cognition [is] dependent upon the kinds of experience that come from having a body with sensorimotor capacities' and both common sense and creativity in cognition 'consist not of representation but of *embodied action*'.[14] The kind of virtues that Levi fosters through his work in the lab are in fact multifold: his is a form of distributed, holistic intelligence in which mental reasoning is combined with the sagacity of smell, touch and the intuitiveness of the eye: '[in the laboratory] other virtues were required: humility, patience, method, manual dexterity and, also, why not, good eyesight, a keen sense of smell, nervous and muscular stamina, resilience when faced by failure' (*Other People's Trades*, p. 88; OII, 812).

The trade of the chemist is not only an intellectual learning process, but also a manual one, through which the young Levi matures into an adult: 'Our hands were at once coarse and weak, regressive, insensitive: the least trained part of our bodies. . . . If man is a maker, we were not men: we knew this and we suffered from it' (*The Periodic Table*, p. 24; OI, 759–60). Manual dexterity is a form of intelligence at its most elementary level, as he tells Tullio Regge: 'manual analysis, like all manual work, has a formative value; it is too similar to our origins as mammals to be neglected' (*Conversations*, p. 62). Furthermore, as Levi explains in the story 'His Own Blacksmith' ('Il fabbro di se stesso'), hands are tools to think with, much like the brain: 'I've also noticed that, as you do things, other things come to your mind in a chain: I often have the impression that I'm thinking more with my hand than with my brain' (*The Sixth Day*, p. 201; OI, 709). And thus to train our hands means to train our brains as well: 'I could see them with my mind's eye, Faussone's hands . . . They had reminded me of distant readings of Darwin, of the artificer's hand that, making tools and bending matter, stirred the human brain from its torpor and still guides and stimulates and draws it ahead, as a dog does with a blind master' (*The Wrench*, pp. 154–5; OI, 1089). The intelligence of the hands becomes the intelligence of the body, as Faussone himself explains: 'after I felt sure of myself as a welder, I felt sure of myself in everything, even the way I walked' (p. 124; OI 1059), pointing to that 'knowledge in action', linked to art or arts, noted earlier. Here, Levi seems also to echo Aldous Huxley's 'muscular morality', 'the kinesthetic sense' which allows us to understand what is 'physical[ly] right and wrong', as explained in Huxley's essay 'The Education of an Amphibian'.[15] And it is no coincidence that Levi famously defined himself in a much-quoted interview as, precisely, 'an amphibian' (*Voice of Memory*, p. 85).

Finally, both Levi's and Bachelard's materialism also overcome the (Aristotelian) duality of 'form' and 'matter': matter is not an undefined substance shaped by abstract forms superimposed from outside. It is rather a multifold entity, that displays an infinite array of behaviour and features according not to a given 'form', but to a given 'combination'. Prevalent in any chemist is an acute awareness of the mixed constitution of matter and things, what Bachelard called the 'conscience mélangeant'.[16] This awareness defies any attempt to discriminate between fixed categories, such as 'pure' and 'impure' (*The Periodic Table*, p. 35; OI, 768), 'identity' and 'difference' (p. 60; OI, 790), 'noble' and 'vile' (p. 181; OI, 895), 'stable' and 'unstable' (*Other People's Trades*, p. 96; OII, 778). 'Discrimination' is here used as both a scientific and ethical term,[17] as Levi's materialism is explicitly an intellectual tool to overcome any form of idealism and any imposition of the spirit over matter, which for Levi has clear political connotations and implications: 'Chemistry, for me . . . led to the heart of Matter, and Matter was our ally precisely because the Spirit, dear to Fascism, was our enemy' (*The Periodic Table*, p. 52; OI, 784).

Technology and communication

From the 'resistance' of matter philosophers of science derive one of the key methodological principles of scientific knowledge, 'empirical verification'. An essential requirement of this principle is that any experiment should be repeatable under given experimental conditions, and be inter-subjective, that is shared and reproduced by a plurality of people, by a given *community*.[18] For Levi, indeed, any trade establishes social links of solidarity: 'the laboratory was collegial, a centre of socialization where one really made friends. As a matter of fact, I remained friends with all my laboratory colleagues. ... Making mistakes together is a fundamental experience' (*Conversations*, pp. 19–20). Knowledge formation, education and indeed culture are themselves collective, communal phenomena.

This is extremely important for Levi, both as a chemist and as a writer, because one of the key ethical element in science and in technical trades is the fact that it provides a common language through which to develop dialogue with others.[19] To build things and objects, to manipulate matter, to practise a trade, means to invent a new language,[20] and to be forced to communicate, to be bound to a common ground for interpersonal dialogue and exchange. Faussone is aware that, 'after all, they were riggers, and we always find a way of explaining ourselves, even if we only use sign language' (*The Wrench*, p. 65; OI, 1001). JoAnn Cannon also reminds us that 'Levi cites the language of the chemists as a possible solution to the fundamental limitation and the constitutive feature of language: the disjunction between the sign and the referent'. The periodic table is 'a means to bridge the gap between words and things ... a universal semantic system, perhaps the closest thing that we will ever have to an Edenic language'.[21] That is why Levi refuses to accept existentialist formulas that stress human 'incommunicability': 'Except for cases of pathological incapacity, one can and must communicate ... To say that it is impossible to communicate is false: one always can' (*The Drowned and the Saved* (*I sommersi e i salvati*, 1986), p. 69; OII, 1059–60).

Communication and dialogue are fostered by technical trades also because of an intrinsic link to storytelling. The problem-solving of practical knowledge equates with the 'troubles overcome' of the Yiddish proverb which opens *The Periodic Table*, 'Troubles overcome are good to tell'. Technical work, rather than being a cold, uninspiring and dehumanizing activity, is a source of inspiration for the writer: 'an illicit advantage *vis-à-vis* my new writer colleagues' ('Ex Chemist' ('Ex chimico'), *Other People's Trades*, p. 176; OII, 642). Specifically, in the chapter of *The Wrench* entitled 'Tiresias', Levi tries to build bridges between his writing activity and Faussone's skills and craft, and in doing so, he unfolds the Greek root of the word *techne*, which translates both art and craft. 'Writing', he agrees in one interview, 'is a technical problem' (*Voice of Memory*, p. 168).

Various elements are shared between the two trades of technology and narrative: a need for symmetry, economy, the form fitting the purpose, careful planning and, crucially, a method of trial-and-error. Unfortunately, 'in the job of writing, the instruments, the alarm systems are rudimentary: there isn't even a trustworthy equivalent of the T square or the plumbline. But if a page is wrong the reader notices, and by then it is too late' (*The Wrench*, p. 48; OI, 985). In relation to this parallelism between the language of science and the language of literature and the borrowing of aesthetic and stylistic principles such as clarity, consistency, concision, Levi adds a category which is seldom used in the realm of literary criticism: *responsibility*. This is a virtue on which Levi lays particular emphasis, at different levels: calling on a government minister to resign, he declares, 'of the many illnesses to afflict us, the most serious is the refusal to accept responsibiliy' (*The Black Hole of Auschwitz*, p. 40; OI, 1220); explaining his admiration for the eighteenth-century poet Parini, he says he was 'responsible for every word he has written' (*The Search for Roots*, p. 42; OII 1396). And in these words, there is a surreptitious polemic against writers and humanists in general, because 'often, unlike technicians, writers feel no responsibility for their "products". A badly made bridge and a faulty pair of glasses have immediate, negative consequences. Not a novel.'[22]

Levi calls for an ethical accountability within creative writing, basing his poetics on a positive notion of the actual practice of writing, with its own tools and methods, which make it intrinsically capable of self-correcting. This attitude is also to be found, according to Daniele Del Giudice, in one of Levi's key models, Joseph Conrad, whom Levi quotes at the end of *The Wrench* (p. 173; OII, 1105).[23] Del Giudice in particular draws on a relatively unknown essay by Conrad, quite revealingly entitled 'Out of Literature', which discusses the so-called 'Notices to Mariners', the instructions that any captain should follow to safely sail his ship into port. Conrad's voice could easily be Levi's also:

> The Notices to Mariners are good prose but I think no critic would admit them into the body of literature. . . . In those compositions which are read as earnestly as anything that ever came from printing press, all suggestions of Love, of Adventure, of Romance, of Speculation, of all that decorates and ennobles life, except Responsibility, is barred.[24]

This is further testimony to the fact that any human activity and trade, including technology and writing, has an intrinsic moral value. As with any other type of *poiesis*, or production, such professions disclose an intrinsic ethical programme:

> ... because they teach us to be whole, to think with our hands and with the entire body, to refuse to surrender to the negative days and to formulas that cannot be understood, because you understand them as you go. And finally our professions teach us to know matter and to confront it: the profession of writing, because it grants (rarely, but it does grant) some moments of creation, like when current suddenly runs through a circuit that is turned off, and a light comes on. *(The Wrench*, pp. 52–3; OI, 989)

NOTES

1. Quoted in OI, 1453.
2. Extensive details of the several chapters he did complete before his death are to be found in Carole Angier, *The Double Bond: Primo Levi, A Biography*, London, Viking, 2002: see index entry, p. 882.
3. See Hannah Arendt, *The Human Condition*, Chicago, University of Chicago Press, 1958, p. 80.
4. See Keekok Lee, 'Homo Faber: The Ontological Category of Modernity', *PSA Annual Conference Papers 1996*, www.psa.ac.uk/cps/1996/klee.pdf (retrieved 20 December 2005).
5. See for instance E. Severino, *Téchne. Le radici della violenza*, Milan, Rizzoli, 2002.
6. The English version of the book, *Other People's Trades*, does not include the essay 'Aldous Huxley', but does include another which discusses the English writer's work, 'Novel Dictated by Crickets' ('Romanzi dettati dai grilli').
7. Quotations taken from Andrew Feenberg, *Questioning Technology*, London, Routledge, 1999, p. 184.
8. Mirna Cicioni, *Primo Levi. Bridges of Knowledge*, Oxford, Berg, 1995, p. 84.
9. See Michela Nacci, *Pensare la tecnica. Un secolo di incomprensioni*, Rome-Bari, Laterza, 2000, pp. 78–85.
10. Edoardo Boncinelli, Umberto Galimberti, Giovanni Maria Pace, *E ora? La dimensione umana e la sfida della scienza*, Turin, Einaudi, 2000, pp. 69–70.
11. See Thomas Kuhn, *The Structure of Scientific Revolutions*, 2nd edition, Chicago, Chicago University Press, 1970, p. 44; Bengt Molander, 'Tacit Knowledge and Silenced Knowledge: Fundamental Problems and Controversies', in Bo Göranzon and Magnus Florin (eds.), *Skill and Education: Reflection and Experience*, London, Berlin et al. Springer Verlag, 1992, pp. 9–31.
12. Gaston Bachelard, *Le Matérialisme rationnel*, Paris, PUF, 1953. See Mario Porro, 'Scienza', in Marco Belpoliti (ed.), *Primo Levi* (Riga 13), Milan, Marcos y Marcos, 1997, pp. 442–55.
13. Arendt, *Human Condition*, pp. 144, 148.
14. Federico Varela, *Ethical Know-How. Action, Wisdom, and Cognition*, Stanford, Stanford University Press, 1999, pp. 11–12, 17.
15. See Aldous Huxley, *Adonis and the Alphabet*, London, Chatto and Windus, 1975, p. 19.

16. Bachelard, *Matérialisme*, p. 15.
17. See Robert S. C. Gordon, *Primo Levi's Ordinary Virtues. From Testimony to Ethics*, Oxford, Oxford University Press, 2001, pp. 85–8.
18. See ibid., pp. 197–239.
19. See Nicoletta Pireddu, 'Towards a Poet(h)ics of *techne*. Primo Levi and Daniele Del Giudice', *Annali d'Italianistica*, 19 (2001), p. 192.
20. Cf. Bachelard, *Matérialisme*, p. 1.
21. JoAnn Cannon, 'Chemistry and Writing in *The Periodic Table*', in S. Tarrow (ed.), *Reason and Light. Essays on Primo Levi*, Ithaca, Center for International Studies, Cornell University, 1990, pp. 107–8.
22. Quoted in *Conversazioni e interviste*, p. 153; not in *Voice of Memory*.
23. Daniele Del Giudice, 'Introduzione', in OI, xlix. The English edition of *The Wrench* has an added explanatory note to the Conrad quotation, by Levi.
24. Joseph Conrad, *Last Essays*, London and Toronto, J. M. Dent and Sons, 1928, pp. 39–40.

7

CHARLOTTE ROSS

Primo Levi's science-fiction

Levi's 'science-fiction' or 'science-fantasy' stories make for fascinating and often unsettling reading. They are stories that slip in and out of conventional genre categories, oscillating between narrating what appears to be purely fictional, and what feels uncannily close to our lived experience. Levi moves from myth and fable to satire and irony; at times he focuses on alternative histories, at others on dystopic futures, in a way that recalls resonantly the range of the science-fiction writer Arthur C. Clarke.[1] Subjects tackled include: robots that compose poetry; duplicator machines; virtual reality devices; cryogenics; test-tube babies; and a sinister, self-generating telephone network. Most of Levi's stories that fall into this rather blurry category are collected in two volumes: *Storie naturali* ('Natural Histories', 1966), and *Vizio di forma* ('Formal Defect', 1971).[2]

Levi first began writing stories of this kind relatively early on in his writing career; the first drafts of 'The Mnemogogues' ('I mnemagoghi'), 'The Sixth Day' ('Il sesto giorno') and 'The Sleeping Beauty in the Fridge: A Winter's Tale' ('La bella addormentata nel frigo') (all from 'Natural Histories', all in *The Sixth Day*), date from 1946, 1946–7 and 1952 respectively. Many stories first appeared in newspapers such as *Il mondo* and *Il giorno* and were reworked for republication in the later collections.[3] They thus run contemporaneous with his testimonial work, and, as will be seen below, act as extensions of Levi's writing about the *Lager*. This chapter, as well as exploring such links, examines the ways in which Levi uses fiction as a vehicle to comment on and think through contemporary and future scientific developments. In this sense the stories are themselves forms of experimental writing. In particular, it looks at his problematization of scientific 'progress' as inevitably beneficial for human life, and explores the moral and ethical concerns that he feels are raised by such developments. It also analyses his engagement with the technologization of social life and the body, as it impacts on individual identity and autonomy, asking finally what suggestions these experiments hold for our own futures.

The 'science-fiction' stories

Any consideration of Levi's stories requires first an exploration of his particular brand of 'science-fiction'. Italo Calvino – Levi's contemporary and a writer with an abiding interest in science and its potential within literature – called Levi's stories 'fantabiological', commending the way in which he cajoled fantasy, poetry and intellectual suggestion from a 'scientific' starting-point.[4] Marco Belpoliti sees traces of the 'fantastic' running through these writings, and through all of Levi's work. He characterizes the science-fiction stories as rooted in the Italian tradition of magic realism, with the result that fantasy gets the better of purely technologically focused sci-fi.[5] Levi himself disputed the label of science-fiction, responding to an interviewer's questions thus: 'No, these aren't science fiction, if by that you mean fiction about the world to come, cheap, futuristic fantasy. These stories are *more possible* than many others. Indeed, they are so possible that parts of them have already come true' (*Voice of Memory*, p. 84).

Although subject-matter and stylistic approach vary considerably, these stories can be linked through their shared focus on the moral and ethical questions raised by the scenarios and individuals described. Indeed, *Il giorno* introduced the stories as 'moral tales disguised as science-fiction'.[6] Levi revealed that they were inspired by his perception of a 'formal defect' afflicting various aspects of our social life and moral framework – a perception that he believed to be relatively widespread (OI, 1434). In building fantastic narratives around what he defines as 'microscopic [*puntiforme*] intuition' (OI, 1434), Levi's aim was with a light touch to raise awareness of these 'defects'; yet his public identity as author of *If This is a Man* (*Se questo è un uomo*, 1947) and *The Truce* (*La tregua*, 1963), was at first disguised. 'Natural Histories' was initially published under the pseudonym 'Damiano Malabaila', for fear that this more light-hearted writing would not be well received by Levi's reading public; as Levi himself asked, 'isn't this a form of con, like selling wine in oil bottles?' (OI, 1435).

Despite this pseudo-anonymity (to careful readers, Levi's 'real' identity was clear from text on the book jacket), Levi simultaneously asserts that a definite bridge does exist linking his science-fiction stories to his testimonial works. He names the Holocaust as the largest of the defects of our age – a 'monster' that comes into being when reason sleeps (OI, 1435). Moreover, he denies that in writing these stories he was in some way betraying his earlier works. In his view, there is a clear resonance between his testimonial and his science-fiction writings. In both we see human existence reduced to slavery, the individual reified, whether through Nazism or through forms of technology. His stories hypothesize about the power of science and knowledge as vehicles that can lead us in diverging directions, linking in to influential discourses in the philosophy of science that question the necessarily teleological character of scientific 'progress'.[7] On the one hand, scientific developments and related change may improve the conditions of human social life; on the other, such change may enslave and imprison us in a nightmare scenario akin to the bleak dystopia described in Aldous Huxley's novel *Brave New World*,[8] where the hyper-rationalization of society quashes individual expression.

By Levi's own definition, the stories hover on the edge of our reality, sometimes actually overlapping with the world we inhabit. Readers were intended to feel an uncanny shiver of truth and recognition when confronting the ostensibly 'other' worlds and societies described. As Sergio Solmi noted in an influential anthology from the late 1950s which Levi knew, 'science-fiction is not prophecy, it is rather an impassioned projection of the present onto a mythical future'.[9] Today, many of the situations Levi conceptualized and many of the questions he posed about the ways in which scientific research was and is conducted remain burning issues in contemporary debate. A careful reading of the texts shows how they interrogate the assumed authority of 'progress', reflect on why and how we are as we are and anticipate future developments with informed circumspection.

'Natural Histories': the temptations of science[10]

The stories in the collection 'Natural Histories' explore a range of situations, questioning scientific practice in the laboratory and hypothesizing about the impact of newly developed technologies on our social life. Six of them are linked, following the career of an American salesman, Mr Simpson, whose own life is ultimately controlled by the products he peddles. Before examining these, I consider four other stories that demonstrate the range of Levi's writing.

'Angelic Butterfly' ('Angelica farfalla') tells of a Professor Leeb, who in 1943 began a series of experiments on four human subjects, in an attempt to demonstrate that human beings were 'neotenic': that is, that human beings exist merely in immature or larval form, and have the potential to develop just as caterpillars become butterflies. We encounter the scene of the experiments, a now derelict building in post-war Berlin, through the eyes of American and Russian investigators and a young German woman who glimpsed the experiment in progress. Events are swathed in sinister secrecy, and abject images of putrid decay abound, contrasting sharply with the allusion among Leeb's papers to Dante's 'angelic butterfly', the form we should assume on ascent to Judgement.[11]

Leeb's experiments are clear examples of the ways in which a brutal process with no clear empirical foundation is passed off as progressive scientific investigation. The callous treatment of the subjects of his experiment – who are obviously Jews, gypsies or some other group deemed inferior or expendable by Nazi logic – is also repeated by some starving German locals who, after Leeb has disappeared, break in to butcher and eat the now contorted, feathered, bird-like frames of the prisoners. This is science as ideology, perpetrated in the name of a deeply twisted sense of 'progress'. The story can be read as alluding to the tacit complicity of German citizens who feigned ignorance of the atrocities perpetrated during the Holocaust. Moreover, the uncertainty surrounding Leeb's apparent death, and the implication that he absconded rather than hanging himself, alludes to the historical figures who eluded capture by staging their own suicides. The story begs us to question our own collusion with such exploitation and cruelty, and implicitly gestures towards the need for a sense of collective responsibility for the fate of our fellow beings.[12]

Another tale of dubious laboratory experiments carried out during the inverted norms of wartime is 'Versamina'. Kleber, a solitary scientist employed in a laboratory, discovers 'versamines', substances that convert pleasure into pain and vice versa, driving whoever consumes them to self-harm and eventually suicide, from which they seem to derive a deep – if not straightforward – satisfaction. The substance is administered to dogs and rabbits, but Kleber also takes it himself, developing an addiction that proves fatal. Aside from the ethical issue of experimenting on animals raised by the disturbing descriptions of the plight suffered by many creatures, and the problems of addiction, the story reveals an even more sinister military use of such a substance. When the American Navy obtains a licence to use versamines, they administer them to Korean soldiers, who act in an abject manner and allow themselves to be killed, offering no resistance now their sense of self-protection has been replaced by a drive for self-destruction. Versamines give false messages to the brain; they are easy to produce and very cheap; 'not more than a few pennies for a gram, and a gram is enough to wreck a man' (p. 51; OI, 473).

In both these stories, key events are related after the fact by a first-hand witness to someone who was not there. They are thus fictional testimonies that seek to bring untold histories to light. Their settings are plausibly real and resonant with recent history, creating discomfort as information emerges; in this, the stories echo the way in which individual and hidden wartime experiences that had previously been suppressed or simply out of view seeped out in the aftermath. The science that Levi presents here is a science that has failed to question its own morality. In a 1986 essay,

'Hatching the Cobra' (*The Mirror Maker*; 'Covare il cobra', *Racconti e saggi*), he warns scientists directly that this lack must be addressed. Pointing out the lurking danger in each new discovery, he beseeches those at the front line to remember that 'what you do when you exercise your profession can be useful, neutral or harmful to mankind'. He continues, prescribing: 'you will agree to study a new medicament, you will refuse to formulate a nerve gas' (p. 175; OII, 992). In the two earlier stories, Levi is issuing a similar warning, but in a more indirect and applied fashion. His critique of exploitation carried out in the name of 'science' is woven together with the idiosyncrasies of individual lives and collective histories, in a cross between contemporary parable and retrieved, silenced histories.

In quite a different vein, 'The Sleeping Beauty in the Fridge: A Winter's Tale', written as a short dramatic sketch, looks to a science of the future that is almost upon us. Patricia is a pioneering subject of cryogenics frozen in 1975, whom we encounter in 2115. She has aged, or lived, less than one year, being unfrozen only on her birthday or to witness what are considered to be important socio-historic events. Unusually for Levi, this story has an undeniably feminist edge, as we witness and are led to condemn the way that Patricia becomes the sexual object *par excellence* for the scientists and men that surround her, controlling and documenting her every move. She is partially unfrozen and systematically raped by her host Peter, and indeed it is only through the sexual attraction she holds for his friend Baldur that she is able to contrive her escape. Aside from these abuses, Patricia also regrets her original decision to be frozen, admitting that she suffers from loneliness and acknowledging that this is part of the deal she struck to gain eternal youth by daring to go so definitively beyond the limits of organic human life.

This drama also offers moments of bleak comedy and satirical light-heartedness, but it is ultimately driven by Patricia's desire to escape her technologized imprisonment. In the cryogenic process human bodies are directly controlled both by machines and apparatuses, and by other humans who are desensitized to issues of human freedom. This is perhaps because the frozen specimen has become for them less than human: Patricia is reified as an object of knowledge, or as a sexual object, rather than being treated as an individual with rights. Many of Levi's stories are concerned with machines and the power they can exert over us if used irresponsibly or for unethical ends. The rapidity of the technological revolution that occurred in the twentieth century has forced us to question whether such developments represent a linear progression towards a 'better' civilization, a notion explored widely in the philosophy of science, in the work of thinkers from Karl Popper and Kuhn to Paul Feyerabend, which Levi here dramatizes effectively.

In some of Levi's stories, the reader is forced to confront nightmare scenarios, in which the drive to advance 'knowledge' has resulted in cruelty, pain and loss of freedom or even lives for his characters. Processes that for many feel like the irrelevant workings of a distant laboratory are shown to impact on our condition as individual beings in localized domestic settings. In some ways, we might see his drive to narrate these cautionary tales as a desire to show how – to adopt a slogan from the second-wave feminist movements of the 1970s – 'the personal is political'; how every aspect of our lives may be affected by events and developments that ostensibly occur at a different socio-political level and in occluded spaces. Levi's work is concerned throughout with human consciousness, with that spirit that makes us human, as the title and epigraph of *If This is a Man* make clear. In these stories we see that this spirit is ever more challenged by the fraught dynamic of our interactions with technology, by what it can do for us, or, more worryingly, what it can do *to* us.

Concern with the growing autonomy of machines, and our dependence on them, is central to Levi's accounts of alienated characters who are effectively replaced by or live in thrall to technological devices. Perhaps the clearest examples are the six stories about Mr Simpson noted above. Simpson is employed by the American company NATCA, an acronym that is never deciphered, rendering the company all the more anonymous, mystificatory and unaccountable. Simpson sells a variety of products ostensibly aimed to enhance and improve our quality of life, but which all lend themselves to questionable application, and have the potential to cause harm. This is evidenced by the warnings and restrictions placed on some of the products, but only after their capabilities have been abused.

For example, 'Il Versificatore' ('The Versifier'; not in *The Sixth Day*) is a robot that can write poetry, which ultimately takes over from its employer, the poet, making him redundant. The 'Mimer', which features in 'Order on the Cheap' ('L'ordine a buon mercato') and 'Some Applications of the Mimer' ('Alcune applicazioni del mimete'), is a duplicating machine used eventually by a certain Gilberto to clone his wife, and finally himself, raising concerns about individual identity and the mass production of human beings. In 'The Measure of Beauty' ('La misura della bellezza'), the 'Kalometer' can be used to obtain beauty ratings for individuals, by registering personal details and comparing them with a male or female ideal standard – which, it goes without saying, is monolithically white and conventional. Finally in 'Retirement Fund' ('Trattamento di quiescenza'), Simpson introduces the Torec, a virtual reality device, and himself succumbs to the addictive lure of vicarious living, replacing reality with serial visions of his own death.

Narration moves between first-person monologue and a dialogue between the first-person narrator and Simpson, a form which Levi used to great effect in other of his works.[13] The narrator and his wife function as sceptical checks against the technological temptations produced by NATCA; for example, the narrator's wife declares the Kalometer a measure of conformity rather than beauty, and the narrator comments on his friend Gilberto: '[He] is a symbol of our century. I've always thought that, if the occasion arose, he would have been able to build an atom bomb and drop it on Milan "to see the effect it would have"' (p. 39; OI, 461).

Levi's 'Simpson' stories narrate a (science-)fictional case study of a firm riding high on the wave of American-style consumerism unleashed in post-war Italy.[14] As critical work on the so-called 'consumerist revolution' makes clear, in the post-war era products were devised, launched and sold on the premise that people – especially women – needed to acquire and use certain technologies in order to keep their homes and their selves in the conditions required by any self-respecting individual. Unprecedented 'needs' were created through advertising and then appeased by new products that fulfilled consumers' dreams in a process that reinforced social docility.[15]

On this issue, Levi's narrator is used to beautiful effect as he is at first uninterested in the duplicator that we all apparently crave: 'A duplicator? . . . I never dreamt about duplicators' (p. 26; OI, 447). However, he then becomes so entranced by its possibilities that he infringes even Simpson's moral sensibilities. It is his questions about acquiring a duplicator with a larger capacity that provoke new stipulations from the company, forbidding the reproduction of '*human beings*, be they living or defunct, or parts thereof' (p. 33; OI, 455; emphasis in original). The hasty cobbling together of this decree has uncanny resonances with recent developments in European law, notably the implementation of new legislation forbidding human cloning as the technology itself becomes a reality. Like NATCA's stipulations after the fact, these clauses did not exist previously to current research on human cloning because it was (naively?) assumed that the various contentious procedures simply would not be put into practice. Yet they can also be seen as the logical and inescapable conclusion of a desire created by the hyper-technologization of society – a conclusion that Levi clearly foresaw.

Levi's stories do away with the 'hypocrisy of neutral science' ('Hatching the Cobra', p. 176; OII, 993), an untenable concept used to justify dubious practices, to dodge accepting responsibility for the research that we, individually or as a society, devise and elect to carry through.[16] This point is made very directly in the 1986 essay, but Levi had already expressed the same concerns in his earlier narratives. His stories also question the ideologies pedalled to an increasingly docile population, one that tends ever more towards passive consumerism rather than active production. Here he raises issues of our objectification and exploitation in the name of 'progress'. Sometimes this occurs in a gender-specific manner, as in the case of Patrizia, or Emma, Gilberto's wife: she is duplicated without her consent because she is 'indispensable to him, and . . . it had seemed a good idea to have two of her' (*The Sixth Day*, p. 40; OI, 462). Levi is sensitive to questions of agency and highlights the concentration of scientific and technological power into often unscrupulous male hands. However, we are clearly all potentially at risk from impositions of this power, the effects of which may steal insidiously upon us, compromising our status as autonomous beings and inching us closer towards a condition of reification.

'Formal Defect': forms of dehumanization[17]

Much of Levi's writing is concerned with the impotence of the individual before unaccountable forces, an anxiety that is palpable in the stories considered above. Impotence is expressed in the 'docile' bodies we encounter. These are bodies subject to what Michel Foucault defined as 'a mechanics of power [which] may have a hold over others' bodies, not only so that they may do what one wishes, but so that they may operate as one wishes, with the techniques, the speed and the efficiency that one determines.'[18] In the stories that make up 'Natural Histories' and 'Formal Defect', we see many examples of such enforced bodily and mental docility as the mechanics of capitalism and the bureacratization and technologization of society impact both on the larger, more amorphous body of social organization and on the individual. The importance of this theme is emphasized by the original title for the collection published as 'Formal Defect': 'Disumanesimo', or 'Dehumanism' (OI, 1441).

Levi discussed the motivation behind the collection, saying that even though he felt he had, in some ways, exhausted himself as a 'witness' and testimonial writer, he had more to say; 'things I could only say in another language, a language some might call ironic, but which I see as shrill, oblique, spiteful, deliberately anti-poetic; anti-human [*disumano*] where my earlier language had been inhuman [*inumano*]' (*Voice of Memory*, p. 88). The results of this urge are several visions of a 'dehumanized' future which raise issues of autonomy and automata, of human freedom, reification and commodification. Two stories clearly exemplify a loss of autonomy: 'Protection' ('Protezione'; not in *The Sixth Day*), and 'Small Red Lights' ('Lumini rossi'). Characters in 'Protection' are required by law to wear protective suits that resemble armour to shield them from the threat of meteorite rain – a threat that may have been devised by car manufacturers to keep up their profits when business slumped. In the second story, Luigi and Maria's daily move-ments are controlled by an average of about 200 red lights situated every-where, from traffic signals to lights implanted in the human body itself. The light between Maria's clavicles indicates her fertile days and thus acts as a contraceptive signal. The docile bodies we see are separated from one another and discouraged from physical contact, either by prohibitive signs or by physically impenetrable layers that obscure the human form. Inevitably, such devices serve to heighten feelings of alienation from one's peers, family and even from one's own body.

In these circumstances, human bodies swiftly become reified, as in 'In fronte scritto' ('Written on Their Foreheads'; not in *The Sixth Day*), in which Enrico and Laura sell their forehead space to an advertising company.[19] Elsewhere, in 'Le nostre belle specificazioni' ('Our Beautiful Specifications'; not in *The Sixth Day*), we hear of an agency that deals in classification, issuing a vast catalogue of specifications of acceptable measurements and qualities. The items listed even include a human being: is it of acceptable dimensions? Is it heat resistant? Fire resistant? Such is the devotion of the manager, Peirani, to his specifica-tions, that he chooses to resign rather than remove this patently absurd, and rather threatening, entry in the catalogue. This is a project of a dehumanized and dehumanizing 'normalization, unification, standardization and the ratio-nalization of production' (OI, 670),[20] one that resonates with Max Weber's notion of the 'iron cage' of rationality. Weber believed that bureaucratic rationality functioned as a cage-like structure in which alienated individuals became imprisoned.[21] Peirani is so trapped within his own irrational ration-ality that he capitulates to the infernal logic of the bureaucracy and condemns himself as an unacceptable specimen.

Aside from autonomy, another concern voiced in many of the stories in this collection relates to technologies of creation and reproduction, viewed from a variety of perspectives and inspired by very different motivations. 'The Hard-Sellers' ('Procacciatori d'affari') narrates a moral choice made by an unborn soul who is to be sent to experience life on Earth. Despite viewing a vividly representative slide-show of the pain and injustice that this might entail, he finally elects to be born at random rather than into a privileged situation, so as not to feel ashamed before his fellow humans who were not given this choice. Continuing in the (then) futuristic vein, 'I sintetici' ('The Synthetics'; not in *The Sixth Day*), introduces the notion of test-tube babies.[22] Schoolboy taunts, partially understood reports of *in vitro* fertilization and conflicting desires to conform whilst retaining indivi-duality lead to heated discussions. We hear that parents can apparently choose their child's features from a menu, as well as choosing its sex by using a red or blue pill, and that the new 'synthetic' race will in time assert its rightful superiority. Although approaching the topic from different angles, both stories highlight the unethical implications of rationalizing the birth process.

Two further 'birth' narratives take us back in time. In 'The Servant' ('Il servo'), a golem is created by Rabbi Ariè in the late sixteenth-century Prague ghetto. Although powerful and a staunch defender of the community, the golem ultimately self-destructs when he is given two contradictory commands – rather like a robot or computer programme might crash or stall.[23] In sharp contrast to the servile golem, the protagonist of 'His Own Blacksmith' ('Il fabbro di se stesso') is just that; the creator of his own form. We read the diary of an individual who is now a man, but whose memory contains the recollections of all his ancestors. Beginning at a time defined as $- 10^9$, Levi's protagonist recounts the changes effected by this first ancestor as he and his wife leave the water and forge a new body able to survive on land, using combinations of carbon, hydrogen and oxygen. This story is dedicated to Calvino since the protagonist is inspired by the character Qfwfq of Calvino's 1965 whimsical science-fantasy work *Le cosmico-miche*,[24] and shares the latter's light and humorous tone, revelling in the impossible yet seductive conceit of a single consciousness whose memory spans an almost inconceivable expanse of time.

These 'creation' narratives are recounted by a series of voices: from solemn prose heavy with biblical allusions, to futuristic modes of techno-logically mediated reproduction, to playful parody of Darwin's theories of evolution. Levi considers the ways in which we do, or might, manage the key moments of our lives from a varied range of perspectives, trying out different hypothetical 'realities' that are alternately less or more resonant with contemporary practices. Many of the stories point towards a common message: our humanity is being eroded by technology. For a significant source of inspiration, we might return to Aldous Huxley, and especially *Brave New World*. In his essay on Huxley in *L'altrui mestiere* (1985), Levi commented:

> [*Brave New World*] contains no elegant deviations nor poetic research and does not even feature flesh and blood characters: it is dry, taut and bitter, but it decidedly deserves a re-reading. It describes with implacable precision a world which back then might have appeared a delirious and arbitrary fantasy, but towards which we are headed today. It is the best of the possible worlds, as it would be if technicians had free rein: a world that is planned in every aspect (even children are born to plan, no longer born in labour but on an assembly line: individuals or batches of identical twins, according to the demands of the market), in which totalitarian hyper-organization and capitalist production converge: Marx, Pavlov, Freud and Ford. (OII, 639)[25]

At times, Levi does indeed assume the implacable tones of Huxley, the 'anti-human' language he described as the contrast to his earlier style; he also engages repeatedly with scenarios like that tackled by Huxley. In these situations, human reproduction becomes a rationalized process on a continuum with the production of potentially autonomous mechanical devices – like the intelligent telephone network that orchestrates its own expansion and controls its human 'managers' by manipulating phone calls in 'For a Good Purpose' ('A fin di bene'). This is what technology can bring us to, and it may happen sooner than we think: Levi quotes Huxley's remarks in 1959 that due to socio-cultural changes, he felt that the events of his novel were now disconcertingly plausible. This is echoed in Levi's letter of January 1987 that prefaces the republication of 'Formal Defect' (OI, 571–2), in which he details which of his hypotheses have been realized and which, thankfully, have not.

The realization or verification of Levi's predictions was a subject of some debate. Levi acknowledged the bleakness of many of his tales, but protested: 'I intended them to be ironic or what you might call conditional catastrophes: we'll end up like this unless we do something about it, but we have the means and the strength and the wit to prevent it' (*Voice of Memory*, p. 89). Stopping scientific research in its tracks was not the answer; Levi emphasizes in 'Hatching the Cobra' that it is imperative for new research to be undertaken (*The Mirror Maker*, p. 175; OII, 992). Furthermore, the description on the back cover of the Italian edition of 'Formal Defect', probably written by Levi, states that although some technologies have caused pollution and become vehicles of oppression, 'the restoration of global order, the healing of the "formal defect", will come from technology, and technology alone' (OI, 1443).[26]

Despite these assertions, however, Levi does not give us any clear indication of how this might be possible. Although they may wish to do so, few of his characters feel strong enough to rise up against dehumanizing forces. We do see a rare rebellion by nature, as the trees in 'Mutiny' ('Ammutinamento') plot together to assert themselves against the mistreatment they have suffered at human hands for centuries, but most of his characters simply become more and more resigned to their loss of freedom and human autonomy. What, then, is the basis of his hopeful vision?

Conclusions

Levi opposed the reification and destruction of the human spirit, perpetrated in the past through the monstrous machinery of war and caused today by 'absurd' developments in science and technology.[27] He described the *Lager* as a new and terrifying 'technological innovation' (*The Black Hole of Auschwitz*, p. 90; OII, 1321). Clearly, Nazi oppression and alienation caused by hyper-technologization figure on a continuum for Levi, and he fears both a recurrence of the atrocities of Auschwitz[28] and an intensification of scientific rationalization in our daily lives. However, technology is by no means necessarily catastrophic: it is like 'Achilles' spear, which may harm or heal depending on how it is wielded, and by whom'.[29] As Levi commented in an interview:

> the greatest error of the applied scientists ... has not so much been capitulation to power, but rather the undervaluing of their own influence and the scale of change unleashed by their work. This is their real 'formal defect'. I don't for a moment think the error is irreversible and I hope that all of the world's scientists understand that the future depends on their return to conscience.
>
> (*Voice of Memory*, p. 90)

Human conscience, then, is one key to redemption – a sense of conscience that might be honed and heightened through the acquisition of productive wisdom. Here we begin to see the ways in which the developments recounted in Levi's stories, although ostensibly bleak, may hold a similar potential to Achilles' spear, suggesting both negative and positive consequences of our actions.

In 'Retirement Fund', the narrator reports, the only book that Mr Simpson can bear to read once hooked on the Torec is Ecclesiastes: a book that announces how 'in much wisdom there is much grief; and he that increaseth knowledge increaseth sorrow' (*The Sixth Day*, p. 124; OI, 567). Yet elsewhere Levi questions why 'our intelligence has increased portentously, yet our wisdom hasn't', and asks, 'how much time, in all the schools of all countries, is devoted to increasing wisdom, that is, to moral problems?' ('Hatching the Cobra', *The Mirror Maker*, p. 175; OII, 992). Wisdom, like technology, like scientific research, like human endeavour of all kinds, can lead to good or evil, to pleasure or pain. The wisdom, or moral concern embedded in these stories, is related to the exercise of restraint or caution. If, as in Huxley's dystopic vision, the technophiles have free rein, our world may indeed resemble that of Simpson or Patricia, a realm in which we wear protective suits and follow red lights in a state of enforced docility. However, we can take heed of Levi's narrative thought experiments and try to differentiate between what we are *capable* of achieving and what we might *elect* to achieve in the best interests of humanity. Levi treats fiction as a realm of possibilities in which to try out our future selves, and from which we can learn. If we are to continue as 'blacksmiths' of ourselves and our world, we have a duty to each other and to future generations to create with conscience.

NOTES

1. Levi included Clarke in *The Search for Roots* (*La ricerca delle radici*, 1981), describing him as 'a living refutation of the commonplace notion that to practise science and to cultivate the imagination are mutually exclusive tasks' (p. 188; OII, 1504).

2. Selections from both collections are in *The Sixth Day*. Other stories in this vein are to be found in a section of *Lilìt e altri racconti* ('Lilith and Other Stories', 1981; *Moments of Reprieve* does not include any of the stories in this section); and *Racconti e saggi* ('Stories and Essays', 1986; selections in *The Mirror Maker*).

3. For more details about date and place of publication of these stories, see OI, 1429–44.

4. Letter dated 22 November 1961, in Italo Calvino, *Lettere 1940–1985*, ed. Claudio Milanini *et al.*, Milan, Mondadori, 2000, pp. 695–6. My translation.

5. Marco Belpoliti, *Primo Levi*, Milan, Bruno Mondadori, 1998, p. 77.

6. OI, 1439. This comment appeared with the story 'Order on the Cheap' ('L'ordine a buon mercato').

7. Thomas. S. Kuhn, *The Structure of Scientific Revolutions*, Chicago, University of Chicago Press, 1970, pioneered the notion of the 'paradigm shift' to challenge perceptions of science as an objective progression towards truth (see chapter 6 in this volume).

8. Levi was a great admirer of Huxley's work and wrote an essay about him in *L'altrui mestiere* (OII, 637–40; not included in *Other People's Trades*).

9. Sergio Solmi, *Le meraviglie del possibile: antologia della fantascienza*, Turin, Einaudi, 1959, p. xx.

10. Unless otherwise stated, stories referred to in this section are from *Storie naturali* and are also included in *The Sixth Day*.

11. *Purgatory*, X, 124–6. See Ilona Klein, '"Official Science Often Lacks Humility": Humor, Science and Technology in Levi's *Storie naturali*', in Susan R. Tarrow (ed.), *Reason and Light: Essays on Primo Levi*, Ithaca, Center for International Studies, 1990, pp. 112–26.

12. For Levi's thoughts on our collective responsibilities to each other see 'Against Pain' ('Contro il dolore', *Other People's Trades*).

13. The richest example is the dialogic novel *The Wrench* (*La chiave a stella*, 1978).

14. See Paul Ginsborg, *A History of Contemporary Italy: Society and Politics 1943–88*, London, Penguin, 1990, pp. 212–26, 247–50.

15. For an example of such a critique, see Betty Friedan, *The Feminine Mystique*, London, Penguin, 1992.

16. Again, Levi's ideas on the false neutrality of science resonate with sceptical philosophies of science, including, for example, Evelyn Fox Keller in 'Feminism and Science', in Evelyn Fox Keller and Helen E. Longino (eds.), *Feminism and Science*, Oxford, Oxford University Press, 1999, pp. 28–40.

17. Unless otherwise stated, stories referred to in this section are from *Vizio di forma* and are also included in *The Sixth Day*.

18. Michel Foucault, *Discipline and Punish, The Birth of the Prison*, London, Penguin, 1977, p. 138.

19. This vision has now become a reality: see John Cassy, 'Students Cash in on "Human Billboards" Plan', *Guardian*, 7 February 2003.

20. My translation.

21. Max Weber's *Economy and Society: An Outline of Interpretive Sociology*, ed. Guenther Roth and Claus Wittich, 3 vols., Berkeley, University of California Press, 1978, vol. II, chapter XI.

22. 'I sintetici' appeared seven years before the birth of the first IVF or 'test-tube' baby: see José Van Dyck, *Manufacturing Babies and Public Consent: Debating the New Reproductive Technologies*, New York, New York University Press, 1995, especially pp. 61–86.

23. Levi actually describes his personal computer as a golem in 'The Scribe' (*Other People's Trades*; 'Lo scriba', *L'altrui mestiere*).

24. In fact, Calvino's 'Cosmicomics' were themselves inspired by Levi's story 'The Sixth Day' ('Il sesto giorno'), and so 'His Own Blacksmith' is part of an ongoing exchange with Calvino; see OI, 1444.

25. My translation.

26. My translation.

27. See Giuseppina Santagostino, 'Destituzione e ossessione biologica nell'immaginario di Primo Levi', *Letteratura italiana contemporanea*, 32 (January–April, 2001), pp. 127–45.

28. See *Voice of Memory*, p. 158.

29. Giuseppe Grassano, 'La "musa stupefatta": Note sui racconti fantascientifici', in Giovanna Ioli (ed.), *Primo Levi: Memoria e invenzione*, San Salvatore Monferrato, Edizione della Biennale 'Piemonte e letteratura', 1995, pp. 164–89, p. 176. My translation.

PART IV

Language and literature

8

ANNA LAURA LEPSCHY AND GIULIO LEPSCHY

Primo Levi's languages

Some readers may feel a sense of unease at treating Primo Levi's work (and particularly his writings about the camps) as literary objects, rather than texts crucial for their ethical, political and historical value. But, as Cesare Segre has argued, 'ethical commitment' is 'among the most important parameters for evaluating a work of art': in both this and the more strictly literary sense, Levi is 'one of the greatest writers of the twentieth century'.[1] Similarly, Daniele Del Giudice notes, in his introduction to Levi's works, that Levi's personal experience of the concentration camp and his ethical commitment to the truth in no way diminish the nature of his account as 'narrative invention' or 'representation' (OI, xiii). His testimonial writing is 'the totally "experimental" and literally unprecedented enactment of a narrative, which was the only way that post-Auschwitz allowed Auschwitz to be recounted' (OI, xxx–xxxi, our translations). It is in this context that this chapter hopes to contribute to a discussion of the role of language in Levi's work. Its emphasis is less on precise textual analysis and more on his own views on language and style and engagement with language and languages, which relate very closely to the core concerns of his writing.

Levi was a writer of a very particular and unusual kind. His relationship to language and to literary language was driven by an intense interest in and enthusiasm for the functioning of different languages and sign systems. His literariness, his style, grew out of what we might call a 'linguistician's mindset'. To understand this mindset and this style better, the following discussion will look in turn at his engagement with idioms beyond Italy, with dialects and varieties of his native language, his style, and their links to the centrality of communication in his testimonial work.[2]

Other languages

Primo Levi was born and grew up in Turin. At the Liceo-Ginnasio he studied Latin and later Greek and French. For a couple of years he attended the

Hebrew school in Turin to prepare for his Bar Mitzvah.[3] He was always keenly interested in languages. In the preface to the school edition of *The Truce* (*La tregua*, 1963) he writes that as a boy he had 'wanted to follow several different paths. Between the ages of twelve and fourteen, I wanted to become a linguist; from fourteen to seventeen I wanted to be an astronomer. When I was eighteen I enrolled at the University for a degree in chemistry' (*The Black Hole of Auschwitz*, p. 13; OI, 1141). He was fascinated by neologisms, language games and the 'linguistic' or semiotic workings of non-linguistic sign systems, such as in his readings of the pavements of Turin in 'Signs on Stone' (*Other People's Trades*; 'Segni sulla pietra', *L'altrui mestiere*, 1985).[4] His 'philological' and 'linguistic' interest in languages emerges frequently in his writings. In the same book, 'Le parole fossili' ('Fossil Words'; not in *Other People's Trades*) describes his disordered passion for etymological dictionaries; he boasts of owning five, for Italian, French, German, English and Piedmontese (the last of which is dearest to him for it elevates his own dialect). The use of languages different from Italian came to the fore particularly through the extreme 'babelic' experience of the *Lager* and recurs explicitly, and in sharp focus, throughout his writings.

Until after World War II French was the most widely known foreign language in Italy, and for an Italian with Levi's cultural and social background an ability to understand some French would have been taken for granted. In *The Drowned and the Saved* (*I sommersi e i salvati*, 1986, p. 75; OII, 1065) Levi tells us that in the *Lager* French-speaking deportees were the natural interpreters for Italian prisoners. And *If This is a Man* (*Se questo è un uomo*, 1947) persistently charts the French individuals and phrases which populate Levi's camp life, from the early lessons '*ne pas chercher à comprendre*' (p. 164; OI, 136), '*Vous n'êtes pas à la maison*' (p. 24; OI, 23), to Jean Samuel, for whom he famously translated Dante into French, to Charles and Arthur, his companions in the last days of Auschwitz.

On rare occasions, Levi also had recourse to that other school-learned language of culture, Latin: in post-war Poland, he conversed in Latin with a local priest, finding no other shared language, as he narrates in *The Truce* (p. 49; OI, 240–1).

English he had studied by himself. It is worth quoting his comments on his first contacts with English (written rather than spoken). This passage is engaging not only for its linguistic implications, but also for what it reveals about Levi's interests and culture. His father, Cesare, who haunted second-hand book stalls in Turin, one day brought home a little volume printed in London in 1846: *Thoughts on Animalcules; or, a glimpse of the invisible world, revealed by the microscope*, by Gideon Algernon Mantell. 'I was fifteen years old, and was immediately transfixed: above all by the illustrations, because I did not know a word of English. But I bought a dictionary and was happily surprised to see that, contrary to Latin, this help was sufficient to understand anything, or almost ...' (*Other People's Trades*, p. 46; OII, 800).

He later translated a few poems from the English, including Kipling's 'The Long Trail'. As he says in a note (OII, 584; not in *Collected Poems*), 'In my intention these translations are more musical than philological, more entertainments than professional works' (our translation). This is borne out in the delightful, simplified opening of this poem: 'There's a whisper down the field where the year has shot her yield' is rendered as 'C'è una voce per i prati, sopra i pascoli falciati', and 'Singing: "over then, come over, for the bee has quit the clover"' becomes: 'Dice: "vieni presto, vieni, si ricoverano i fieni"' (OII, 599).

After the 1938 Racial Laws, like many Italian Jews, he sensed the importance of knowing English, and so also took private lessons in 1939 from Gladys Melrose, a Londoner who taught at the Berlitz School and later kept in touch with him until her death. The precision of Levi's knowledge of English was later borne out in interviews, but also in his close attention to the English translations of his works, starting with his regular collaboration in 1958–9 in Turin with Stuart Woolf, the young translator of *If This is a Man*.[5]

As for German, Levi's comments are, as to be expected, more frequent and impassioned, since knowing German or not frequently implied the difference between life and death in the camps. He stresses the chasm between the educated variety he had learned from his scientific texts, such as the chemistry textbook by Ludwig Gattermann he includes (translating the extract himself) in his anthology of formative readings, *The Search for Roots* (*La ricerca delle radici*, 1981, pp. 74–6; OII, 1422–5), and

> the German of the *Lager* – skeletal, howled, studded with obscenities and imprecations – ... only vaguely related to the precise, austere language of my chemistry books, and to the melodious, refined German of Heine's poetry that Clara, a classmate of mine, would recite to me ... It was a variant, particularly barbarized, of what a German Jewish philologist, Klemperer, had called *Lingua Tertii Imperii*, the language of the Third Reich ... It is an obvious observation that when violence is inflicted on man, it is also inflicted on language
>
> (*The Drowned and the Saved*, pp. 75–6; OII, 1066)

It included changes in value, such as *völkisch*, charged with nationalistic pride, or *fanatisch*, with a positive, appreciative meaning; Levi offers frequent examples of this variant, such as *fressen* employed in place of *essen*, as the ordinary verb for 'eating', or *hau' ab* (from *abhauen*) not in the usual sense of 'cut off', but as a demotic expression for 'beat it', 'get lost'. He mentions the surprise of some German business acquaintances after the war when he used the latter expression, and then explained, to their embarrassment, that 'I had not learned German in school but rather in a *Lager* called Auschwitz ... I also realized later that my pronunciation is coarse, but I deliberately did not try to make it more genteel; for the same reason, I have never had the tattoo removed from my left arm' (*The Drowned and the Saved*, p. 77–8; OII, 1067–8).

As a contrast to the German of brutality, Levi turned to the poetry of Heine, from whose *Buch der Lieder* he translated a selection of poems (OII, 583–98). In 1983, he also contributed a version of Kafka's *Trial* to the Einaudi series 'Scrittori tradotti da scrittori' ('Writers Translated by Writers'). This recovered relationship to an acquired language is in striking contrast to the corrupted relation of German native-speaker survivors to their mother tongue, such as Paul Celan or Jean Améry, as Levi was acutely aware. Of Améry, he comments in *The Drowned and the Saved* that he suffered the brutalization of his language

> in a different way than we who, not knowing German, were reduced to the condition of deaf mutes: in a way, if I may put it like this, that was spiritual rather than material. He suffered from it *because* German was his language, because he was a philologist who loved his language ... therefore the suffering of the intellectual was different in this case from that of the uncultivated foreigner. For the former, the German of the *Lager* was a language he did not understand and this endangered his life; for the latter, it was a barbaric jargon that he did understand but that scorched his mouth when he tried to speak it.
>
> (pp. 108–9; OII: 1097)

Following the foreign languages of which Levi had some knowledge before his *Lager* experience we now move on to those that he heard from other prisoners, passing from the more recognizable Romance and Germanic (Romanian, Dutch), to East European (Hungarian, Polish and Russian), to Yiddish and Hebrew, and come full circle with those nearest to home in Piedmont.

Of Romanian he says: 'I don't have the good fortune to know Romanian, a language beloved of philologists' (OII, 732). In *The Truce* (*La tregua*, 1963) he mentions 'a delicate philological pleasure at such names as Galati, Alba Iulia, Turnu Severin' (p. 210; OI, 385), and he observes the contrasting elements of that language, 'well known roots and terminations, but entangled and contaminated in a millenary common growth alongside others of a strange wild sound; a speech familiar in its music, hermetic in its sense' (p. 200; OI, 376).

Dutch, another language Levi does not know, is mentioned as an example of a language whose words and sounds heard on a particular occasion Levi remembers with uncanny accuracy, without any sense of meaning, even years after liberation; evidence of the trauma and almost automatic 'mechanical' recall experienced by survivors ('A Mystery in the Lager', *The Mirror Maker*; 'Un "giallo" nel Lager', *Racconti e saggi*, 1986, p. 66; OII, 909).[6] He talks in similar terms of his complete aural memory of phrases in Hungarian and Polish, calling this uncanny recall 'almost an unconscious preparation for the task of bearing witness' (*Voice of Memory*, p. 255).

Hungarian is mentioned frequently by Levi: for instance in 'A Disciple', the Hungarians at Auschwitz 'communicated with us in a curious dragged-out German, and communicated with each other in their odd language, which bristles with unusual inflections, and seems to be made up of interminable words, pronounced with irritating slowness, and all with the accent on the first syllable' (*Moments of Reprieve*, 'Un discepolo', *Lilít e altri racconti*, 1981; p. 50; OII, 24). Hungarian is evoked in different contexts as well, for instance apropos of the etymology of *electricity*, from the Greek *electron*, which means 'amber': 'Only the Hungarians have coined a neologism which says, more logically, the "force of the lightning bolt", i.e. *villamosság*, formed from *villám* "lightning" and two suffixes, the adjectival *-os-* and the collective *-sag-*' (*Other People's Trades*, p. 126; OII, 759). Hungarian, however, is unlikely to have appeared completely exotic to him, since his father, a graduate in civil engineering, had worked in Budapest from 1911 to 1915 and then again in 1918–19.[7]

Although Levi noted that Oświęcim is less fearful than its German version, Auschwitz, Polish is often associated with violence, described as unintelligible, 'a rough Polish, full of swearing and imprecations that we couldn't understand; it was truly the language of hell ... And I was deeply struck, last night, by the drunken Poles in the hotel lift, who were speaking the language I remember, not like all the others around us: they were swearing, spitting out what seemed like a stream of consonants, a genuinely infernal language' (*Voice of Memory*, p. 209). This is best confirmed in *The Truce*, which ends with great power on the horrific return of the dawn wake-up call of the camp, '*Wstawać*' (p. 222; OI, 395). These evocations have obviously more to do with context, situation and sense impression than with a linguistic evaluation, as is also confirmed by the following:

From the background racket of my first days of imprisonment there immediately emerged, with insistence, four or five expressions that were not German; they must, I thought, indicate some basic object or activity such as work, water, and bread. They became engraved in my memory ... Only much later a Polish friend unwillingly explained to me that they simply meant 'cholera', 'blood of a dog', 'thunder', 'son of a whore' and 'screwed'; the first three having the function of exclamations.　(*The Drowned and the Saved*, p. 78; OII, 1068)

Russian, by contrast, is considered sympathetically, on the many occasions on which it is mentioned, particularly in *The Truce, If Not Now, When?* (*Se non ora, quando?*, 1982), and *The Wrench* (*La chiave a stella*, 1978). We shall limit ourselves to a humorous passage of *The Truce* (pp. 138–40; OI, 321–3), full of fascination for language in general, in which Cesare and Primo try to barter some of their earthenware dishes in exchange for a chicken, only to discover that they cannot convey what they want to a group of Russian peasants. 'Cesare, deep down, had never really accepted that Germans speak German, and Russians Russian, except out of gross malice.' Notwithstanding the fact that Russian is an Indo-European language, and that chickens must have been known to Indo-Europeans, describing this animal proved beyond their linguistic and mimic abilities:

[Cesare] rather half-heartedly, glowering and sullen ... put on a very second-rate imitation of the habits of the chicken, crouching on the ground, scraping first with one foot and then with the other and pecking here and there with his hands shaped like a wedge. Between one oath and the other, he also cried 'coccode-e-eh'. But this rendering of the chicken's cry is of course highly conventional; it is only to be heard in Italy and has no currency elsewhere.

Only when Levi draws on the ground a hen and an egg is the mystery resolved and an old woman shouts with delight '*kura! kúritsa*'. There are other wry linguistic asides, as when a Russian soldier tries to teach Levi Russian, in spite of his conviction (parallel to Cesare's, who felt that not understanding Italian was bloody-minded) that if 'a man, adult and normal, cannot speak Russian, which means he cannot speak, it must be out of insolent arrogance' (*The Truce*, p. 166; OI, 347).

Yiddish, 'that extraordinary, wondrous language which is unknown in Italy' (*Voice of Memory*, p. 268), has a special place in Levi's work, especially in its later stages. Levi first encountered Yiddish in the *Lager*:

Yiddish was *de facto* the camp's second language ... Not only did I not understand it, I only vaguely knew about its existence, based on some quotation or joke heard from my father who had worked for a few years in Hungary. The Polish, Russian, and Hungarian Jews were astonished that we Italians did not speak it: we were suspect Jews, not to be trusted ... Yiddish is substantially an ancient German dialect, different from modern German, both in lexicon and pronunciation. It caused me greater anguish than Polish, which I did not understand at all, because I should have understood it'

(The Drowned and the Saved, p. 78; OII, 1068–9)

There is a striking, and often quoted, passage in *The Truce*, in which Cesare and Primo approach two young girls who are speaking Yiddish:

> That night everything seemed easy to me, even understanding Yiddish. With unaccustomed boldness I turned to the girls, greeted them, trying to imitate their pronunciation, asked them in German if they were Jewish, and declared that we four were also Jewish. The girls (they were perhaps sixteen or eighteen years old) burst out laughing. '*Ihr sprecht keyn Jiddisch; ihr seyd ja keyne Jiden!*' 'You do not speak Yiddish; so you cannot be Jews!' In their language the phrase amounted to rigorous logic. (p. 117; OI, 302)

Later Levi devoted himself to reading as much as he could about Yiddish, 'the unifying spoken language in the archipelago of Jewish communities' of Eastern Europe,

> the *Mamaloshen*, as it was affectionately called, that is 'mama's language' . . . In any case, Yiddish itself, a fascinating language for linguists (and not only for them) is intrinsically a multi-language . . . It is the language of a wandering people, driven by history from country to country, and it bears marks of each of its stations. And its evolution is not finished . . .
> *(Other People's Trades*, pp. 73–4; OII, 817, and cf. OII, 1286)

Yiddish plays a central role in *If Not Now, When?*, a book which is in fact a linguistic *tour de force*, partly because familiarity with Yiddish culture and the Yiddish language itself for Levi came late in life. As he explained in a revealing autobiographical sketch of 1982, *Itinerario d'uno scrittore ebreo* ('Itinerary of a Jewish Writer', *The Black Hole of Auschwitz*, pp. 155–68; OII, 1213–29):

> it was not my culture. My own experience and knowledge were not enough, and a period of study was indispensable. Before beginning writing I dedicated almost a year to collecting and reading documents and books . . . I studied a little Yiddish grammar and vocabulary because it is difficult to reproduce a social environment and make characters speak when you do not know their language . . . This is perhaps the only time I have found myself confronted with a real (but unusual) linguistic problem: I had to give the reader the impression that the dialogues between my characters, which were obviously in standard Italian, were translated from Yiddish, a language which I know badly and which the Italian reader does not know at all. I do not know whether I succeeded in this or not: it is for my readers who know enough Yiddish to make that judgement. (p. 167; OII, 1226–7)

Behind his self-mocking modesty, however, one can feel a passionate commitment. Elsewhere, Levi had said that he nourished the ambition of being the first Italian writer to describe the Yiddish world (*Voice of Memory*, p. 21). The idea of writing dialogues in standard Italian 'as if' they had been translated from Yiddish, which might appear at first sight an absurdity, on further reflection turns out to have relevant parallels. One only has to think of Giovanni Verga's great naturalist novel *I Malavoglia* (1881), a masterpiece of Italian literature using standard Italian 'as if' it were translated from Sicilian. Levi manages to introduce, as the occasion arises and with a light touch, the explanations which may be needed by readers unfamiliar with Yiddish and its culture. Sometimes certain expressions are clarified contextually rather than literally translated, which contributes to their effectiveness without blunting their value as strange-making devices. For instance: 'Mendel told Dov that Leonid had had a difficult life, but Dov answered him with a single syllable, looking into his eyes: "*Nu?*" In Novoselki this wasn't any excuse. Who didn't have a difficult life behind him?' (*If Not Now, When?*, p. 66; OII, 269).[8]

As for Hebrew, it seems difficult to ascertain how much knowledge Levi had of this language. As a child he must have learned some elements, at least for his Bar Mitzvah. In 'Le parole fossili' ('Fossil Words', *L'altrui mestiere*, OII, 819; not in *Other People's Trades*), he mentions being struck, while reading Mario Rigoni Stern's *Il sergente nella neve*, by the question obsessively repeated in dialect, in the night, by the freezing river Don: 'Sergentmagiú, ghe rivarem a baita?', i.e., 'Sergeant Major, will we make it back to base?' *Baita* is annotated by Levi as 'haven, asylum, safety, home'. He also observes that it is similar to the Hebrew *bait*, which means 'house'. The etymology of *baita* is debated, and current etymological dictionaries still mention the possibility of a link with the Hebrew word.

In 'Itinerary of a Jewish Writer', Levi writes: 'I adapted to the condition of being a Jew only as the effect of the Racial Laws passed in Italy in 1938 when I was nineteen years old, and following my deportation to Auschwitz in 1944 ...' Like the majority of Jews of ancient Italian descent his relatives were 'profoundly integrated into the life of the country in terms of language, customs and moral attitudes'.[9] It is interesting that the observations which follow in this article concern not Hebrew, but the Italian dialect varieties prevalent among Jews in various Italian towns: 'curious dialectal variants, with Hebrew insertions which had been more or less distorted to local phonetic patterns ... the pathetic survival of biblical language in the speech of family and dialect speech.' Elsewhere Levi writes: 'I am implicitly criticized for being assimilated. I am. There do not exist Jews in the Diaspora who are not, to a greater or lesser degree, if for nothing else than for the fact that they speak the language of the country in which they live'.[10] On occasion, however, Levi showed he was not immune to a fascination with Israel: in *If Not Now, When?* he stresses the difference between the 'liturgical embalmed Hebrew of the synagogue', and the 'flowing living Hebrew that has always been spoken in Palestine' (p. 302; OII, 486).

Italian, its dialects and varieties

Two idioms rooted in Levi's home territory were particularly dear to Levi, Judeo-Piedmontese and Piedmontese. The chapter 'Argon' in *The Periodic Table* is devoted to the traditions of Piedmontese Jews and to their speech, which reveals 'an unsuspected phonetic analogy between Hebrew and the Piedmontese dialect' (p. 6; OI, 743), and their 'particular jargon', which 'has now almost disappeared; a few generations back it still numbered a few hundred words and locutions, consisting for the most part of Hebrew roots with Piedmontese endings and inflections ... Its historical interest is meagre, since it was never spoken by more than a few thousand people; but its human interest is great, as are all languages on the frontier and in transition' (pp. 8–9; OI, 746). Levi observes that it has a great comic energy deriving from the contrast between the sober, laconic, dry manner of the Piedmontese dialect and the sacred and solemn remoteness of the ancient language of the Bible. It is a contrast which reflects the one between the everyday wretchedness of exile for Diaspora Jews and the fidelity of the chosen people to their covenant, and perhaps the one, in the human condition, between flesh and mind, matter and spirit, and the resulting sceptical, ironic wisdom, and the laughter, which is lacking in the Bible and the Prophets:

> It pervades Yiddish, and, within its modest limits, it also pervades the bizarre speech of our fathers of this earth, which I want to set down here before it disappears: a skeptical, good-natured speech, which only to a careless examination could appear blasphemous, whereas it is rich with an affectionate and dignified intimacy with God – Nôssgnôr ('Our Lord'), Adonai Eloénô ('Praised be the Lord'), Cadòss Barôkhú ('Dear Lord'). (p. 9; OI, 746)

This chapter offers in fact, in a light-handed manner, a valuable collection of words and expressions of this language whose survival is endangered.

Piedmontese is one of the dozen or so main regional dialects in Italy. 'Piedmont was our true country', says Levi in *The Periodic Table* (p. 51; OI, 783). The use of the dialect is one of the main components of his sense of belonging to this *piccola patria* (little homeland). Levi was in a situation of what linguists call 'diglossia', that is, the coexistence in society of two languages side by side. In Italy, until the second half of the twentieth century, people were native speakers of their own regional dialect: the 'Low Variety' used in speech, prevalently at home, in the family, and in informal contexts. Italian, the 'High Variety', was used in writing, and in public, official contexts (school, bureaucracy, administration, the law etc.). For most people the dialect was the mother tongue and Italian, learned at school, for the majority remained an idiom used in a slightly awkward and artificial way. On the other hand, amongst the middle classes, more familiarity with standard Italian was to be expected. Nevertheless, this diglossic situation had certain inescapable consequences also for the literary language. The distinction between spoken and written was more marked than in other European languages such as English and French, and in narrative, when a conversation was reported, the exchanges were felt to be 'translated' from an 'original' which was likely to have been in dialect.

Levi often makes moving comments on his native dialect: he regrets (with interesting resonances with his use of Yiddish) the awkwardness of his Piedmontese which, 'correct in form and sound, is so smooth and enervated, so polite and languid, that it does not seem very authentic. Instead of a genuine atavism it seems the fruit of diligent study, burning the midnight oil over a grammar and dictionary' (*The Periodic Table*, p. 170; OI, 885). And again: 'this dialect of ours which I speak badly but which I love with the "due love" which ties us to the place where we were born and grew up and which we miss when we are far away' ('Fossil Words', OII, 821; our translation); and in an essay published the year before his death:

> I love this dialect, that incidentally does not contain the verb 'to love'; I am sad to see it decline, I admire those who go on using it with spontaneity and elegance, but I am so unsure of my pronunciation that I dare not speak it in public ... I know that it is neither more nor less noble than other Italian dialects, all of which are destined to a speedy extinction in the face of lifeless television Italian; but it is mine, it belongs to my childhood, my father used it with my mother, and my mother with shopkeepers; it was even spoken in defiance of the Fascist school programme by my sweet little teacher in elementary school, who died a centenarian a few years ago.
>
> ('"Bella come una fiore"' ('A Girl as Lovely as a Flower'), *Racconti e saggi*, OII, 987; not in *The Mirror Maker*; our translation)

The emotional bond to the dialect extends into his description of his own Italian, 'the only language I know well', as he described it (*The Black Hole of Auschwitz*, p. 159; OII, 1218). Elsewhere he qualifies, adding a crucial regional touch: 'I speak Italian, standard Piedmontese Italian' (*Voice of Memory*, p. 236). And when he describes hearing Lorenzo's voice in Auschwitz, he comments: 'I wasn't dreaming: he had spoken Italian and with a Piedmontese accent' ('Lorenzo's Return' ('Il ritorno di Lorenzo'),

Moments of Reprieve, p. 152; OII, 61). It is thus all the more significant to note, as many have done, that Levi's Italian strikes one for its 'normality': it is rooted in the sort of educated standard language that tends not to call attention to itself, nor to reveal its regional origin or to appear stylistically marked. In the Italian cultural tradition this is by no means an obvious and expected feature: it comes from a studied, deliberate choice of a cultural and an ethical kind. In this it bears comparison with one of the authors who belong to Levi's pantheon; Alessandro Manzoni, the early nineteenth-century writer and father of the Italian novel, was a native speaker of Milanese and the modern language with which he was most familiar was French. His novel *I promessi sposi* (1840) was studied in Italian schools for generations, and treated as a model of modern Italian usage. Its characters spoke not like the seventeenth-century Lombards they were but used instead an idiom which the author had fashioned adapting literary Italian to what he imagined was the educated Florentine of his own time – an idiom which was certainly not his mother tongue.[11] Levi too created a literary language rooted in the standard language, but enriched by all the many and varied idioms and languages we have seen.

A very particular and historically important instance of Levi's use of Italian and its varieties is represented by *The Wrench*. Linguists designate as 'popular Italian' a colloquial form of the national language, used in speech, which gradually spread during the twentieth century. In writing, it usually conveys a lack of familiarity with the written register. Traditionally, until the second half of the last century, what people used in speech was their own dialect, not popular Italian. *The Wrench* has been described as the first important work in Italian literature to be rooted and produced in popular Italian. What Levi does is to present conversations between himself, in standard Italian, and a Piedmontese technician, Faussone, a mechanical rigger, who travels round the world, from Russia, to India, to Alaska, setting up enormous cranes and other metal structures. As Beccaria observes,

> the creation of Faussone's language is both new and important. Pavese and Fenoglio have given us lofty examples of 'illustrious Piedmontese' with country roots. With Levi instead we have a popular Italian with city roots ... with a bold and well-judged originality, Primo Levi does not give us a translation from dialect into Italian, but rather an Italian which has been "thought" in dialect, and whose dialect nature emerges more in the syntax than in lexis or idioms.[12]

To quote a few examples (using our own translations): 'ciau' (OI, 947) instead of the more standard *ciao*, 'hello/goodbye'; ''na fija' vs 'ragazza' (OI, 979), 'a girl' in Piedmontese and in Italian; 'leggergli la vita' (OI, 979), 'to criticize, to gossip about';[13] 'boie panatere' (OI, 998) instead of the standard *scarafaggi*, cockroaches; for syntax: 'non c'è uno che si osi' (OI, 947), 'there's no-one who dares', used as if it were reflexive; 'io sono uno di quelli che il suo mestiere gli piace' (OI, 1071), 'I am one of those who like their work', in the standard 'uno di quelli a cui piace il loro mestiere'; 'averne un po' basta' (OI, 1095), 'to have had enough', in the standard 'averne abbastanza'; and for spelling, with renderings of foreign words in popular Italian pronunciation: 'un brait gai' (bright guy) (OI, 994), 'ghestrúm' (guest room) (OI, 995), 'chetuòk' (cat walk) (OI, 1042).

Style, rhetoric, communication

Levi's interest in, and varied engagement with, languages interacts with his writing style in many ways. We have already noted the 'Babelic' nature of the concentration camp as a source for his 'multilingualism', for example: 'The confusion of languages is a fundamental component of the manner of living here: one is surrounded by a perpetual Babel, in which everyone shouts orders and threats in languages never heard before and woe betide anyone who fails to grasp the meaning' (*If This is a Man* p. 35–6; OI, 32). Levi praises the authors of the Canadian radio-drama version of *If This is a Man*, who 'had understood full well the importance in the camp of a lack of communication, exacerbated by the lack of a common language, and they had bravely set their work within the framework of the theme of the Tower of Babel and the confusion of languages' (*The Black Hole of Auschwitz*, p. 26; OI, 1160–1).

In contrast to the impression of Babelic chaos, Levi uses a firm, formal and lucid prose style which has often been noted by critics. Mengaldo stresses the 'classic' quality of Levi's writing, with its economy, lightness, elegant formality, paratactic structures and its preference for striking and ironic juxtapositions.[14] To give an idea of this, we shall analyse, as an example of Levi's writing, the Italian opening of *Se questo è un uomo* (with Stuart Woolf's translation), the book where his prose is at its most formal:[15]

> Ero stato catturato dalla Milizia fascista il 13 dicembre 1943. Avevo ventiquattro anni, poco senno, nessuna esperienza, e una decisa propensione, favorita dal regime di segregazione a cui da quattro anni le leggi razziali mi avevano ridotto, a vivere in un mio mondo scarsamente reale, popolato da civili fantasmi cartesiani, da sincere amicizie maschili e da amicizie femminili esangui. Coltivavo un moderato e astratto senso di ribellione. (OI, 7)

> [I was captured by the Fascist Militia on 13 December 1943. I was twenty-four, with little wisdom, no experience, and a decided tendency – encouraged by the life of segregation forced on me for the previous four years by the Racial

Laws – to live in an unrealistic world of my own, a world inhabited by civilized Cartesian phantoms, by sincere male and bloodless female friendships. I cultivated a moderate and abstract sense of rebellion.   (p. 3)]

The first point to note is the subtle use of past tenses: the past perfects (*ero stato catturato . . . mi avevano ridotto*), the imperfects (*avevo . . . coltivavo*) immediately suggest a distancing from the events mentioned, and an attempt at interpreting them and offering their background. In the English rendering this particular aspect is absent: the past historic ('I was captured') might introduce a fact as if it were a new event rather than background. The narrative dynamic is different in the two languages. The Italian original is still open and conveys a sense of expectation: this is the preliminary information introducing the reader to events which have not yet been mentioned. In English the narrative tension is different: the text is more closed and the facts are presented as new events and do not prepare us for something that is yet to happen.

The use of traditional rhetorical devices is also noticeable in its unobtrusive and yet effective way. To give four examples, with the technical terms in each case: there is a careful use of zeugma (in which one verb governs several different, often oddly juxtaposed elements) in '*Avevo ventiquattro anni, poco senno, nessuna esperienza*', which is obviously lost in the English ('I was twenty-four, with little wisdom, no experience'). There is a triple anaphora, that is, a repeated grammatical form underlined by the syntactic parallelism of three complements introduced by '*da*' ('*popolato da . . ., da . . . e da . . .*') and by the tripartite structure of each colon consisting of a noun and two adjectives. The first and second colon with the same syntactic structure (Adjective + Noun + Adjective): '*civili fantasmi cartesiani*', '*sincere amicizie maschili*'. The second and third are linked by the anaphora of the nouns and the accompanying antithetical adjectives ('*amicizie maschili . . . amicizie femminili*') and by their chiastic structure (i.e. reversed-order, such as Adjective + [Noun-Adjective] . . . [Noun-Adjective] + Adjective): '*sincere amicizie maschili . . . amicizie femminili esangui*'. These features too are absent in the English, where the distribution of nouns and adjectives is different. Noticeable also is the use of oxymoron (i.e., linking of antithetical elements): a sense of '*ribellione*', which is however '*moderato*'.

The paragraph overall is symmetrically structured. It consists of three sentences. The first and the last are short and simple clauses, of ten and eight words respectively, syntactically straightforward.

The second sentence is a long one (forty-nine words), with a complex structure consisting of a main clause ('*Avevo . . .*') which includes an object ('*una decisa propensione*'). This introduces an infinitive which governs its own complements. After the noun *'propensione'*, before the prepositional infinitive which depends on it (*'a vivere ...'*), a parenthetical clause is inserted with a qualifying passive participle, also depending on *'propensione'* (*'favorita dal regime di segregazione ...'*) on which a relative depends in its turn (*'a cui ... le leggi razziali mi avevano ridotto'*).

To sum up, we have a main verb (*'avevo'*) on whose object (*'propensione'*) two secondary verbs depend (*'mi avevano ridotto'* and *'a vivere'*). What is immediately striking is the simplicity and readability of a structure which turns out to be, when one produces a grammatical analysis, rather involved and complicated. This is in fact an example of the characteristic we have mentioned above: a highly literary verbal texture which nevertheless produces an impression of limpidity and transparency.

The impression of clarity is one Levi deliberately strived for – part of an enlightened, indeed Enlightenment, reasonableness – as he makes clear in essays such as 'On Obscure Writing' ('Dello scrivere oscuro', *Other People's Trades*, p. 157–63; OII, 676–81). There, Levi makes some vivid statements concerning the unintelligibility of certain contemporary writers, including philosophers and poets. The critique is not straightforward, for obscurity may be not an extrinsic defect, but an essential feature of the message. It is hard, however, not to sympathize with Levi's attitude, whether one calls it his poetics or his philosophy of life:

> The effable is preferable to the ineffable, the human word to the animal whine. It is not by chance that the two least decipherable German poets, Trakl and Celan, both died as suicides, separated by two generations ... For Celan above all ... we must speak with more seriousness and greater responsibility. It is evident that his song is tragic and noble, but confusedly so ... This darkness grows from page to page until the last inarticulate babble consternates like the rattle of a dying man, and in fact that is just what it is ... If his is a message, it gets lost in the 'background noise': it is not a communication, it is not a language, or at most it is a dark and truncated language precisely like that of a person who is about to die and is alone, as we all will be at the point of death.
>
> (pp. 160–1; OII, 680)

Communication is the key here. In *The Drowned and the Saved* he writes: 'I never liked the term "incommunicability", so fashionable in the 1970s, first of all because it is a linguistic horror, and in the second place because of more personal reasons' (p. 68; OII, 1059). The personal reasons, he explains, are that 'We saw incommunicability in a more radical manner' (p. 70; OII, 1061). Preventing the deportees from communicating with each other, with prisoners put into groups speaking different and reciprocally unintelligible languages, was an important element in the demolition of the personality and in the dehumanization imposed by the *Lager*. So too was the 'non-verbal' language, the brutalized semiotics of violence: 'the blows fell, and it was obvious that they were variants of the same language: use of the word to communicate thought, this necessary and sufficient mechanism for man to be man, had fallen into disuse' (p. 70–1; OII, 1061). He goes on to note how, in Mauthausen, 'the rubber truncheon was called *der Dolmetscher*, the interpreter: the one who made himself understood by everybody' (p. 71; OII, 1062; and cf. p. 55; OII, 1048).

Levi's comments on the 'language' or 'semiotics' of the blow suggests that his reaction to Celan, for instance, author of some of the greatest and most tragic poems of the twentieth century, should not be taken as mere rejection. A more careful reading reveals a deeper level of sympathetic understanding in Levi for the darker side of language. For all his clarity, balance and equanimity, Levi was always aware of the impossibility of overcoming the traumatic experience he had undergone, of its 'untranslatability', one might say, into linguistic form. For this reason, Levi's commitment to the role of language, and his analysis of different idioms and their effects, can be seen as central to the moral and historical substance of his work.

NOTES

We are grateful to the editor, Robert Gordon, for his comments and suggestions.
1. Cesare Segre, *Tempo di bilanci. La fine del Novecento*, Turin, Einaudi, 2005, pp. x–xii.
2. Within the literature on Levi's work, many items touch on questions of language, although only a few examine them in detail. See the essays by Cesare Cases, Cesare Segre and (especially) Pier Vincenzo Mengaldo, written for the first Einaudi edition of Levi's work (3 vols., 1987–90) and now in Ernesto Ferrero (ed.), *Primo Levi. Un'antologia della critica*, Turin, Einaudi, 1997, pp. 5–33, 91–116, 169–242; and the important computer analysis: Jane Nystedt, *Le opere di Primo Levi viste al computer. Osservazioni stilolinguistiche*, Stockholm, Almqvist and Wiksell, 1993.
3. See Ian Thomson, *Primo Levi. A Life*, London, Hutchinson, 2002, pp. 68, 44.
4. See Stefano Bartezzaghi, 'Cosmichimiche', in Marco Belpoliti (ed.), *Primo Levi* (Riga 13), Milan, Marcos y Marcos, 1997, pp. 267–314; and chapter 9 in this volume.
5. See Thomson, *Primo Levi*, p. 100, 266.
6. Levi later translated a Dutch novel, although possibly not directly from the Dutch: Jacob Presser, *La notte dei girondini*, Milan, Adelphi, 1976. See Alexander, chapter 10 in this volume.
7. Thomson, *Primo Levi*, pp. 15–16.
8. See similar occurrences of the same '*nu*' elsewhere, for instance pp. 81, 294, 304 (OII, 284, 479, 488).
9. *The Black Hole of Auschwitz*, p. 155–6; OII, 1213–14. Translation adapted from published version.

10. From Levi's reply to a critical American review of *If Not Now, When?*: Primo Levi, 'To the Editor of *Commentary*', *Commentary*, 81, 2 (February 1986), pp. 6–7, p. 7; OII, 1293.

11. For Levi on Manzoni, see *Other People's Trades*, pp. 135–40; OII, 699–703; *The Drowned and the Saved*, p. 29; OII, 1023.

12. See the school edition of Primo Levi, *La chiave a stella*, ed. Gian Luigi Beccaria, Turin, Einaudi, 1983, 'Letture per la scuola media', n. 65, pp. x–xi.

13. Levi wrote a fascinating etymological essay on this phrase in *L'altrui mestiere* ('"Leggere la vita"', OII, 682–4; not translated).

14. See note 2 above.

15. On the formality of *If This is a Man*, see Cases in Ferrero (ed.), *Primo Levi*. Later works, from *The Truce* onwards, use more informal, colloquial and demotic elements.

9

MIRNA CICIONI

Primo Levi's humour

'If I were asked to define the writer in a single word,
I would say he was a humorist.'
(Massimo Mila)

'Argon', the story which opens *The Periodic Table* (*Il sistema periodico*, 1975), contains an important and often-quoted digression. While sketching the history of the Jews in Piedmont, and the mixture of Piedmontese dialect and Hebrew expressions used in the various communities, Levi points out that what makes this mixture funny is the intrinsic cultural and structural contrast between the two languages. From there he goes on to identify contrasts and conflicts as a central component of all Diaspora Jewish cultures and their humour; and then he generalizes even further, attributing contrasts to all human nature, and therefore – implicitly – to all humour:

> It [Jewish-Piedmontese] contains an admirable comic force, which springs from the contrast between the texture of the discourse, which is the rugged, sober, and laconic Piedmontese dialect ... and the Hebrew inlay, snatched from the language of the fathers, sacred and solemn ... [T]his contrast reflects another, the essential conflict of the Judaism of the Diaspora ... torn between their divine vocation and the daily misery of existence;[1] and still another, even more general, the one which is inherent in the human condition, since man is a centaur, a tangle of flesh and mind, divine inspiration and dust.
>
> (*The Periodic Table*, p. 9; OI, 746)

The assertion that to be a human being is to be a tangle (*groviglio*) of incompatible elements which cannot be reconciled seems partly to contradict another of Levi's frequently quoted statements, that his writing is a deliberate progression 'from darkness to light'.[2] The notion of linear movement towards the 'light' has been consistently refuted by Levi research in the past ten years: scholars have revealed the complexities within his work, providing insights into his ambivalent views on communication, science, writing, Jewishness and more. The notion of 'tangle' seems useful in this context, because it is recurrent in Levi's writings, and can have ethical, cognitive and linguistic implications: two among many instances are the narrator's tangle [*groviglio*] of 'contradictory feelings' when he first glimpses captured Germans after liberation at the beginning of *The Truce* (*La tregua*, 1963) (p. 56; OI, 246); and the statement in *The Drowned and the Saved* (*I sommersi e i salvati*, 1986) that psychologists 'have pounced upon the tangles [of ex-deportees] with professional avidity' (p. 64; OII, 1056). Tangles are also useful in an analysis of Levi's humour, because Levi's implicit acknowledgement that most tangles must remain knotted is often the basis of his humour, irony and occasional excursions into word-play.

Several scholars of Levi's work have examined his humour, from different perspectives: from its literary and biblical connections[3] to its ethical dimensions;[4] from a purely linguistic viewpoint,[5] a cognitive viewpoint[6] or with eye to the interplay of order and chaos in producing humour.[7] All have usually argued that its origins lie in what Levi, in a 1981 interview, calls his 'hybrid nature':

> I really believe that my inevitable destiny (my stars, as Don Abbondio would say) is to be a hybrid, to be split. Italian, but Jewish. A chemist, but a writer. A man who has been deported, but does not (or not always) choose to complain or whine.[8] (my translation)

My examination of Levi's humour focuses not so much on the (auto)biographical notion of his 'hybrid nature' as on the cognitive notion of 'tangles': the uncertainty experienced when facing cultural or ethical tangles usually leads to gaining new knowledge, which in Levi's perspective is the main purpose of life ('We are here for this – to make mistakes and to correct ourselves,' *The Periodic Table*, p. 75; OI, 804). In the ellipse-shaped diagram which opens *The Search for Roots* (*La ricerca delle radici*, 1981) there are four possible pathways through the works which most influenced Levi's writing: the two outside pathways, which define and surround the others, are 'la salvazione del riso', 'salvation through laughter', and 'la salvazione del capire', 'salvation through knowledge' (*The Search for Roots*, p. 9; OII, 1367). The word *salvazione* is a secular appropriation of a religious concept: in the Christian culture dominant in Levi's Italian background, it had the spiritual connotations of individual preservation from the powers of evil. In Levi's own secular perspective, the only two possible forms of *salvazione* are through knowledge (*capire* how nature, technology and relations between people work) and laughter (*riso* at the awareness of their flaws, contradictions and tangles). The Italian word *riso* is a traditional, all-encompassing term, covering comedy, irony, sarcasm and humour. Levi's *riso* takes different forms – puns, Jewish jokes, proverbs, juxtapositions of different languages, parody, pastiche, irony, sarcasm – but it remains firmly rooted in his consciousness of being Italian: it is based on ironic or playful intertextual dialogues with Italian literary classics, and his love for the varieties of language within

Italy. I will trace some of these linguistic and cultural connections, including Levi's debt – already visible in the quotation from the 1981 interview – to the humour of Alessandro Manzoni's masterpiece *The Betrothed* (*I promessi sposi*, 1840–2).

Although the literature on humour and irony is vast, both terms elude classification and categorizations: the border between them is generally acknowledged to be blurred, and their ethical, political and cognitive dimensions cannot be explained by any single theory. All theories, however, identify a feature common to humour and irony, namely the momentary confusion caused by the simultaneous presence of two conflicting paradigms. In humour this double presence takes the form of incongruity, and in irony it becomes a gap between expectations and experience; the resulting destabilization can be interpreted as cognitive loss (the loss of order and certainty) or as cognitive gain (overcoming the fear of chaos, and accepting ambiguities, contradictions and multiplicity of discourses).[9]

Other people's words: laughter and code-mixing

Multiple or opposing views of experience can also clash, producing humorous effects, through different linguistic codes coming into contact. Mikhail Bakhtin, in his analysis of the dialogical relation between languages, pointed out that 'the mutual illumination of a native language and a foreign language underscores and objectifies the "conception of the world" facet of both languages, as well as their internal form, and their respective systems of values'.[10] In the context of theories of humour, what Bakhtin calls 'mutual illumination' could be related to Arthur Koestler's 'bisociation', the coming together of two separate frameworks for interpreting reality; and to what Victor Raskin calls 'opposing scripts', differing cognitive structures which have been internalized by the speakers of a language and which come together in a humorous text.[11] In the language of Piedmontese Jews, the 'bisociation' and the 'opposing scripts' come from the encounter of the biblical 'language of the Father', with its sacred status, and the dialect of the region where Levi's ancestors had settled over four centuries earlier, with its earthy domestic role. The tensions between the cultural values and the linguistic structures of both languages produce humorous effects through what linguists call *code-mixing*: using lexical items and grammatical features from two languages within the same communicative act, so as to give emphasis, add an aside or a figure of speech, or express solidarity.[12] 'Argon' provides numerous examples of this mixing, with biblical sources of each Hebrew term carefully quoted and glossed before the domestic Piedmontese usage is given and explained. Some particularly humorous ones are *fé sefòkh*, a genteel reference to the vomit of children, based on the Hebrew *shafòkh*, 'which is equivalent to "pour" and appears in Psalm 79 ("Pour out Thy wrath upon the heathen that have not recognized Thee, and upon the kingdoms that have not invoked Thy name")', and the curse *medà meshônà*, literally 'strange death', used by one of Levi's ancestors in the 'inexplicable imprecation "*C'ai takeissa 'na medà meshônà fàita a paraqua*" ("May he have an accident shaped like an umbrella")' (*The Periodic Table*, pp. 12–13; OI, 749–50).[13] The integration of Hebrew and Piedmontese becomes in Levi's text a symbol for the mostly successful integration of Italian Jews in the various regions of Italy; however, this integration is also shown as being in constant tension, because the idiom is also said to be

> a crafty language meant to be employed when speaking about *goyim* in the presence of *goyim*; or also, to reply boldly with insults and curses that are not to be understood, against the regime of restriction and oppression which they (the *goyim*) had established. (*The Periodic Table*, p. 8; OI, 746)

Aspects of code-mixing between Hebrew and an Italian dialect are also present in *The Truce* (*La tregua*, 1963). This book – which, between its sombre opening and its haunting conclusion, contains a variety of Levi's best comic and ironic scenes – also contains numerous linguistic tangles resulting from attempts to communicate between speakers of many different languages. The use Levi makes of multilingualism in *The Truce* achieves effects similar to what Ezio Raimondi, in his analysis of Manzoni's humour, has called 'polyphonic irony': 'the awareness, while voices are clashing, that "man sees only a part of things, and never *la vérité entière*"'.[14] Encounters between languages in *The Truce* highlight the importance of free communication in the ex-deportees' process of rediscovery of themselves and their cultures, but also reveal that under certain circumstances any communication is fraught with uncertainties, ambiguities and potential conflicts. In the character of Cesare – a monolingual speaker of the dialect of the Roman ghetto – Levi represents both the humour and the 'secret language' function of another Jewish-Italian variety. In the market of the Polish town of Katowice, Levi's narrated self helps Cesare sell an unsuspecting local a shirt with a hole. The scene, an extended comic masterpiece, has a particularly funny ending:

> 'Come on, lad. Let's hop it [*famo resciutte*], before he puts his hand through the hole [*sennò questi svagano er búcio*].' So, fearful lest the client discover the hole too quickly, we hopped it. (*The Truce*, p. 85; OI, 273–4)

No English translation of this passage can fully convey the humour of the code-mixing between three varieties of Italian. These are Cesare's *giudeo-romanesco* (*famo resciutte* consists of the Roman *famo*, 'let's get', and *resciutte*, phonologically adapted from the Hebrew *rishut*, permission); Cesare's *romanesco* (*svagare*, to detect, *er búcio*, the hole); and the author's affectionate mockery of their non-standard status through the use of a formal paraphrase in standard Italian: Levi's original text ends with an explanation which also provides an explicit contrast: 'we hopped it (*that is, we took our leave*)' (my italics).

The contrast between the language of the uneducated and the language of the educated is also – as it frequently is in Manzoni's *The Betrothed* – the interplay of two different, and differently limited, visions of the world, with a humorous distancing effect. *The Wrench* (*La chiave a stella*, 1978) is constructed on the basis of this interplay.[15] Levi's occasional metalinguistic comments on the language of the book's hero, the fitter Faussone, light-heartedly emphasize the tension between the need for spoken language to reflect the speaker's local origin and the need for written language to be in a code accessible to more than one community:

> 'But if the job proceeded badly, with all those delays, the fault was also partly mine. Or rather, a girl's.'
> Actually, [Faussone] used the dialect expression, *'na fijia*, and indeed on his lips the proper Italian word, *ragazza*, would have sounded forced, unnatural; but it sounds equally forced to translate this term.
>
> (*The Wrench*, p. 43; OI, 979–80)

Some problematic aspects of communication are foregrounded in a brief scene of *The Truce* where a verbal interaction, although successful, turns out to be a tangle of historical and political uncertainties. In the centre of Cracow, needing directions and not speaking a word of Polish, Levi's narrated self addresses a Catholic priest in the one language they have in common: Latin. The *lingua franca* of the Catholic Church, Latin was also familiar to all Italians who – like Levi – had attended the academic secondary school *liceo classico*. Communication is successful as long as the topic of conversation is the whereabouts of the soup kitchen (*mensa pauperorum*), but problems arise when the exchange moves on to the experiences of Levi's narrated self. Since their common language lacks terms for 'concentration camp' (*castra*, army camp, is obviously inadequate), the two men have to resort to another shared language, German: *Lager* is immediately understood by both (*The Truce*, p. 49; OI, 241–2). The cognitive gain here could be seen in terms of tragic irony: the language of the common enemy is the only one available to a Polish Catholic and an Italian Jew to refer to a new horror for which no other language has a name. Alternatively, the cognitive gain could be interpreted in the light of the well-known theory of humour developed in a 1908 essay by the playwright Luigi Pirandello. This theory postulates humour as a two-stage process: the laughter provoked by incongruity (*l'avvertimento del contrario*, the detection of incongruity) is followed by painful awareness (*il sentimento del contrario*, the comprehension of the reasons for incongruity and the reasons why it cannot be reconciled).[16] In Levi's scene, the *avvertimento del contrario* (two people successfully communicating in a dead language) is quickly replaced by the *sentimento del contrario* at the irony of words from a living language being the most suitable to talk of extermination; readers at the same time laugh at and sympathize with the two people caught in the tangle.

Other people's works: parodies and pastiche

The 1981 interview quoted above contains other self-revelations. The interviewer makes a general reference to Levi's 'humour', contrasting it with the image critics had of him as a very serious writer. Levi replies:

> Sometimes, when facing the blank page, I find myself in what I would call a Sabbath mood: then I enjoy writing quirky stuff ... It is true that some critics, and many readers, prefer my serious works; they're entitled to it, but I am entitled to step over boundaries ...

This statement contains a Jewish cultural reference – the Sabbath, a pause from everyday concerns, which is also study and meditation – as well as a defensive distinction between 'serious' and 'quirky' writings. In Levi's work the 'stepping over boundaries' often takes the form of parody or pastiche; the works parodied or quoted – usually well-known literary texts – are recontextualized into different discourses, and humour is the result of an intertextual tangle of respect, conflict and distance. The poem 'Pio' ('Pious'; OII, 581, not in *Collected Poems*) meets the definitions of parody given by Linda Hutcheon ('repetition that includes difference [and] imitation with critical ironic distance') and Margaret Rose (who argues that 'most successful parodies may be said to produce from the comic incongruity between the original and the parody some comic, amusing, or humorous effects').[17] 'Pio' is an explicit dialogue, which becomes an open confrontation, with the poem 'Il bove' ('The Ox') written in 1872 by the poet and academic Giosuè Carducci and subsequently memorized by generations of Italian schoolchildren. Carducci addresses the ox with the familiar *tu* ('T'amo, o pio bove', 'I love thee, o pious ox') and constructs him as 'pious' in the classical Roman sense of 'dutiful', meek and content to be subservient to the superior species, man. In Levi's poem the ox becomes the neutered victim who, speaking in the first person, asserts his own subjectivity and questions the claims to authority of the oppressor's discourse. The title acquires bitterly ironic connotations in the initial anaphora, and the speaking subject distances himself from the poet by angrily addressing him with the polite *Lei*,

> Pious ox my foot. Pious by compulsion,
> Pious against my wishes, pious against my nature,
> Pious by pastoral cliché, pious by euphemism.
> . . . Pious yourself, Professor. . . .
> Had you been present when they made me pious
> You would have lost all desire to write poetry
> And to eat beef for your midday meal. (my translation)

The last two lines of the poem make the ox into a collective metaphor by the insertion of the at first sight incongruous and alien (and not evidenced by italics) *Oy gevalt!*, the Yiddish cry of shock and protest before a greater power:

> Oy gevalt! Unheard-of violence
> The violence of making me non-violent. (my translation)

The parody not only becomes a specific historical reference, but targets any political discourse which represents the victims as passively consenting.

Parody is a textual strategy also appropriate to and typical of science-fiction, a genre which questions the past and the present by describing the future. Levi's parodic use of Italian and European literary heritage is demon-strated in a number of his stories. Some of these – possibly deemed too culture-bound – have not been translated into English: the most interesting are 'Il Versificatore' ('The Versifier') from *Storie naturali* ('Natural Histories', 1966; OI, 413–33) and the two-story sequence 'Lavoro creativo' ('Creative Work') and 'Nel parco' ('In the Park') from *Vizio di forma* ('Formal Defect', 1971; OI, 651–60, 671–80). In 'Il Versificatore', a verse-writing machine produces 'poems' which are creditable parodies of Italian poetry from different periods and genres. 'Lavoro creativo' and 'Nel Parco' – a variation on Rabelais' Elysian Fields, depicted in chapter 30 of Book Two of *Gargantua and Pantagruel* – encourage multiple frames of reference by recontextualizing fictional characters, mainly from European literature, into a supernatural 'Park' where they are allowed to dwell as long as they remain known to the reading public:

> [T]he chubby and greasy one with the three-day stubble is the good soldier Svejk:
> he is drinking but hasn't paid. The elderly gentleman on the left, with the top hat
> and the tiny spectacles, who is drinking and has paid, is Pickwick. The last one,
> with eyes like pieces of coal, a leathery skin and his shirt open on his chest, who

hasn't paid and is not drinking or singing, or listening to the others, and is telling tales no one is listening to, is the Ancient Mariner. (OI, 674; my translation)

The play 'Il sesto giorno' ('The Sixth Day'), from *Storie naturali* (and the title piece of the English translation), engages with social discourses through the juxtaposition of different registers of the same language. At a meeting of a supernatural Executive Board an outstanding project – Man – needs to be completed. Various proposals are evaluated in the various registers of different managerial departments. The Comptroller threatens his colleagues in colloquial language ('if [Man] is going to be bigger than a stag beetle, I won't be responsible for anything, and you'll have to see about the budget', *The Sixth Day*, p. 95; OI, 536). The Psychology Adviser is concerned about the new being's intelligence, particularly in view of the fact that some of the requisites are to be 'a particular aptitude for the creation and utilization of tools' and 'a certain degree of preference for social life' (*The Sixth Day*, p. 92; OI, 532–3). Opposing points of view are expressed by two gods of Persian mythology, Ahriman (the god of darkness; Arimane in Levi's text) and Ahura Mazda (the god of knowledge; Ormuz in Levi's text). Arimane, in polite yet inflexible corporate jargon, encourages his colleagues to agree that Man should belong to the snake species. Ormuz, worried about the potential dangers that Man may cause to his future environment, warns in prophetic terms that 'the one who is about to be born will be our judge. Not only our errors but all his or her errors through centuries to come will fall on our heads' (*The Sixth Day*, p. 104; OI, 545). After the Board finally decides that the creature-to-be should be a bird, it is notified that higher authorities 'upstairs' have already created the new being out of clay and formed the female from one of his ribs. The higher authorities are constantly referred to as 'they', as if they were a superior committee: the story closes in a mood of ambiguity as to whether God is absent, plural or an unapproachable CEO.

Two brief pieces (also not translated into English), 'In fronte scritto' ('Written on the Forehead') from *Vizio di forma* and 'Le sorelle della palude' ('Sisters of the Swamp') from *Lilít e altri racconti* ('Lilith and Other Stories', 1981) are not so much parody as lightweight pastiche: their humour results from recontextualizing recognizable quotations from Italian literature into completely incongruous settings. The title 'In fronte scritto' belongs to a quatrain, familiar to and quoted by most Italian speakers for over 200 years, by the eighteenth-century poet Pietro Metastasio:

> If the inner woes of people
> Could be seen writ on their foreheads
> Many objects of our envy
> Would be objects of our pity. (my translation)

Metastasio's line is placed in a dystopian future where growing numbers of people have consumer or political slogans tattooed on their foreheads. In 'Sisters of the Swamp', the leader of a community of leeches attempts to convert her sisters to temperance by positing all living beings as part of Divine Providence's plan for the protection of their species. Her speech reproduces, in an almost word-by-word quotation, a speech in chapter 24 of Manzoni's *The Betrothed*, where the converted villain, Innominato, tries to convince his henchmen to give up their evil ways. The story also looks forward to a series of humorous dialogues and poems written in the final period of Levi's life, in which animals and other organisms (bacteria, seagulls, giraffes, spiders, moles, mice, snails, etc.) are given voice to narrate and describe their lives and habitats.[18]

A more subtle example of Manzoni's influence on Levi is discernible at the end of the story 'Tin' ('Stagno') in *The Periodic Table*, set in the late 1940s. Levi's narrated self, while dismantling a makeshift workshop, comes across an eighteenth-century *grida* (local edict)

in which F. Tom. Lorenzo Matteucci, General Inquisitor of the Ancona District, especially delegated against the heretical depravity, with much complacency and little clarity 'orders, prohibits, and severely commands, that no Jew shall have the temerity to take Lessons from Christians for any kind of Instrument, and much less that of Dancing'.   (*The Periodic Table*, p. 190; OI, 903)

Levi's use of the term *grida* and his reproducing of the key passage with its archaic syntax and vocabulary echo several passages of *The Betrothed*, where Manzoni ironically quotes and glosses many unheeded *gride* against nobles abusing their power. Manzoni's novel, written in the optimism of the Risorgimento, represents the seventeenth century as a time when oppression continued unopposed despite being formally forbidden by the law; *The Periodic Table*, written thirty years after the Holocaust, provides evidence that Italian history also had a constant component of legalized antisemitism. The intertextual dialogue, through irony, suggests that there never is a clear connection between laws and justice.

Another important source of ironic quotations is the Bible, which Levi first studied in the period of shock and fear which followed the Race Laws of 1938 and rediscovered later in life as a cultural rather than religious text. Many biblical references significantly appear in various contexts of *The Periodic Table*, recontextualized in secular settings. The craft of varnish-making is presented as 'ancient and therefore noble' because Noah coated his Ark with molten pitch (Genesis 6.14), and as 'subtly fraudulent' like cosmetics (Isaiah 3.16) (p. 148; OI, 867–8). Levi's father is represented as someone who, 'when he sat at home, when he walked by the way, when he lay down and when he got up', read books, instead of repeating the fundamental Jewish prayer, as commanded in Deuteronomy 6.7 (*The Search for Roots*, p. 4; OII, 1362). The intertextual dialogue thus becomes an ironic rewriting of divine utterances in secular terms, as encouragements to increase human knowledge. This implicit dialogue becomes an explicit parody when Genesis is paraphrased in the story 'His Own Blacksmith' (*The Sixth Day*; 'Il fabbro di se stesso', *Vizio di forma*). The narrator – a being coded as male, who has inherited the memory of all his ancestors – describes in colloquial terms his evolution, from the aquatic stage to the Neanderthal stage, as if it were the result of a series of deliberate design choices made by himself and his 'wife':

> I had told her so. 'Now, listen, I don't care whether the children are three meters long or weigh half a ton, or are able to crush a bison's femur with their teeth; I want children with prompt reflexes and well-developed senses, and above all alert and filled with imagination, who in due time will perhaps be able to invent the wheel and the alphabet. So they'll have to have quite a lot of brain, and therefore a large skull, and so how will they manage to come out when the moment arrives to be born? It'll end up that you will have to bring them forth in pain.'   (*The Sixth Day*, p. 198; OI, 705)

The tension between multiple discourses, which represent multiple perspectives on historical and cultural experiences, is usually left unresolved, since no discourse clearly prevails over the others. Cognitive gain (acceptance of multiplicity) and cognitive loss (constant uncertainty) coexist dialectically.

'A persistent, healthy doubt': irony

In Linda Hutcheon's formulation, irony 'happens in the space *between* (and including) the said and the unsaid; it needs both to happen'.[19] The 'space between the said and the unsaid' in Levi's works contains tangles which are more readily identified if examined from a mainly cognitive perspective. Levi's own definition of irony has to do with destabilization: 'it is typical of the best irony to ironize about itself ... so as to arouse in the reader a persistent, healthy doubt'.[20]

The 'space between the said and the unsaid' is emphasized by another textual strategy which suggests Manzoni's influence: the use of comments in parentheses, which establish an internal dialogue within the text by breaking the syntax and argument in order to question or emphasize a point. In *The Betrothed*, the author intervenes to stress the gravity of some kinds of historical or personal behaviour or to challenge stereotypes: 'When an honest man faces an evil one, people (I am not saying everyone) usually like to picture the former with his head held high' (chapter 5, my translation). Levi's interventions jolt readers into questioning beliefs or drawing unexpected connections between areas of experience.[21] He uses this strategy most frequently in *The Periodic Table* and *The Drowned and the Saved*, the two books where the narrating self looks back on the past to draw lessons from it. Sandro, the narrated self's friend in the story 'Iron' ('Ferro'), 'did not belong to the species of persons who do things in order to talk about them (like me)' (*The Periodic Table*, p. 44; OI, 777): the brief aside is ironically self-deprecating, yet also, ironically, asserts the narrating voice's right to narrate, and thus – in the context of this story, and of most of Levi's work – to allow memory to be preserved. The crematoria of Auschwitz 'were designed, built, assembled and tested by a German company, Topf of Wiesbaden. (It was still in operation in 1975, building crematoria for civilian use, and had not considered the advisability of changing its name)' (*The Drowned and the Saved*, p. 5; OII, 1001). The ironic understatement links the past and the present to jolt readers into realizing that the end of Nazism did not mean the end of institutions and people who had prospered by participating in genocide. Similarly, in the story 'Il mitra sotto il letto' ('The Tommy-Gun under the Bed') – a humorous story where the eponymous weapon is a symbol of various kinds of desire for social renewal – the aside which defines post-World War II Polish authorities as 'perhaps slightly allergic to our surname Levi' (*Racconti e saggi*, 'Stories and Essays', 1986; selections in *The Mirror Maker*, p. 77; OII, 918) conveys centuries of antisemitism through one word of understatement.

Moments of ironic understatement are found in the chapter 'The Journey' ('Il viaggio') in *If This is a Man* (*Se questo è un uomo*, 1947) and in the story 'A Disciple' in *Moments of Reprieve* ('Un discepolo', *Lilít e altri racconti*). In the former, a 'degenerate German engineer' allows the parents of a three-year-old girl to wash her with water drawn from the engine of the train which is taking them to Auschwitz (*If This is a Man*, p. 26; OI, 14). In 'A Disciple' the eponymous character, the inexperienced new deportee Bandi, initially does not heed the advice of Levi's narrated self to work as little and steal as much as he can get away with, but eventually hands him a radish with the proud words 'I've learned. This is for you. It's the first thing I've stolen.' (*Moments of Reprieve*, p. 54; OII, 27). In the first example, the negative word *degenerate*, one of the favourite Nazi terms of abuse, is at the same time right according to the Nazi superiors of the engineer and wrong from the humanist point of view of the narrator and his implied readers. In the second example, Bandi's theft shows that he has finally understood the camp's multiple system of ironies: certain kinds of behaviour are wrong according to ethics outside Auschwitz and are an offence according to the camp regulations, but from the deportees' point of view they are acts of self-preservation and therefore acts of resistance against the camp's purpose of destruction.

Multiple perspectives are also central in 'Argon', in another of the anecdotes about Levi's Piedmontese ancestors. One of his great-uncles fell in love with the cheeky, illiterate *goy* housemaid; his parents went wild with rage when he announced that he wanted to marry her, whereupon he 'took to his bed. He stayed there for twenty-two years' (*The Periodic Table*, p. 17; OI, 753). Lucidly and economically, Levi presents two incompatible perspectives, the Jewish law which forbids mixed marriages, and his uncle's attraction to a woman deemed unsuitable. The unexpected outcome does not coincide with either of the two sets of values: Levi's uncle does not submit to his law, nor does he break it outright; rather, he opts for a solution which is a clever compromise, since his bed is occasionally visited by the housemaid in question.

The ironic attitude to traditional values is evident also in a passage from *The Wrench*, where Faussone recalls that his father, a village coppersmith, together with some friends who, like him, were disillusioned veterans of World War II,

> decided to make a monument and give it to the town, but it was going to be a monument in reverse: iron instead of bronze, and instead of all the eagles and wreaths of glory and the charging soldier with his bayonet, they wanted to make the statue of the Unknown Baker, yes, the man who invented the loaf. . . . They actually made it, and it was good and solid, all right, but as for looks, it didn't come out too well. So the mayor and the priest wouldn't accept it, and instead of standing in the centre of the square, it's rusting in a cellar, among the bottles of good wine. (*The Wrench*, pp. 73–4; OI, 1009–10)

Here irony brings together elements belonging to two opposite values – nurturing and killing – juxtaposing them under the single comprehensive notion of monuments and celebrations. Its function is simultaneously cognitive and ethical: it exposes and questions the paradox of the unethical activity being chosen for celebration and the ethical activity being ignored by those who have the power to decide.

Levi's autobiographical writings play on the cognitive aspect of irony in a self-deprecating way: the younger, narrated self 'ought to have known better' and the older, narrating self points out his delusions and errors. In *The Truce* and *The Periodic Table* comic effects result from the contrast between the narrated self's assumptions and the circumstances in which he makes them. In *The Truce*, the narrated self, who wants to buy a chicken from some Russian peasants, reasons that – since Russian is an Indo-European language and since Russians are doubtlessly familiar with chickens – his attempts to say 'chicken' in several languages will be understood, and is surprised when they are not.[22] *The Periodic Table* also contains comic effects, but in many cases the two incongruous perspectives coexist, with neither having the upper hand.

At sixteen, the narrated self is constructed as naively arrogant, yet ultimately in the right: he blows up a glass jar when he lights a match to see whether it contains hydrogen and returns home shaking but proud to have identified 'the same element that burns in the sun and stars, and from whose condensation the universes are formed in eternal silence' ('Hydrogen' ('Idrogeno'), *The Periodic Table*, pp. 27–8; OI, 763). At twenty-seven, he tries to synthesize a lipstick ingredient from a nitrogen compound found mainly in chicken and snake droppings. The narrating self ironizes on the narrated self's proud comparison – emphasized by Latin terms – between his attempts and those of alchemists: 'the idea of obtaining a cosmetic from excrement, that is, *aurum de stercore* ("gold from dung") amused me and warmed my heart like a return to the origins' ('Nitrogen' ('Azoto'), *The Periodic Table*, p. 182; OI, 895–6). Then the irony focuses on the gap between the narrated self's aspirations and his daily reality: 'I informed [my wife] that the next day I would leave on a business trip: that is, I would get on my bike and make a tour of the farms on the outskirts of town ... in search of chicken shit' (p. 181; OI, 896). At fifty, the narrated self is represented as unwilling to face his own tangle of contradictions when faced with a German colleague who had been his supervisor in Auschwitz. At the same time he longs to confront him as a representative of his former oppressors, admits his own survivor's shame, and yet deliberately underplays his state of mind: 'he had a past to overcome and I didn't: I wanted from him only a discount on the bill for the defective resin' ('Vanadium' ('Vanadio'), *The Periodic Table*, p. 217; OI, 927).

Laughing at oneself has often been interpreted as double-edged: apparently self-critical, in fact a self-protective strategy.[23] In the specific context of Jewish humour, drawing attention to one's weaknesses is usually seen as a defence mechanism: Jewish laughter mocks the majority's prejudices and builds bonds of solidarity.[24] Levi presents laughing about oneself as an aspect of the general human need for the 'refreshment of laughter' (*The Periodic Table*, p. 205; OI, 915). When he refers to 'autoironia ebraica', Jewish self-disparaging irony, he sees it as part of Eastern European Jewish culture, connected to traditional rituals, an element in the fascinating Otherness of Ashkenazi Jews.[25] When he draws attention to his own wrong assumptions and delusions, he constructs them as part of his – and metonymically of humanity's – process of learning by trial and error, and of the human right 'to make mistakes and to correct ourselves'.

'The uncontaminated delight of the *dilettanti*': language play

In two essays published in *L'altrui mestiere* and not translated into English, 'Le parole fossili' ('Fossilized Words') and 'Leggere la vita' ('Reading Lives'),[26]

Levi admits to his 'weakness' for dipping into other people's areas of expertise just for fun, with 'the uncontaminated delight of the *dilettanti*' (OII, 820), and his particular fondness for '"playing philologists", just like, as children, we "play doctors" or "play tea-parties"' (OII, 683). Bending the rules of language causes words to change and generate other meanings, destabilizing the readers' assumptions; therefore the laughter that comes from looking at tangles of meaning is cognitive as well as playful.[27] Levi introduces his readers to folk etymologies – ways in which scientific or technical neologisms are altered by uneducated speakers so as to seem more 'transparent' – and explains them as mistrust and mocking of the innovations denoted by the original terms: replacing 'aria *condizionata*', air conditioning, with 'aria *congestionata*', congested air, 'is the product of an attitude which rejects all the diabolical tricks of progress: innovative architects, blocks of flats with too many floors, windows you can't open' ('L'aria congestionata', OII, 667). Occasionally he describes the new words created by folk etymologies as acts of communication, which at first produce estrangement, then imaginatively connect specialized terms to everyday experience: 'iniezioni *indovinose*' (guessing injections) for 'endovenose', intravenous, are called that 'because you need to guess the vein, and don't always succeed first time around' (OII, 665). At other times he dwells on his love of tracing etymologies in all the languages he knows, particularly in Piedmontese, 'which I speak badly, but which I love with the "long-due love" which binds us to the place where we were born and grew' ('Le parole fossili', OII, 821). Ironically, Levi's tribute to his dialect includes a quotation from the 'father of the Italian language', Dante, and specifically from the Canto of Ulysses, which Levi's narrated self in *If This is a Man* had chosen as a symbol of 'Italianness' in the middle of Auschwitz.

Through the character of Cesare in *The Truce*, Levi makes creative use of the resources of Italian to produce new meanings and to domesticate foreign cultures. Cesare addresses a group of Russians as *russacchiotti*; the lexical creation is humorous because it incongruously adds to *russi*, Russians, the domestic and affectionate suffix – *acchiotti*, used in household words such as *orsacchiotti* (teddy-bears) or *fessacchiotti* (twits). He also integrates Russian and Polish words into Roman dialect, by means of common Italian suffixes: *curizetta*, *ribbona* and *cosciuletta* (respectively, from the Russian *kuritsa*, little hen, and *ryba*, fish, and from the Polish *koshula*, shirt).

Existing words can also be used humorously in word-play when they are piled up in lists where the connections are tenuous or nil – a technique almost as frequent in Levi as it is in Rabelais' *Gargantua and Pantagruel*. The humour (and the cognitive gain) come from the awareness that 'reality ... rarely lies on one level' (*The Periodic Table*, p. 218; OI, 928) and that some aspects of experience are bound to occur together without being reduced to one single meaning. In the story 'Psicofante' from *Vizio di forma* ('Psychophant', *The Sixth Day*) the narrator and his friends experiment with the eponymous machine: it produces objects which represent 'the inner image' of whoever inserts a hand into it. The 'inner image' of the narrator is a tin of paint which contains:

> a needle, a seashell, a malachite ring, various used tickets from streetcars, trains, steamers and airplanes, a compass, a dead cricket and a live one, and a small ember, which however, died out almost immediately.
>
> *(The Sixth Day,* p. 181; OI, 688)

In the essay 'Tradurre ed essere tradotti' ('Translating and Being Translated', which, ironically, was not translated for *Other People's Trades*), Levi lists the conflicting emotions he attributes to any translated living author:

> He feels, sequentially, or at the same time, flattered, betrayed, ennobled, X-rayed, castrated, scraped, raped, adorned, killed ... [and would gladly send to his translator], sequentially or at the same time, his carefully packed heart, a cheque, a wreath, or his seconds. (OII, 734; my translation)

For Levi, language is humanity's toybox as well as the building blocks of its achievement: his love for language play is evidence of this. He manipulates its elements so as to create incongruous juxtapositions between cultures, or to foreground tangles within them and within himself. The result is laughter, playfully cognitive and enticingly intertextual.

Although linked to his Jewishness and rooted in his Italian culture, Levi's laughter steps over the boundaries of compartmentalized knowledge: it establishes dialogues between linguistic systems, between literary works, and between his own reflections upon his areas of expertise and the areas into which he enjoys dipping. It questions assumptions and values, constantly moves back and forth between certainty and uncertainty when highlighting the tangles of human experience, and reveals that reality cannot be organized into an integral whole; it becomes an instrument of salvation because it points the way to acknowledging and accepting differences and contradictions.

NOTES

1. The original Italian has '*esilio*', 'exile' here.
2. 'Translating Kafka', in *The Mirror Maker*, p. 106 ('Tradurre Kafka', *Racconti e saggi*, 1986; OII, 939).
3. Mirna Cicioni, ' "Un riso che direi sabbatico": aspetti dell'umorismo di Primo Levi', *Italian Culture*, 18, 2 (2000), pp. 183–93.

4. Robert S. C. Gordon, *Primo Levi's Ordinary Virtues. From Testimony to Ethics*, Oxford, Oxford University Press, 2001, pp. 257–90.
5. Pier Vincenzo Mengaldo, 'Lingua e scrittura in Levi', in Ernesto Ferrero (ed.), *Primo Levi: un'antologia della critica*, Turin, Einaudi, 1997, pp. 169–242.
6. Massimo Rizzante, 'Dell'ibrido: osservazioni su Primo Levi', in Ada Neiger (ed.), *Primo Levi. Il mestiere di raccontare, il dovere di ricordare*, Fossombrone, Edizioni Metauro, 1988, pp. 45–52.
7. Domenico Scarpa, 'Chiaro/oscuro', in Marco Belpoliti (ed.), *Primo Levi* (Riga 13), Milan, Marcos y Marcos, 1997, pp. 230–53.
8. Interview with Giovanni Tesio, 'Credo che il mio destino profondo sia la spaccatura', *Nuovasocietà*, 208, 16 January 1981; reprinted in M. Belpoliti (ed.), *Conversazioni e interviste*, Turin, Einaudi, 1997, pp. 185–7, p. 186.
9. On cognitive loss, see e.g. Linda Hutcheon, *Irony's Edge. The Theory and Politics of Irony*, London and New York, Routledge, 1994, p. 14. On cognitive gains, see e.g. Peter Berger, *Redeeming Laughter. The Comic Dimension of Human Experience*, Berlin and New York, Walter De Gruyter, 1997, pp. 208–9.
10. Quoted in Tzvetan Todorov, *Mikhail Bakhtin: The Dialogical Principle*, Manchester, Manchester University Press, 1984, pp. 61–2.
11. Arthur Koestler, *The Act of Creation*, New York, Dell, 1969, pp. 32–8; V. Raskin, *Semantic Mechanisms of Humour*, Dordrecht and Boston, Reidel, 1985, pp. 99–100.
12. Pieter Muysken, *Bilingual Speech: A Typology of Code-Mixing*, Cambridge, Cambridge University Press, 2000, p. 1.
13. I am indebted to my student Liam Neame for giving a plausible explanation of this 'inexplicable curse': a 'death shaped like an umbrella' opens and hangs over the head of the person in question.
14. Ezio Raimondi, 'L'ironia polifonica in Manzoni', in G. Manetti (ed.), *Leggere i Promessi Sposi*, Milan, Bompiani, 1989, p. 205.
15. See Mengaldo, 'Lingua'; and essays by Marcello Verdenelli and Gian Luigi Beccaria in Giovanna Ioli (ed.), *Primo Levi, memoria e invenzione*, San Salvatore Monferrato, Edizioni della Biennale 'Piemonte e letteratura', 1995, pp. 121–46, 157–63.
16. See Luigi Pirandello, *L'umorismo* [1908], Milan, Mondadori, 1986, p. 135.
17. Linda Hutcheon, *A Theory of Parody. The Teachings of Twentieth-century Art Forms*, New York and London, Methuen, 1985, p. 37; Margaret Rose, *Parody: Ancient, Modern, and Post-Modern*, Cambridge, Cambridge University Press, 1993, p. 45.
18. OII, 1332–40; 562–73; five are in *The Mirror Maker*, English edition only, as 'Five Intimate Interviews', later integrated into *Il fabbricante di specchi*.
19. Hutcheon, *Irony's Edge*, p. 12.
20. Review of the book *Parliamo itangliano* by Giacomo Elliot (pseudonym of the engineer, scientist and writer Roberto Vacca), OI, 1225, my translation.
21. Gordon, *Primo Levi's Ordinary Virtues*, p. 270. See also Marina Mizzau, *L'ironia*, Milan, Feltrinelli, 1984, pp. 47–50.
22. The episode also contains further allusions to Manzoni: Cicioni, 'Un riso', pp. 186–7.
23. E.g. Hutcheon, *Irony's Edge*, pp. 47–50; D. C. Muecke, *The Compass of Irony*, London, Methuen, 1969, pp. 56–7.

24. See 'Introduction', in Avner Ziv (ed.), *Jewish Humor*, New Brunswick and London, Transaction, 1998, pp. 54–5 and Cesare Musatti, *Mia sorella gemella la psicoanalisi*, Rome, Editori Riuniti, 1982, p. 123.
25. See *If Not Now, When?* (*Se non ora, quando?*, 1982), p. 82 (OII, 299), and the much-quoted essay 'Il rito e il riso' ('Ritual and Laughter') in *Other People's Trades*.
26. Translations from these essays below are mine.
27. See David Crystal, *Language Play*, London, Penguin, 1998, pp. 1–2.

IO

ZAIA ALEXANDER

Primo Levi and translation

Early on in the 1984 book-length dialogue between astrophysicist Tullio Regge and concentration-camp survivor and chemist Primo Levi, Regge mentions his interest in comparing the Hebrew and Italian versions of the Bible. Levi is immediately struck: 'is your passion born from a linguistic, philological interest, or from something else?' (*Conversations*, p. 3). This opening talk is, surprisingly, not about science, which was the intended topic of their dialogue, nor even about Levi's experiences in Auschwitz-Monowitz, but rather about problems of translation, between Hebrew, Greek and Italian, and interpretation of the Bible, from Dante to the Talmud. Levi's perceptive observations about the intricacies of Bible translation and interpretation (a topic that lies at the core and historical origin of translation studies) reminds us that translation was not only a trade he practised, but also a subject he studied and thought about in some depth, part of a large, intense interest in language and language systems in general terms. The conversation with Regge continually navigates between linguistics, etymology and translation (among other topics) and this pattern can be observed throughout his many interviews as well as his own written work.

While Levi's career as a scientist and writer and his experience as a writer-survivor have been well documented, his rich and varied career as a translator has remained largely unknown and unanalysed.[1] Levi translated parts of a four-volume chemistry textbook in the 1950s, works of anthropology by Mary Douglas and Claude Lévi-Strauss, Holocaust narratives, poetry by Heine and Rudyard Kipling and several diverse fragments of novels, works of history and science for his own anthology, *The Search for Roots* (*La ricerca delle radici*, 1981).[2]

The neglect of this body of work and the reflections that went on around it, and indeed of the broad significance of translation in Holocaust memory, is surprising, given that questions of translation overlap with and complicate in often unseen ways many of the already daunting problems – 'truth' and evidence, language and the unsayable, historiography and the 'limits of represenation'[3] – that have beset Holocaust studies; to say nothing of the pragmatic reality that so much Holocaust testimony is mediated and disseminated by the work of translators. Levi rejected the notion of incommunicability, and his extensive activity as a practitioner and theorist of translation informed his belief that even the most daunting problems of communication can be solved (see *The Drowned and the Saved* (*I sommersi e i salvati*, 1986), pp. 68–9; OII, 1059–60).

Indeed, there is evidence from Levi himself that already in the 1940s, before his deportation to Auschwitz, he was engaging with the threat of Nazi antisemitism and the 'Final Solution' and using translation as a tool. In 1971, he gave evidence at the trial of Friedrich Bosshammer, an SS officer in Italy, indicating what he knew about the camps in the period 1942–3, listing one source as: 'a "White Paper", published by the English government, on the German atrocities in the extermination camps, a brief work that I had got hold of secretly *and that I myself had translated from English to Italian.*'[4]

This chapter considers Levi's practice and ideas of translation first through examining his experience of being translated and then through close readings of three representative texts: an essay, a narrative about translation itself and one of Levi's own experiences in the field of translation. The essay is 'Tradurre ed essere tradotti' ('On Translating and Being Translated'), from *L'altrui mestiere* (1985; OII, 730–4; not in *Other People's Trades*), a kind of summation of his theoretical reflections on the matter.[5] The narrative is the famous chapter 'The Canto of Ulysses' from *If This is a Man* (*Se questo è un uomo*, 1947), which allegorizes the vicissitudes of translating and signals metaphorically how so much survivor testimony remains lost in translation. Finally, I will examine Levi's anguished, indeed depression-inducing, commentaries about the process of translating Franz Kafka's *Der Prozess* (*The Trial*) for Einaudi in the early 1980s.

Being translated

Aside from translating through most of his post-war career, Levi was also widely and increasingly being translated, a process on which he commented vocally and by no means always in positive terms. Already in 1946, shortly after finishing the manuscript of *If This is a Man* and *prior* to locating an Italian publisher, Levi asked his cousin Anna Yona to search for an American publisher.[6] He went on to work closely with his English and German translators in the late 1950s (Stuart Woolf and Heinz Reidt, in the first instance). With the latter, he even had a special clause written into his contract that allowed him final say in the finished product:

I did not trust my German publisher. I wrote him an almost insolent letter: I warned him not to remove or change a single word in the text, and I insisted that he send me the manuscript of the translation in batches ... I wanted to check on not merely its lexical but also its inner faithfulness.

(*The Drowned and the Saved*, p. 139; OII, 1126)

In fact, Levi went on to develop a close and fruitful relation with Heinz Reidt, confounding his initial mistrust. Nevertheless, the forcefully worded letter to Einaudi shows the depth of Levi's obsession about issues of accuracy and *word-for-word* fidelity, and conveys his desire to control the memoir's reception beyond Italy's borders, especially in Germany. The scope of his concern is borne out by the fact that, throughout his life, Levi not only obsessively kept track of the various translations of his memoirs, but with the help of dictionaries and grammar books, sought to measure their fidelity against his original text.[7] Levi was aware that future generations would receive information about the extermination camps from survivor-witness testimonies and, in its widest sense, through the correct translation of those memoirs and memories. In the late 1950s, when relatively little was known about the camps and there was no crystallized and commonly known category of 'the Holocaust', a translator's close contact with the author-survivor as informant was a precondition for an accurate and authentic rendering.

Contrary to the successful collaborations in England and Germany, Levi was particularly dissatisfied with the French translation of his memoir, calling it 'rushed and unreadable'.[8] And if the poor reception of his work in France (in his lifetime at least), with its inappropriate and inaccurate title *J'étais un homme* (I Was a Man), is any indication, his concern for translation was more than warranted.[9] Not only do bad translations and bad translators produce, in Levi's terms, an 'unreadable text', they affect the transmission of memory as authentic evidence:

Experience then taught me that translation and compromise are synonymous, but at that time I was driven by a scruple of superrealism; I wanted that in that book, particularly in its German guise, nothing should be lost of its harshness and the violence inflicted on the language, which for that matter I had made an effort to reproduce as best I could in my Italian original. In a certain sense, it was not a matter of a translation but rather of a restoration: this was, or wanted to be, a *restitutio in pristinum*, a retroversion to the language in which events had taken place and to which they belonged. More than a book, it should be a tape recording.   (*The Drowned and the Saved*, pp. 141–2; OII, 1128)

From his first memoir, published in 1947, to his final work, published in 1987, Primo Levi described daily life in Auschwitz as a battle of languages and, already in *If This is a Man*, he speculated that had the war and the *Lager* lasted longer, a 'new harsh language would be born' (p. 123; OI, 119). Four decades later, Levi described in detail the new idiom, or language indigenous to the concentration camps, calling it the *Lagerjargon* (*The Drowned and the Saved*, pp. 74–9; OII, 1064–9). On nearly every page of his memoirs he inserted a wide variety of translation strategies – literal, adaptive, foreignizing, domesticating – to decode that camp language for us, with the ultimate goal of preserving the sound and authenticity of the original expressions, drawn and distorted from many source languages, as they were used and developed in Auschwitz. It is almost as if we have a 'glossary' of the language set out in his texts. Levi's intense interest from the earliest date in being translated suggests that perhaps already within the original language and 'translation' strategies embedded in *If This is a Man*, he was anticipating and containing the risks of future translations and transmissions of his own testimony, subverting or circumventing what is lost in translation. This role of translation *within* Levi's original conception of writing is also apparent in the three key texts we will now examine.

'On Translating and Being Translated'

Immediately after finishing his translation of Franz Kafka's *The Trial* (see below), Levi wrote a summation of his views on translation in 1985 and included it in *L'altrui mestiere* (OII, 730–4). His witty, sardonic, and at times brutal essay contains few original insights into the craft of translation, but it does offer a concise description of several major points of concern expressed by translators and theorists of translation. What makes this essay particularly interesting, however, is the compelling argument it contains for viewing Levi's testimonial writing (and perhaps testimony in general) through the lens of translation.

Levi begins with a discussion of the 'Babelian' curse, relating it to Man's original sin and expulsion from paradise, and he concludes that 'from earliest times linguistic difference had been considered a malediction' (OII, 730). Here, Levi follows a long tradition of writing on translation that seeks to understand the origin of difference in language,[10] and indeed the original newspaper title for the essay in *La stampa* in 1980 had been 'Lasciapassare per Babele' ('Passport for Babel'). Of course, the word 'Babel' initially had appeared in Levi's first book, in 1947, where it served as a functional description of Auschwitz: 'The confusion of languages is a fundamental component of ... living here: one is surrounded by a perpetual Babel' (*If This is a Man*, pp. 35–6; OI, 32). The linguistic challenge of understanding one's fellow prisoners, where in Buna alone 'fifteen to twenty languages are spoken' (p. 81; OI, 67), was exacerbated by the difficulty of translating into words traumatic experiences that had no precedent or terminology. Deciphering that world (with its multitude of languages, code of ethics and rituals) was an essential component of the experience and later testimony, during and after the war. While translation theorists such as Walter Benjamin, Jose Ortega y Gasset, and George Steiner[11] see in Babel a touchstone for everything that is possible and impossible in man's linguistic existence, Levi sees in it, beyond confusion of language, remnants of the ancient curse:

> The Carbide Tower, which rises in the middle of Buna ... was built by us. Its bricks were called *briues, tegula, cegli, kamenny, mattoni, téglak* and they were cemented by hate; hate and discord, like the Tower of Babel, and it is this that we call it: – *Babelturm, Bobelturm*; and in it we hate the insane dream of grandeur of our masters, their contempt for God and men, for us men.
>
> (p. 81; OI, 68)

Levi's pessimism on this score remains in 'On Translating and Being Translated', where he links the Babelian curse to our own time: 'It continues to be a malediction to this day, as anyone knows who has had to live or, worse, work in a country where he did not know the language' (OII, 730).[12] Levi knows first hand the stakes of living and working as a foreigner and slave, and though much of the essay reflects on the humorous side of cultural and linguistic difference, the opening paragraphs reveal the sombre origins of his musings:

> Furthermore, there are many people who believe, more or less consciously, that a person who speaks another language is *an outsider* by definition, *a foreigner, strange*, and hence, a *potential enemy*, or at least a *barbarian* that is, etymologically, a stutterer, a person who doesn't know how to speak, *almost a nonperson*. In this way, linguistic friction tends to turn into racial and political friction, another of our maledictions.   (OII, 730; emphasis mine)

Levi probes the darkest side of the curse – the 'friction' engendered by difference in language and race – allowing his readers to surmise where that erosion leads. In his later chapter 'Communicating' ('Comunicare') in *The Drowned and the Saved* Levi returns to the idea that difference can lead to the murderous notion that the 'other' is a barbarian or beast.

> Whoever did not understand or speak German was a barbarian by definition; if he insisted on expressing himself in his own language – indeed, his nonlanguage – he must be beaten into silence and put back in his place, pulling, carrying, and pushing, because he was not a *Mensch*, not a human being. (p. 71; OII, 1062)

Considering Levi's observation that the purposeful turning of 'the other' into a non-human was essential for murder, the ability to communicate with his oppressors 'man to man' was a necessary strategy for survival. The Nazi's deception in the form of euphemisms and outright lies added yet another layer of fragmentation and confusion to the experience, and since dissimulation made killing go more smoothly, decoding their opaque terminology was a matter of survival; tragically and ironically, 'knowing German meant life' (p. 74; OII, 1065).

In contrast to his memoirs of Auschwitz, which embed in the narrative definitions of *Lagerjargon*, idioms, and euphemisms, along with cues for their successful translation (regardless of the target language), 'On Translating and Being Translated' is made up almost entirely of untranslatable, idiomatic expressions only native speakers could appreciate. Raising the stakes even higher, his word-plays, jokes and idioms illustrate the pitfalls of translation, while simultaneously performing them. Despite some humorous examples of the baffled translator confronted by God's cursed task, even here the Holocaust-driven origins of his earliest musings on the craft are not entirely forgotten.

Beyond the clear references to Auschwitz of the first three paragraphs (Babel, the foreigner as beast, racial and political friction leading to crimes of hate, translator as slave labourer), the essay is dotted with phrases suited more to paranoid writing than to a treatise on translation. Translation is like crossing a difficult, perilous border. It is 'capricious', deceptive, rooted in historical misunderstandings. Even seemingly harmless dictionaries 'constitute a dangerous font of illusion', where the meaning of terms continually 'slip in a different direction' (OII, 730–2). The process is depicted as a series of traumas inflicted not only upon text and author, but upon the unsuspecting translator who must negotiate his/her way through a virtual minefield of 'pitfalls', 'traps' and 'snares lying in wait, invisible, but with their jaws wide open'. Significantly, Levi is both victim and oppressor in this unhappy marriage, playing each role – author and translator – in equal measure.

Levi's pained allusions virtually jump from the page, the layers of trauma encoded in the text. He compares '*envie*' in French to both Latin and Italian's '*invidia*', which contain 'hatred', 'aversion', stemming from '*veder male*' or 'evil eye', noting along the way the 'discomfort we feel when looking at a person we "despise"'(OII, 731).

In his next example, he traces the transformation of the word 'chair' to 'stool'; '*Stuhl* in German means chair, [but] through a chain of metonymic senses that would be easy to reconstruct, it came to mean "excrement" as well' (OII, 731). Like Walter Benjamin, Levi argues that literal translation is impossible because all words contain an entire chain of culturally determined metonymic associations.[13] However, where Benjamin chooses a rather commonplace word like the German *Brot* and French *pain* to illustrate his point (i.e. *Brot*/bread meaning something entirely different to a German than *pain*/bread means to a French person), the words Levi proffers, 'hatred' and 'excrement', belong to the vocabulary associated with the extermination camp experience. Of course, bread was a crucial element of Levi's account of the camps in *If This is a Man* – and of the prisoners' survival there – and he used it also as a token of the multilinguistic confusion there: he uses the example of bread to capture the Babelic multilingualism of the place: 'bread-Brot-Broid-chleb-pain-lechem-keynér, the holy grey slab which seems gigantic in your neighbour's hand, and in your own hand so small as to make you cry' (p. 36; OI, 33).

Translation, then, is depicted in Levi's essay as nothing short of 'a super-human task' (OII, 733), fraught with insurmountable risks and difficulties; and yet, in the end, Levi offers a way out of the treacherous maze, a fighting chance for survival. He writes that 'the most potent weapon for a translator is a sensitivity for linguistics', an ability that seems to have helped Levi to survive Auschwitz. Despite the rhetoric of impossibility, of 'speaking the unspeakable', Levi firmly believed in the power of communication, which he considered not a choice, but a moral obligation. 'Whoever practises the trade of translation or acts as an interpreter ought to be honoured for striving to limit the damage caused by the curse of Babel' (OII, 730). His vision of the translator as hero is suggestive (even if there is neither recognition nor compensation to be gained in that singularly altruistic act), and it sheds an important light on his relentless quest to communicate experiences many deemed untranslatable.

Drawing a line between the extermination camps and our own world was important to Levi, and though he insisted on its incommensurability, he continually sought ways to bring Auschwitz into meaningful dialogue with us. He could not afford to alienate his readers to the point of incomprehensibility (as, in his view, was the experience of readers of the poetry of fellow survivor Paul Celan),[14] yet domesticating the experience, making it too accessible, would distort and trivialize its reality. As many survivors aver, if we can understand what happened, they failed to convey the true horror.

'The Canto of Ulysses'

Whilst in several chapters of *If This is a Man* Levi portrays translation as literally a matter of life and death, in 'The Canto of Ulysses' ('Il canto di Ulisse') he signals metaphorically what happens to texts as they traverse history and geography and are rewritten according to their time, place and language. On the surface, Levi's intent is to recuperate Dante's words (and his pre-camp self) from oblivion, but like all translations and acts of remembrance, the Ulysses speech (from *Inferno*, canto 26) rendered in

Auschwitz cannot but bear the imprint of the moment. Like Dante, who rewrites the traditions of the Ulysses/Odysseus legend according to his needs, Levi rewrites Dante through the prism of the camps. Levi's background activity in the chapter of transporting soup from the kitchen to his work detail functions as a metaphor for what happens when words are transported from one shore to another, from past into present.

If throughout the book Levi acts as our Virgil, lucidly guiding us through the zones of Hell, here he introduces us to one of his own 'guides', his shrewd companion Jean the Pikolo. Mirroring previous descriptions of Auschwitz as a modern-day Babel, Levi's allegory begins with Jean entering the gloomy underground petrol tank and being bombarded with questions from his multilingual co-workers. Only German and French, Jean's languages (he is from Alsace), but also two of Levi's principal 'second languages', are transcribed in the original. '"*Also, Pikolo, was gibt es Neues? Qu'est-ce qu'il y a comme soupe aujourd'hui?*"' (literally, So, Pikolo, what's new? What kind of soup is there today?) (p. 128; OI, 105). Levi does not decode the foreign sentences and this gesture, peppered throughout the book, reminds us that daily life in Auschwitz, often, consisted of untranslatable moments. Jean takes a detour through the camp, allowing the two prisoners time to reminisce about life before Auschwitz, 'of the books we had read, of what we had studied, of our mothers' (pp. 130; OI, 107).

Upon passing an SS guard, Levi marvels at his comrade's 'equal facility' to speak (and curse) in his native French and in German, which again he does not translate. '*Sale brute, celui-là. Ein ganz gemeiner Hund*' ('A dirty brute that one. A real mean dog') (p. 130; OI, 107). Jean wishes to learn Italian and Levi, attuned to his partner's aptitude for learning languages, agrees to begin teaching him immediately. His first lesson begins with a conversation; the topic of discussion (presumably as usual) is soup. 'Pikolo listens carefully, picks up a few words of our conversation and repeats them, smiling: "*Zuppa, cam-po, acqua*"' (p. 130; OI, 108). The message has been deciphered and received, the body language of the man with his soup bowl, together with the repetition of familiar words, illustrates language acquisition and translation in Auschwitz at its most basic.

Immediately after, there is a break in the text indicated by a skipped line and an ellipsis. A fragment has been lost that would bridge Jean's first words in Italian to Levi's sudden inspiration to translate, into broken French, Dante's *Inferno*: '... The canto of Ulysses. Who knows how or why it comes into my mind?' (pp. 131; OI, 108). The implication is that the very momentum of the translation and language-teaching exchange brings him almost inexorably to this point. Levi struggles painfully to recall not only the original passages from Dante's *Commedia* that he had learned at school, but also his pre-war life. He knows he is a flawed translator, that his French is inadequate to the task; he calls his attempts 'wan', 'pedestrian', 'rushed' (p. 133; OI, 110). His memory fails him, in both source and target languages, in different ways. There is always a remainder or residue, linguistic and experiential, that resists translation.

There is no time to translate or to explain what lies behind Dante's verse: 'How many things there are to say ... I am in a hurry, a terrible hurry' (pp. 132; OI, 109). He has little time to transmit the deeper implications of Ulysses' speech to either of his two audiences, Jean in Auschwitz, and the present-day reader. The pressing need to translate Dante increases proportionately to the proximity of the kitchen. In the last heartbeats before stepping into the soup queue, he implores a final time:

> It is late, it is late, we have reached the kitchen, I must finish ... I keep Pikolo back, it is vitally necessary and urgent that he listen, that he understand this ... before it is too late; tomorrow he or I might be dead, or we might never see each other again. (pp. 134; OI, 110–11)

Rather than responding to the sight of the (barely) life-sustaining liquid, Levi concentrates on his task of remembrance and translation. The dual activities of retrieving soup for bodily sustenance and retrieving memory as spiritual regeneration signal how entwined eating and translating are to Levi, both keys to survival. The conflation of both forms of nourishment is crystallized in Levi's confession that '[he] would give today's soup to know how to connect' two lines of the canto (134; OI, 110).

Crucial to Levi's purpose here is his receptor. At each successfully remembered and translated line of the canto, Levi underscores his need to be understood by Jean (and consequently by us) and this passion to communicate made of Levi a resourceful and zealous translator. He opts for a translation strategy of maximum effect in a minimum amount of time, speedily evaluating which passages of the Ulysses speech need to be translated, elaborated with commentary, or omitted altogether. Considering the lack of time, vocabulary and memory, Levi focuses on his goal: making immediate sense to his target audience(s) and recuperating what is lost linguistically through culturally equivalent selections.

> He has received the message, he has felt that it has to do with him, that it has to do with all men who toil, and with us in particular; and that it has to do with us two, who dare to reason of these things with the poles for soup on our shoulders. (p. 133; OI, 110)

Using the same strategy he adopted to link the world of the camps with our own, he links the *Inferno* to their shared experience as slave labourers in

Auschwitz. To do so, translation must be supplemented by (or even consist in) commentary and interpretation: he begins the task of translation by asking 'Who is Dante? What is the Comedy?' (131; OI, 108). A page later, Levi returns to his earlier queries, realizing that not only Dante and the *Commedia* had been transformed by the fact of Auschwitz; so too, had he. The translation into French does not alter Dante's original words or meaning; the change occurs mediated through Auschwitz, because his translation was created there and from there emerged his final interpretation of his source, the 'reason for our fate, for our being here today' (p. 134; OI, 111).

The various levels of translation from the source language to the target language and back again function metaphorically as multi-layered acts of remembrance and it creates a time-machine effect that transports us into three different time and space zones: the *liceo* of his youth, Auschwitz and post-war Turin as he writes. Crucially, although French words and sounds are frequent presences in the book and in the camp as we have seen, Levi almost entirely omits the French of his translation (except for '*Je me mis*' for Dante's '*misi me*', 'I set out', pp. 131–2; OI, 109). It is as though we are reading a retranslation into Italian, or an indirect re-evocation in Italian of a translation. What we also have is a description of the translation process, as a subjective and impassioned, urgent task, with a meaning and value prior to the end product. But the impression is unclear: like the vanished memories and voices, like the unachieved 'perfect' translation he is attempting, his lost French version of the canto symbolizes on many levels the destruction that occurred in the camps and the difficulties of language, memory and transmission.

Before Levi can explain to Jean his sudden flash of insight, 'the reason for their being there today', the chapter ends as it began, with a multilingual queue of workers (including a return to French), hungering to know the contents of their daily ration of soup: '"*Kraut und Rüben? Kraut und Rüben*" … "*Choux et navets*" "*Kaposzta éa répak*"' (p. 134; OI, 111). Levi never does provide Jean with an answer to the reason for their fate. Retrieving Dante in Auschwitz reflects Levi's present-time difficulty in post-war Turin, of remembering/translating a time and place he would as much prefer, at one level, to forget. The interface between suffered memory and translation recurred for Levi many years later, as he translated Kafka.

The Trial

After the publication of *If Not Now, When?* (*Se non ora, quando?*, 1982) Levi received a commission to translate Franz Kafka's *The Trial* for Einaudi's newly established series 'Scrittori tradotti da scrittori' (Writers Translated by

Writers). In addition to his 'Translator's Note' in the published work (OII, 1208–10), Levi discusses the difficulty of translating Kafka in a number of interviews (*Voice of Memory*, pp. 10–11, 42–3, 155–60) and in an article for *La stampa* entitled 'Kafka with a Knife in his Heart'.[15] The abundance of translator's notes is significant not only for their insights into Kafka, but because they allow us to see the evolution of his views on translation.

Levi locates his translation of Kafka's *Der Prozess* between two previous translations of the work – Giorgio Zampa's 1973 interlinear version, which Levi criticized for being too faithful, and Alberto Spaini's adaptive version of 1933.[16] According to Sandra Bosco Coletsos, who has compared all five Italian translations of the work, Levi's version, while being perhaps the most readable, is least faithful in terms of retaining Kafka's trademark ambiguity.[17]

In his translator's note Levi defends his less than faithful rendering by claiming that the heavy German syntax was too dense to reproduce for an Italian reader. His solution was to change the text: 'in other words, to correct, to stretch lexical choices, to superimpose my way of writing on to Kafka' (OII, 1209). Characteristic of his own style, Levi edited superfluous words, producing what he considered to be the essence of Kafka's intent. At other times he added phrases to clarify obscure meanings, and in a sense this 'improvement' constitutes a fundamental betrayal of Kafka's intended ambiguity.

Sensing the danger of losing his authorial voice, Levi eschews word-for-word fidelity to Kafka as a form of self-defence against what he calls this 'pathogenic book' (*Voice of Memory*, p. 10) and opts for a free translation so as not to 'distort myself [*mutilarsi*] too much as a writer' (*Voice of Memory*, p. 158). Nevertheless, the task of translation was like a 'sickness' (OII, 1208) and Levi's relationship to Kafka never failed to be ambivalent at best:

> Translating *The Trial* I have understood the reason for my hostility towards Kafka. It is a form of defence born of fear. Perhaps for the very particular reason that Kafka was a Jew and I am a Jew. *The Trial* opens with a surprise and unjustified arrest and my career, too, opened with a surprise and unjustified arrest. Kafka is an author I admire – I do not love him, I admire him, I fear him, like a great machine that crashes in on you, like the prophet who tells you the day you will die. (*Voice of Memory*, p. 156)

Here, Levi shuns the conceit of self-effacing translator, setting the equal, agonistic stage for author and translator, original and translation; and he fairly warns the reader that his version will be anything but faithful. 'I must confess that I was constantly at war with myself, split between my philological conscience that said I must respect Kafka and my personal reflexes, my own personal habits as a writer – what is called style' (*Voice of Memory*,

p. 155). Reversing the commonplace idea that an author's hidden text is often revealed in translation, one might question whether Levi discovered his own hidden text buried in Kafka's original – albeit as 'rough version' or rejected draft. In this sense, Kafka as prescient voice, rather than being 'superimposed' by Levi's Italian, actually caused Levi to ventriloquize his own latent, unspoken words, refracted through his *Doppelgänger*'s original.

Contrary to Einaudi's expectation, that the union between Levi and Kafka would be ideal, the combination proved distressing for Levi. Whereas Kafka delighted in lucidly detailing the absurd and prosaic nature of a lethal bureaucracy, Levi insisted on elucidating the reason and purpose of even the most outrageous behaviours of man. Where Kafka obscured, Levi was compelled to illuminate; where Kafka's characters became inextricably entangled in hopelessly bizarre machinations, without hope of escape from 'an abject and inscrutable, tentacular tribunal that invades the city and the world' (p. 107; OII, 940), Levi sought liberation through order and reason.

In his interview with Germaine Greer, Levi confesses that the Kafka translation was 'difficult', 'painful', even 'anguishing', and it induced in him a depression that lasted the entire six months he worked on the book (*Voice of Memory*, pp. 10–11). Surrendering to suffering – in life or in writing – was anathema to Levi: elsewhere he warned would-be writers of fiction against taking their personal anguish out on their readers (*Other People's Trades*, pp. 157–8; OII, 678). Creating clarity out of confusion was a personal mission for Levi. He refused Kafka's 'inability to communicate' much as he refused to surrender to the silence which plagued many fellow survivors.

> I have always strived to pass from the darkness into the light, as . . . a filtering pump might do, which sucks up turbid water and expels it decanted: possibly sterile. Kafka forges his path in the opposite direction; he endlessly unravels the hallucinations that he draws from incredibly profound layers, and he never filters them. The reader feels them swarm with germs and spores.
>
> (*The Mirror Maker*, p. 106; OII, 939)

As before, the language Levi uses – of infection, germs, and bacteria – is highly telling. Precisely the same terms that had been used by the Nazis to describe Jews.

The final sentence in *The Trial* reads, 'es war, als sollte die Scham ihn überleben'[18] ('it was as if the shame would survive him'), which Levi translates faithfully as 'e fu come se la vergogna gli dovesse sopravvivere'. In his essay on translating Kafka, Levi concludes with the words, 'e Josef, col coltello giá piantato nel cuore, prova vergogna di essere un uomo' (OII, 941) ('and Josef, with the knife already planted in his heart, feels the shame of being a man'). In creating a suggestive word-play, derived from the title of his first memoir, *Se questo è un uomo*, and looking forward to a key essay on survival in *The Drowned and the Saved*, entitled 'Shame' ('Vergogna'), he symbolically conflates his personal memoir with Kafka's fiction through his translation. The shift Levi operates is subtle but powerful: from the individual, intrinsic sense of Josef K's guilt to Levi's personal shame of having survived even though he no longer felt fully constituted as a human being ('if this is a man?'), to a further collective level of species shame, for belonging to a species capable of such crimes. This core insight of Levi's work emerges by way of his practice of translation.

Despite the seemingly insurmountable problems of linguistic, cultural or moral equivalence between the world and language of Auschwitz and our own reality, Levi's strategy as a translator was to emphasize the alien, dehumanizing universe while simultaneously teasing out similarities to our own world. Throughout his work, Levi employed a variety of translation strategies to communicate experiences which many survivors and theorists described as impossible to articulate. He rejected the notion of incommunicability, which he called 'frivolous and irritating', and he asserted that 'any human experience can and must be communicated' (*The Drowned and the Saved*, p. 68; OII, 1059). Whether alternating between paraphrastic and literal or foreignizing and domesticating translation procedures, Levi's intent was to find a balance that would bring the camps closer to his readers without trivializing or betraying the experience, and he proved that through translation he could say in language precisely what trauma tends to silence. In view of the *Sprachkrise* or 'language crisis' haunting Holocaust testimonials, Levi's search for lost words via his own acts of translation – from the 1940s to the 1980s – is a bold assertion of his belief in the possibility of communication, regardless of the obstacles. In the same measure that Levi's stories, regardless of genre, revolve directly or indirectly around his experiences in Auschwitz, the theme and practice of translation appear with remarkable persistence in all his books, fiction and non-fiction alike, and it remains a defining feature of his writing. Translation is not only fundamental to understanding Levi's testimony and fiction; it is integral to his philosophy of communication and language.

APPENDIX: LEVI'S TRANSLATIONS

Gilman, H. (ed.), *Chimica organica superiore*, vols. I–IV, tr. P. Levi and G. Anglesio, Turin, 'Edizioni Scientifiche' Einaudi, 1955–60, from *Organic Chemistry. An Advanced Treatise*, London, Chapman & Hall, 1943–53

Presser, J., *La notte dei Girondini*, Milan, Adelphi, 1976, from *De nacht der Girondijnen*, Amsterdam, Vereeniging ter Bevordering van de Belangen des Boekhandels, 1957

Douglas, M., *I simboli naturali. Sistema cosmologico e struttura sociale*, Turin, Einaudi, 1979, from *Natural Symbols*, New York, Pantheon, 1970

Kafka, F., *Il Processo*, Turin, Einaudi 'Scrittori tradotti da scrittori', 1983, from *Der Prozess*, Berlin, Schmiede, 1925

Lévi-Strauss, C., *Lo sguardo da lontano. Antropologia, cultura, scienza a raffronto*, Turin, Einaudi, 1984, from *Le Regard éloigné*, Paris, Plon, 1983

Lévi-Strauss, C., *La via delle maschere*, Turin, Einaudi, 1985, from *La Voie des masques*, Geneva, Skira, 1975

For *The Search for Roots* (*La ricerca delle radici*, 1981), Levi translated extracts from the following:

Eliot, T. S., *Murder in the Cathedral*, London, Faber, 1935 (OII, 1510–12)

Gatterman, L., *Die Praxis der organischen Chemikers*, Berlin, Walter de Gruyter, 1939 (OII, 1423–5)

Langbein, H., *Menschen in Auschwitz*, Vienna, Europa, 1972 (OII, 1519–23)

Rosny, J. H., *La Guerre du feu*, Paris, Plon, 1911 (OII, 1393–5)

ASTM D 1382–55 T, from *Annual Book of ASTM Standards*, Philadelphia, American Society for Testing Materials, 1955 (OII, 1493–5)

Ad ora incerta (1984) includes a section of poetry translations (OII, 583–601), from a Scottish ballad, Heine and Kipling.

NOTES

My thanks to Michael Henry Heim, Efraín Kristal, Arnold J. Band, Emily Apter, ARAS and Sophie Alexander for their valuable insights.

1. An exception is Marco Belpoliti's informative note 'Primo Levi traduttore' in OII, 1582–9. See also Lina Insana, 'Translation "alla rovescia": The Metaphor and Practice of Translation in Primo Levi's Holocaust Writings', Ph.D dissertation, University of Pennsylvania, 2000.
2. For a full list, see 'Appendix: Levi's translations' at the end of this chapter.
3. See Saul Friedländer (ed.), *Probing the Limits of Representation. Nazism and the 'Final Solution'*, Cambridge, MA, Harvard University Press, 1992.
4. Quoted in Liliana Picciotto Fargion, 'Le informazioni sulla "soluzione finale" circolanti in Italia nel 1942–1943', *Rassegna mensile di Israel*, 55, 2–3 (May–December 1989), pp. 331–6, p. 336 (emphasis added).
5. The essay is not included in *Other People's Trades*. It has appeared in English as Primo Levi, 'On Translating and Being Translated', tr. Zaia Alexander, *Los Angeles Times Sunday Book Review*, 27 April 2003, pp. 12–13.
6. Marco Belpoliti, *Primo Levi*, Milan, Bruno Mondadori, 1998, p. 178. According to Ian Thomson, *Primo Levi. A Life*, London, Hutchinson, 2002, p. 228, Yona translated 'The Canto of Ulysses' as a sample to show US publishers, with little success. For a survey of translations of his work, see OII, 1590–99.
7. Belpoliti, *Primo Levi*, pp. 178–9.
8. Ibid., p. 179.

9. Primo Levi, *J'étais un homme*, Paris, Corréa, 1961. See Robert S. C. Gordon, 'The Centaur's Ghastly Tale', *Times Literary Supplement*, 4984, 9 October 1998; Michel André Bernstein, 'A Yes or a No', *The New Republic*, 27 September 1999, p. 35.

10. See, for example, George Steiner, *After Babel: Aspects of Language and Translation*, 3rd edn, Oxford, Oxford University Press, 1998.

11. See samples in Lawrence Venuti (ed.), *Translation Studies Reader*, New York, Routledge, 2000.

12. This observation refers us to the narrative setting of *The Wrench* (*La chiave a stella*, 1978), which is, among other things, a narrative of the journeyman worker travelling away from his home country.

13. Walter Benjamin, 'The Task of the Translator', in Venuti, *Translation Studies*, pp. 15–23.

14. See 'On Obscure Writing' ('Dello scrivere oscuro'; *Other People's Trades*); and *Voice of Memory*, p. 42.

15. Primo Levi, 'Kafka col coltello nel cuore', *La stampa*, 5 June 1983; as 'Translating Kafka' (*The Mirror Maker*; 'Tradurre Kafka', *Racconti e saggi*, 1986).

16. Franz Kafka, *Il processo*, tr. Alberto Spaini, Milan, Frassinelli, 1933; tr. Giorgio Zampa, Milan, Adelphi, 1973.

17. Sandra Bosco Coletsos, 'La traduzione di *Der Prozess* di Franz Kafka', *Studi tedeschi: annali dell'Istituto Universitario Orientale*, 1–3 (1985), p. 249.

18. Franz Kafka, *Der Prozess*, Berlin, Schmiede, 1925, p. 401.

I I

JONATHAN USHER

Primo Levi, the canon and Italian literature

Primo Levi holds an 'insider-outsider' place in Italian literature, which continues to exercise critics, just as it exercised Levi himself, who labelled himself 'the writer who is not a writer' (*The Black Hole of Auschwitz*, pp. 101; OI, 1202). But this apparently single, lengthy debate about where to place him in the canon actually covers many separate issues, pertinent to other authors besides Levi. Amongst the hotly debated questions are: was he primarily an Italian writer or part of a wider or narrower community – in Levi's case scientific, Jewish, moralist, rationalist, memorialist? Was he a writer of fictions or rather an essayist, autobiographer or chronicler? Was he a great writer, or somebody destined to write about great things?

Recent critical writing on Levi, in Italy and beyond,[1] reveals that the commonest topic is Memory, almost exclusively Levi's position in the memorial literature of the Holocaust. Slightly less frequent are discussions of Levi as a moralist. Again the focus is on keeping alive the lessons of a chronologically receding, but morally ever-pertinent, personal and universal wrong. After these 'great' themes, whose terms are often dictated by external values and militant agendas Levi himself sometimes rejected, we finally reach intellectual and artistic concerns with which the author was explicitly engaged: the role of reason and science in life and literature, the value of work and place, the hidden trace of language as clue to our past, the fragile nature of artistic creativity. On Levi's craft as a writer, and on his literary standing, there is surprisingly little. Even the three major biographies in English, by Angier, Anissimov and Thomson,[2] concentrate on the extraordinary aspects of his life (including the challenge of being 'ordinary'), rather than on the culture of his writing. He is arguably the victim of mass selective memory, remembered for why he wrote, particularly at the beginning and end of his career, rather than how he wrote.

On the canon, too, more discernment is called for. One the one side is Levi's gradual entry into, and continuing place in, the Italian *and* world canon; and on the other is Levi's own personal conception or reuse of the canon, Italian or otherwise. In Italy as elsewhere, the significance of the Holocaust only gradually seeped into mass consciousness over the post-war period, and then only because of outside events (such as the trial of Adolf Eichmann in Jerusalem in 1961). Partly influenced by this process, and partly for internal Italian reasons, Levi's entry into the Italian canon was also gradual and belated and to a significant degree driven by external, international popularity which forced a reassessment back in Italy. In this respect, at least, he belongs to a disparate camp of Italian writers – including Carlo Levi, Ignazio Silone, Giorgio Bassani and even perhaps Giuseppe Tomasi di Lampedusa and Umberto Eco – all of whom were propelled to higher visibility at home in Italy by foreign acclaim. Conversely, some of Levi's works, such as *If Not Now, When?* (*Se non ora, quando?*, 1982), initially well received in Italy, were only grudgingly appreciated in the United States. There is, in other words, an Italian canon for foreigners, which coincides only imperfectly with the internal one.

Further, and again illustrative of particular cultural conditions of Italy, Levi became a middle-brow read, a best-selling author and also a school 'set text' long before critical acceptance within the literary pantheon.[3] Popular and commercial success in this field delayed Levi's cultural acceptance as 'author' rather than mere 'writer'. Levi, as an outsider, is therefore a litmus test for the evolution of both elite and middle-brow tastes in Italy; and this applied equally to the tastes of Levi's readers as to his own tastes as both writer and reader.

In 'Phosphorus' ('Fosforo') in *The Periodic Table* (p. 111; *Il sistema period-ico*, 1975, OI, 834–5), Levi describes leaving the isolated asbestos quarry, where he had been working clandestinely, for the Swiss-run pharmaceutical lab where he was to research diabetes treatments. He takes along his essential belongings, a strange and revealing list: his bicycle, Rabelais, Folengo's *Macaroneae*, Pavese's translation of *Moby-Dick*, a few other books, climbing equipment, a slide-rule and a recorder. This jumble is simultaneously poignant and revealing. Levi's nourishment was varied and unselfconscious. Other intellectuals edited their culture in a ruthlessly unidirectional way. Levi was happy to present himself as a 'centaur', in literary as well as other terms. He was middle-brow as well as high-brow and formed his own varied and eclectic canons.

There are two examples of quite explicit canon-formations, however partial: his translations both in prose and in verse[4] and his commented anthology of his favourite books, *The Search for Roots* (*La ricerca delle radici*, 1981). The latter texts, though marking intense moments in Levi's life, are not all necessarily formative for his own writing, with one or two exceptions. A useful parallel could be drawn with Levi's avowedly uneducated preferences in music, acoustic tokens of particular experiences, rather than informed musical culture (*Voice of Memory*, pp. 47–56).

Beyond these explicit examples, Levi used his own personal canon of authors and texts to inscribe himself into the literary universe and to feed his imagination creatively. His texts are full of borrowings, conscious and unconscious, not only physical components of his texts, but also ready-made psychological structures which the borrower assumes, sometimes ironically. The borrowings were drawn widely, from both Italian and foreign literatures, but it is perhaps with the former that Levi's creative engagement with canonical literature is most evidently at play.[5]

Dante, Petrarch, Boccaccio

The most famous borrowing in Levi's work is the Ulysses episode in *If This is a Man* (*Se questo è un uomo*, 1947), where the surface narrative, attempting to recall Dante's lines, hides a deeper set of parallels between the Levi-character and Dante's enigmatic intellectual in the *Commedia*. The enduring role of Dante in Levi's fiction has been intensely studied, though there are still many individual passages to identify.[6] The most revealing quotes occur in non-fictional contexts, concerning the act of creativity directly, such as when, in the essay 'Why Does One Write?' (*Other People's Trades*; 'Perché si scrive?', *L'altrui mestiere*, 1985), Levi uses a fragment of Dante's famous definition of the *dolce stil novo* from *Purgatorio* 24, 51–4, '[Love] dictates within', to talk about the impulse to write and the question of authenticity and authority of voice. Dante's definition is an attempt to set himself apart from those who ape the formal motions of poetry, whereas he himself was writing from his inner core. Levi gives this inner reason first amongst his nine reasons to write.

Dante informs also Levi's moral divisions. In the occasional essay 'Così fu Auschwitz' ('This Was Auschwitz', not translated; OI, 1990–3), he compares Italian and German Fascism, branding them as equally guilty, but different in their expression of evil: fraud or violence. It sounds like a distinction drawn from *Inferno* 11, where Virgil differentiates between the two forms of malice, vulpine fraud and leonine violence.

Traces of Dante are also in the 1947 poem 'Il testamento del vicecapolaboratorio' ('The Assistant Lab Chief's Last Will', not translated; OI, 1366–7),[7] marking Levi's departure from the DUCO factory. Levi ends the ambiguously light-hearted piece with a conventional signing-off: 'I lived in DUCO under the good Debove at the time of the false gods and Zanardi', echoing Virgil's greeting to Dante in *Inferno* 1, 70–2, 'I lived in Rome under the good Augustus, / at the time of false and lying gods'. Behind the apparent humour is a sinister hint: Dante has Virgil say these words just after he has announced, "'I am not a man, though man I once was.'" As Levi had been writing *If This is a Man* during his lunch-breaks at the DUCO factory, the omitted Virgil remark perhaps betrays a wider self-questioning of Levi's survivor or guide status, as though he too were ghost-like.

That Dante remained a constant presence for Levi can be seen in 'Incontri ravvicinati con astuzia' of 1978 ('Canny Close Encounters', not translated), where Levi discusses the science-fiction film *Close Encounters of the Third Kind* with writer Mario Soldati. Levi despises the glycerine political correctness of the film, with its facile message of 'love the Other'. He argues it is more important to love one's direct neighbours, paraphrasing Dante's famous remark (*Paradiso* 22, 151) about earth viewed from space: 'it is not space which makes us fierce, but this small threshing-floor' (OI, 1232). The quote exemplifies an important facet of Levi's intertextuality. The images he draws on typically have some striking visual parallel, as if he stored and retrieved them in graphic form rather than as text. Indeed, sometimes they are so reliant on image, rather than actual word, that the reader must employ visual memory to retrieve the intertext.[8] For example, in a short story about famine relief, 'Recuenco: The Nurse' (*The Sixth Day*; 'Recuenco: la nutrice', *Vizio di forma*, 1971), the arrival of a high-tech Rafter is described as if it looked like Dante's angel-driven ship of souls arriving on the shores of Purgatory, gradually becoming clearer and more defined as it approaches (p. 183; OI, 690).

If Levi 'films' his quotes, the moral or intellectual aspect is still important. In his review of *Close Encounters*, the choice of quote, given Dante's detached viewpoint (looking down from space), implies that Levi identified with the aliens of the film. The same sympathy for outsiders can be seen in the choice of a short passage from Fredric Brown's *Sentinel* in the chapter 'We are the Aliens' in *The Search for Roots* (p. 172; OII, 1491–2). In Levi, citational strategies are not neutral and require careful reading.

But Dante, though omnipresent throughout Levi's writing, was *not* one of the authors chosen for *The Search for Roots*, precisely because Levi felt that this inheritance was one which all Italians of his generation shared. He claimed it would be like entering 'two eyes' as distinguishing marks for his identity card. Indeed, the selection formula for *The Search for Roots* has to be understood in oppositional terms: the choices advertise Levi's conscious divergence from what he considers is the common culture of Italian writers.

Petrarch had a more superficial, uneasy impact on Levi. He is there in a poem for a school magazine uncovered by Carole Angier,[9] but the creative use of his unease is most evident in the story 'Breve sogno' (*Lilít e altri racconti*, 1981, OII, 200–5; 'Brief Dream', not in *Moments of Reprieve*).

Riccardo, a hack copywriter (a wry dig at Levi's own self-assessment), encounters on a train a foreign girl, who is reading the 1916 catalogue of a famous Cornell University collection on Petrarch. Both fall asleep, and Riccardo dreams he is Petrarch. Petrarch's coronation on the Capitol becomes the contemporary Strega prize, which Levi himself had nearly won in 1963 for *The Truce* (*La tregua*, 1963), and would win for real with *The Wrench* (*La chiave a stella*, 1978). The triumphal train returning him to Vaucluse (actually Petrarch rode on horseback, to Parma) is decorated with Napoleonic as well as royal insignia. The laurels, which Petrarch at his coronation had stressed were evergreen, are now shrivelled. But the unresponsive 'Laura', asleep on the seat opposite, is, in her indifference, unadulteratedly Petrarchan.

When the girl wakes up, the train has reached Pisa: she spontaneously quotes Dante, 'Pisa, shame of the peoples' (*Inferno* 33, 79), and Riccardo, on automatic pilot, completes the citation. The situation parallels the Ulysses episode in *If This is a Man*, only now the purpose is humorous. The girl, still sleepy, asks whether she can stretch her limbs, using a precious, dated expression which recalls for Riccardo a famous Petrarch poem (*Canzoniere* 126). In that poem, Petrarch admits his imaginings have created a vision of his lady far removed from physical reality, just as Riccardo has constructed the girl of his dreams out of a tubby English student. Again, Levi's source are not only in precise quotes, but also in what has been left out.

As the pair separate at Naples station, their mutual attraction never voiced openly, the girl makes one more quote, from the last line of Petrarch's opening sonnet: 'Worldly pleasure is but a brief dream [*sogno*]'. She cannot pronounce the palatalized 'gn' in 'sogno'. Riccardo's last, despairing gallantry is to correct her pronunciation. The irony is that the girl really lives Petrarch, despite defective command of spoken Italian, whereas the native speaker has a shallow appreciation of the poet. Despite its bitter-sweet humour, 'Brief Dream' is a hymn to the power of the girl's imaginative reading (a theme Levi shared with his contemporary Calvino).

The story indicates that Levi was fully conscious of the modelling effect of the classics. His Riccardo suffers from an anxiety of influence – indebted to Petrarch and Dante, even for his vicarious identity as writer, but aware of his own shortcomings and of the gap between fantasy and reality.

The story's opening widens the range of literary sources considerably: Riccardo, on the arrival of the student in his compartment, starts thinking about train stories he has read by a wide range of authors: Tolstoy, Maupassant, Calvino, Conan Doyle. The reference to Calvino as a railway writer is sly here, for Levi's own story is a subtle reworking of one of the most erotic novellas of Calvino's *Difficult Loves* (1970), 'The Adventure of a

Soldier', in which a young soldier seduces (or is seduced by) an apparently impassive widow on a train. Of course, the first two books Levi had himself published, *If This is a Man* and *The Truce*, were themselves prime, if tragic, examples of 'railway literature'.[10]

Finally, Petrarch is sometimes the model even when Levi is apparently talking about somebody else. In 'Dear Horace' (*The Mirror Maker*; 'Caro Orazio', *Racconti e saggi*, 1986), a letter addressed to the Roman poet, Levi gives an update on what has changed, and what hasn't, since the classical author's time. The source of this idea of anachronistic correspondence can be found in Petrarch's own letters to the ancients in *Familiares* 24. In fact, Levi's letter to Horace is more closely modelled on Petrarch's to Virgil (24, 12), rather than on the epistle to Horace (24, 10). Nevertheless, Levi admires Horace: the *Ars Poetica*, with its approachable, no-nonsense poetics of clarity, underlies two essays in *Other People's Trades*, 'To a Young Reader' ('A un giovane lettore'), in its precepts and mode of address, and 'On Obscure Writing' ('Dello scrivere oscuro').

Boccaccio is less of an obvious source of inspiration, unless one considers the microcosms of humanity amidst the madness and cruelty of Levi's Holocaust works as a reworking of the Plague frame of the *Decameron*. In a 1981 interview, Levi announced playfully that for him there was no hierarchical distinction between studying Boccaccio or transistors.[11] One instance of direct contact can perhaps be discerned in the short-story 'Uranium' ('Uranio') in *The Periodic Table*. Levi's description of the manifest faults in Bonino's storytelling technique uncannily parallels the list of narratological failings in Boccaccio's tale of Madonna Oretta (*Decameron* VI, 1). Levi's interest in such 'bad' storytelling receives a fascinating twist in the opening pages of *The Wrench*, where Faussone gives the narrator-author figure his express permission to rework his rough-edged stories, just as a machinist might 'finish rough mouldings'. The technological vocabulary used by Faussone humorously transposes the classical precept from Horace of '*labor limae*' (filing away excess), and though used here by Faussone, it is almost expresses a fragment of Levi's own poetic.

From the Renaissance to the twentieth century

From Renaissance and Counter-Reformation literature, authors such as Ludovico Ariosto, Galileo Galilei and Teofilo Folengo stand out for Levi (along with Rabelais, if we include other literatures). In his interview with Tullio Regge, Levi agrees that Ariosto is a comic-strip writer *ante-litteram* (*Conversations*, p. 17). The comment is not dismissive: Levi, himself no mean cartoonist, admires Ariosto's ability to enchain stories, tragic or rocambolesque, within an epic scope and structure. Galileo, on the other hand, is respected for his ability to turn scientific discoveries and arguments into lucid text (something Levi admired in the Roman writer Lucretius, too). Levi even imagines himself as Galileo in a poem of 1984, 'Sidereus Nuncius' (*Collected Poems*, p. 67; OII, 578), whose title reproduces that of Galileo's most famous treatise of 1610. The poem's theme is the moment during the Inquisition when Galileo is obliged to renounce heliocentrism. Levi compares Galileo's predicament to that of Prometheus, his liver consumed as punishment for bringing the secret of fire to humanity. In a chilling twist, reminiscent of his take on ordinary Germans' participation in the Holocaust, Levi implies that Galileo's tormentors were not gods, but mundane human beings, only doing their job. Teofilo Folengo's *Macaronee* (first published in 1517 and a great influence on Rabelais), on the other hand, interested Levi not for its digressive content, but rather for its elaboration of a personal, hybrid language, made up of Italian and Latin. Levi would privilege later writers, too, who trod this individualistic linguistic path, and his own *The Wrench* was as much an experiment in language as an essay in storytelling.

The elaborate baroque aesthetics of the seventeenth century did not seem to interest Levi, no doubt for his aversion to unclear writing, non-linearity and unreason. One important though undeclared influence, however, may be at work in the short-stories 'Lavoro creativo' ('Creative Work') and 'Nel parco' ('In the Park') from *Vizio di forma* ('Formal Defect', 1971; OI, 651–60, 671–80, not in *The Sixth Day*), which recount a limbo in which characters from literature are kept in suspended semi-animation by continued readership. The stories have something of the joyous, gossipy fun of Traiano Boccalini's *Ragguagli dal Parnaso* (1612), where fame, in the form of continued readership, kept authors alive after their deaths, living petty, jealous lives on Parnassus.

From the eighteenth and early nineteenth centuries, poet and satirist Giuseppe Parini is warmly admired in *The Search for Roots*, but Levi's admiration is for his social satire, and for plain, unostentatious communication, not art. He is somebody with whom Levi would have liked to have shared a 'moderate' drink of wine, not somebody whose poetic had had a great impact. Alessandro Manzoni and Giacomo Leopardi, however, can be singled out as especially influential. Manzoni is one of the authors explicitly mentioned by Levi whom it was unnecessary to include in *The Search for Roots*, in that he, like Dante, was the cultural property of all Italians. But Manzoni also merits an extraordinary essay, 'Renzo's Fist' ('Il pugno di Renzo', *Other People's Trades*), about what strikes Levi upon an adult rereading of Manzoni's 1840 novel *The Betrothed*. Some of what Levi rediscovers is immensely positive, if somewhat predictable: the humanism and the wisdom.

Some is less so, as in the perceptive remarks on Manzoni's recreation of the micro-society and mentality of the '*monatti*' (corpse-gatherers), implicitly described by Levi as if they were the *Sonderkommando* assigned to the gas-chambers and crematoria of the *Lager* (a link he made again later in *The Drowned and the Saved* (*I sommersi e i salvati*, 1986)). But then the encomium stops jarringly. Levi subjects Manzoni to a relentlessly logical, provocatively non-literary analysis. Renzo's acrobatics, as Manzoni tries to lend him a physical expression of emotion, are minutely examined and found mechanically wanting. Even Friar Cristoforo's indignation at Don Rodrigo's designs on Lucia, one of the high points of Manzoni's writing, is taken apart: it is mediocre theatre, not immediate experience. Authenticity does not come second hand. Intellectually and morally, Levi is on the side of direct observation, whether in science or literary creation.

Levi noted in a 1981 interview that Leopardi was not one of his favourite authors, on account of his programmatic pessimism in his poems and philosophical dialogues (*Voice of Memory*, p. 100), but – much as with Kafka, another pessimist who both repelled and fascinated him – Leopardi was deeply integrated into his literary consciousness. The most obvious literary by-product is the 'Dialogue of a Poet and a Doctor' ('Dialogo di un poeta e di un medico', *Lilít e altri racconti*; OII, 114–16; not translated). In it, an unnamed poet, suffering from depression, pours his heart out to a sympathetic young doctor, before refusing a therapy that might limit his freedom to create/be unhappy. The situation is analogous to the one described in Levi's short-story 'Westward' (*The Sixth Day*; 'Verso occidente', *Vizio di forma*) where the Arunde refuse the drug which would have saved them from lucid suicide. The short text in *Lilít* (not technically a dialogue, but called such in tribute to Leopardi's *Operette morali*, 1827) is a masterpiece of concision, an exemplary encyclopedia entry on Leopardi's cosmic pessimism: rational despair relieved by short idyllic moments. The doctor asks him about his love-life, and the poet, after embarrassment, explains that he is caught between an incurable tendency towards idealizing women and falling into impossible loves without reciprocity. It is the same dilemma Riccardo-Petrarch feels in the train compartment, as he transforms his English student into a Laura. The Leopardi of the *Operette* also inspires, in *Other People's Trades*, 'The Most Joyful Creatures in the World' ('"Le più liete creature del mondo"'), where Levi produces a scientifically qualified commentary on Leopardi's assertion that animals which cannot reflect on their fate are happy, whereas Man, conscious of destiny, is doomed to sadness.

Perhaps the most telling example of Leopardianism in Levi is to be found in the fragments of Levi's last and unfinished book, *Il doppio legame* (The Double Bond) described by his biographer Carole Angier.[12] She notes that

Levi admits to reading Leopardi 'as no one else has ever read him, hoping to see myself in him'. However, Angier's description of Levi's own love-life as portrayed in the book seems to fall, wittingly or unwittingly, into a Leopardian paradigm: he falls in love with the girl he sees doing the ironing in the house across the road. Even the slightest acquaintance with Leopardi's poetry reveals this as a reworking of the poem 'A Silvia'. But Levi humorously breaks the spell. The young laundress sexually exposes herself, causing the young man to fall ill with shock. Levi's final comment, in the first person, was 'From that day on I kept the curtains over that window carefully closed', a clear echo of Francesca's famous remark in Dante's *Inferno* (V, 138), when reading Arthurian romance has led to a kiss, and 'That day we read no further' (V, 138). One wonder, then, if the narrator of *The Double Bond* is really Levi, as Angier thinks, or a more fictionally distanced creation, filtered through Leopardi and Dante.

Leopardi was not just a poet of thwarted love and cosmic despair. He would be a source of inspiration to Levi even when writing on scientific and moral matters. In an article on control engineering, homeostasis and entropy, in which technical problems and procedures are used as a metaphor for a Lucretianesque treatment of life as a struggle with matter, Levi quotes from Leopardi's poem 'A se stesso', including in the title of the article 'The Ugly Power' (*The Black Hole of Auschwitz*; 'Il brutto potere', pp. 136–40; OII, 1203–7). He makes a point of disagreeing with Leopardi's cosmic pessimism, before providing his own, scientifically disguised one.

Giuseppe Gioacchino Belli, the nineteenth-century Roman dialect poet, figures in *The Search for Roots*, largely for his espousal of Roman dialect, a moral gesture in Levi's eyes (something he notes also in the Milanese Carlo Porta). Nevertheless, aspects of Belli's writing seem to be pretty close to Levi's own. From the small selection Levi makes in his anthology, he singles out 'Dying' ('Se more'), on the death of a donkey, grossly overloaded and beaten by its owner (*Search for Roots*, pp. 159–62; OII, 1481–3). The sentiment is similar to that displayed by Levi in his poem 'Pio' ('Pious', OII, 581; not in *Collected Poems*), on human cruelty to animals, and by implication from man to man. In a 1984 interview, Levi, when asked about the privileged place of animals in his poetry, replied: 'Each one of them is a metaphor, a hypostasis of all the vices and virtues of mankind'.[13]

Late nineteenth-century Italian writing seems to have had relatively little creative impact on Levi. Giosuè Carducci's famous sonnet 'Il bove' ('The Ox', *Rime nuove* 25) informs the first line of Levi's poem 'Pio', but the ideology is diametrically opposed. Carducci's servile animal is now a victim of intolerable violence, and Carducci himself is denounced, despite his Nobel prize, for having obscured the true state of affairs, where the world is ruled by 'Gevàlt' (brute force) and injustice. Amongst the prose writers working at the turn of the century, Italo Svevo, with the famous description of Zeno's father's slow death agony in *The Conscience of Zeno* (1923), furnishes an important model for rereading the passage in *If This is a Man* (pp. 202–4; OI, 166–7) describing the last hours of Sòmogyi, investing the episode with a much more ambiguously desperate humanity.

Luigi Pirandello was a major source of ideas. The concept of characters interacting with their authors, and acquiring a life of their own, albeit doomed to repeat itself, clearly appealed to Levi. The most striking examples are the short-stories noted above as possibly echoing the baroque Boccalini: 'Creative Work' and 'In the Park'. The intertextuality with Pirandello is much stronger and instructive, with affinities to both Pirandello's *On Humour* (1908) and the preface to his 1921 play *Six Characters in Search of an Author*, which portrays figures like Dante's Paolo and Francesca condemned to re-enact their tragedy each time a reader dips into *Inferno* V. But this is not a simple case of dependency. Instead, Levi actually develops the Pirandellian concept of character autonomy. The character created by the author in turn writes a version of the author, threatening to trap him into the stasis (and paradoxical immortality) of a literary creation. The only solution is to make one's self into a character, by writing an untrue autobiography, whose subject has done far more interesting things than its author.

When Levi discusses his own relationship with his characters, the Pirandellian paradigm is clear to see. In a 1982 interview, Levi admits that his original plan for *If Not Now, When?* had been undermined by the revolt of his characters, hijacking the novel, imposing their own solutions. He tells the interviewer that he now understands the Pirandello of *Six Characters in Search of an Author* (1921) (*Voice of Memory*, p. 107). Whilst one of the strands of Pirandellism is the autonomy of the character and the impotence of the author, the other is the permanence of literary creations compared with the ephemeral nature of real life. Levi is exceptionally interested in this second aspect. Already in 'Dear Horace' he had noted the way in which literary works acquired longevity, citing Horace's dictum, 'I have built a monument more durable than bronze'. In 'In the Park', it is the characters who become durable. Levi imagines that the author, Riccardo, now a fictional character by virtue of liberties in his own autobiography, has achieved literary immortality, inducted into a 'hall of fame', essentially an international canon of fictional characters. Perhaps this is an ironic reflection on Levi's part-imposed, part-deliberate manufacture of his own literary persona, very different from the private individual.

The approach to the park is up a river, which makes one initially think of Aeneas' navigation up the Tiber in the *Aeneid*, but towards the end of the story, Levi reveals that the river was the Congo. This seemingly irrelevant detail illustrates that Levi's character (and perhaps Levi himself), like Calvino and many others of their generation, had begun his literary career under the sign of Joseph Conrad. It also hints that *Heart of Darkness* may also be more operative as an ominous intertext than the facile literary humour of 'In the Park' first suggests. Indeed, a Conradian notion of struggle, work and self-mastery runs throughout Levi's work, especially in *The Periodic Table* and *The Wrench*.

'In the Park' delights in creating a gossipy promiscuity between heroes and heroines of different genres, cultures and epochs. One wonders whether Levi was familiar with Philip José Farmer's 'Riverworld' science-fiction books, where such anachronism, in just such a setting, dominates.[14] Sometimes the same personalities in the park have been imagined by different authors, so characters come in multiple versions, leading to confusion and rivalries. Though the intention is ironic, it does provide an extensive catalogue of Levi's reading, when characters are matched to the books they come from. The literary list is something of a tic in Levi, who produces his own, and has his characters produce them too.[15] The one in 'In the Park' yields interesting results. For instance, Levi's father's ban on reading the hugely popular adventure-story writer Emilio Salgari had had no effect, on the young Levi, since his most famous hero, Sandokan, is a denizen of the park. Similarly, Giovannino Bongeri's and Barberina's presence only underlines the importance of their creator, Milanese dialect poet Carlo Porta, in Levi's literary treasurehouse. (Porta is also in *The Search for Roots*.) In choosing a character to include here from Boccaccio's *Decameron*, Levi favours the foolish comic character Calandrino over any of his more serious-minded characters or the tragedy of the terrible plague that provides the *Decameron*'s backdrop. Conversely, Dante's lady, Beatrice, is mocked for her petulant demands for apotheosis in a wonderful pastiche of neon, plastic and consumer electronics.

Towards the end of the story, the autobiographical character begins to become translucent and finally fades away. He has been forgotten by the public.[16] If Barthes preached the death of the author, supplanted by the creative primacy of the reader, Levi now indicates that the reader had a power over the characters as well. But the question of literary creation and dissolution is one which Levi returns to again and again, whether in essays and short-stories on computers, or in subtle disquisitions on the difference between real people and the characters they inspire. A case in point can be found in the short-story 'La ragazza del libro' ('The Girl of the Book'; in *Lilít e altri racconti*, OII, 175–9; not in *Moments of Reprieve*), where a recluse of advancing years is compared, and compares herself, with the dashing, erotic and ebullient woman she had once been and has now lost.

Contemporaries

Levi is difficult to map onto the contours of post-war Italian literature. The dominant Catholic–Communist polarity which conveniently pigeonholed many writers, and also the critical reactions to them, is inapplicable. He was not an 'engaged' writer in the group sense. He was not even fully integrated into the strange but fertile conventicle of the Einaudi publishing house. Starting simultaneously with the neo-realists in the late 1940s, he spans an arc of time which takes him past the politically committed writing of the 1950s, past the neo-avant-garde and experimentalism of the 1960s, and past the literary theory and semiotics of the 1970s and early 1980s. Though he was aware of changes, his voice rarely picked up their inflections or ran contrary to them, free from the ideological choosiness which the more integrated writers showed. And yet Levi read adventurously and was creatively engaged with his contemporaries as he was with earlier figures in Italian and other literatures.

Cesare Pavese has been linked to Levi simply because both were suicides. But the points of contact run deeper. Pavese had actually taught briefly at Levi's school[17] and he was famously party to the rejection of *If This is a Man* by Einaudi in 1946. As we saw, it was Pavese's translation of Melville's *Moby-Dick* that Levi carried around in his 'survival pack' during the semi-clandestine years before deportation. Pavese's championing of instinct and tactility over intellect, his metaphors of life as 'hunt' and as 'survival test' (from Melville and Conrad), were clearly influential in Levi's philosophy (and poetic) of practicality and experience.

Elio Vittorini, like Pavese a strong model for young post-war writers, had some impact. For Levi, like many of his generation, there was a lot of catching up to do culturally, after the years of Fascism and war. In a 1976 article (OI, 1194–5; not translated), Levi writes that of Vittorini's work he was only acquainted with *Uomini e no* (1945). It must have had a considerable effect. The short resistance story of 1949 'Fine del Marinese' ('Marinese's End'; OI, 1109–12; not translated), in which a captured partisan blows himself up with a lorry full of his captors, is an able fusion of two scenes from *Uomini e no* – the bombing of a truckload of Fascist soldiers and the final deadly sacrifice of the partisan EnneDue. Vittorini's highly poetic, iterative prose, especially in *Conversazione in Sicilia* (1941) and *Uomini e no*, may well have informed the repetitive rhetoric of Levi's poem 'Monday' (*Collected Poems*; 'Lunedì', p. 11; OII, 527) with its deceptively simple, mesmerically direct questions. The final title of Levi's first book, *If This is a Man*, also contains an echo of Vittorini's resistance novel's title, but via a line from Levi's poem 'Shemà' (*Collected Poems*, p. 9; OII, 525), chosen by the original publisher, Franco Antonicelli. Perhaps a more important, if less trumpeted, influence on Levi's early writing was Umberto Saba, the Triestine Jewish poet, and in particular the prose fragments and aphorisms in *Scorciatoie e raccontini* ('Short-Cuts and Tiny Tales', 1946).

As Levi became more sought after, his stories appeared regularly in newspapers, particularly the Turinese daily *La stampa*. Whilst they provided an outlet for his writing, and offered additional income, they did impose a rhythm hard for a non-professional to match. Perhaps this is why Levi latched onto the master of the genre, Dino Buzzati, whose stories appeared regularly in the *Corriere della sera*, before being collected in book form. Substantial traces of Buzzati's technique and even story-lines surface in Levi's science-fiction stories. To give only a handful of examples:[18] ' "Cladonia rapida" ' (OI, 442–6; not in *The Sixth Day*), an account of an epidemic affecting automobiles, is unmistakably modelled on Buzzati's 'La peste motoria' ('Engine Plague'), though, as usual, Levi's take is very different from his source, concentrating on a novel pathology rather than the sinister public health measures Buzzati described. Levi's tale of telephone malfunction 'For a Good Purpose' (*The Sixth Day*; 'A fin di bene', *Vizio di forma*) derives from Buzzati's 'Sciopero dei telefoni' ('Telephones on Strike'), but whereas Buzzati deals with the social effects of unpredictable connections, Levi deals with the technical challenges for hard-pressed engineers. Similarly, Levi's account of a patent for a time-machine, 'Time Checkmated' (*The Mirror Maker*; 'Scacco al tempo') reproposes Buzzati's 'La macchina che fermava il tempo' ('The Machine that Stopped Time'), but without Buzzati's disastrous coda in which the time-machine fast-forwards into the future. Stopping and starting time also recur in 'In the Park' and in two pieces from *Storie naturali* (1966; both in *The Sixth Day*); the disturbing fairy-tale 'La bella addormentata nel frigo' ('The Sleeping Beauty in the Fridge: A Winter's Tale') and (mediated through Philip K. Dick's 1966 novella 'We Can Remember It for You Wholesale') 'Trattamento di quiescenza' ('Retirement Fund'), where Simpson's over-use of vicarious experience with the Torec leads to premature aging.

Perhaps the only foreign author reworked by Levi in a comparable way to Buzzati was the Argentinian Jorge Luis Borges, not uncoincidentally also a crafter of short-stories, more than large-canvas novels, who displayed a wide interdisciplinarity (although Levi professed himself to be uninterested in him).[19]

Calvino's influence on Levi, and Levi's on Calvino, has been amply written about.[20] Though most of the attention has been paid to their common interests in scientific thinking and expression (including collaboration on the translation of Raymond Queneau's *Petite Cosmogonie Portative*) and the sequential cross-fertilization between their science-fiction and fantasy, it is worth noting that in the afterlife of 'In the Park', one of the prominent figures is Pin, the juvenile hero of Calvino's first novel *Il sentiero dei nidi di ragno* (*Path to the Spider's Nest*, 1947). Levi and Calvino had shared space in their very first *La stampa* review in 1947 and this fortuitous pairing was an important milestone for Levi (see 'With the Key to Science', *The Black Hole of Auschwitz*, pp. 169–70; OII, 1274–5). It is legitimate to ask whether Levi sometimes felt that his first book ought to have been classified as part of that extraordinary outpouring of testimonies on the resistance, rather than a moral and historical exception, a classic of a separate Holocaust tradition.

Calvino's 1964 preface to the new edition of *Path to the Spider's Nest* seems also to have been the model for Levi's own preface to the theatre version of *If This is a Man* (*The Black Hole of Auschwitz*, pp. 23–6; OI, 1158–62), where the need to tell one's life-story in any company, at any time, becomes imperative. Sometimes Calvino, like Buzzati, offered a ready-made narrative framework which Levi took in directions not envisaged by the original author. Levi's account, for instance, of employing insects for nanotechnology on the cheap, 'Full Employment' (*The Sixth Day*; 'Pieno impiego', *Storie naturali*) depends, in setting, on Calvino's 1952 'La formica argentina', but develops the material in a comic, practical-scientific, rather than metaphorical direction. Even here, however, Levi's ants and other insects remind us of the industrial slavery practised in the camps, and link us to the Dante-titled poem 'Dark Band' ('La schiera bruna', *Collected Poems*, p. 43; OII, 557), in which colonies of ants toil and are crushed in close and uncaring proximity to civilization.

The 1960s flourishing of experimental avant-garde literature in Italy known as the *neo-avanguardia* movement demonstrably left Levi cold. His rational approach to writing, and his frequently expressed preference for clarity, privileging transmission of content over expression, meant that he was not attracted to some of the more impenetrable exercises of the group. A hint of his antipathy can be seen in some of the computer doggerel composed by ' Il Versificatore' (*Storie naturali*, 1966; OI, 413–33; not in *The Sixth Day*), which cruelly apes the language of Edoardo Sanguineti's *Laborintus* (1956). Levi would even publish, in *La stampa*, a manifesto, 'On Obscure Writing' (*Other People's Trades*; 'Dello scrivere oscuro') championing his own polemically 'commonsense' poetic. Giorgio Manganelli, the brilliant and mercurial experimental writer, felt he was being singled out for criticism, and replied with a virulent piece in *Repubblica*. Though Manganelli's replique was intemperate, it made an important point, exposing a weakness in Levi's argument. Sometimes, in order to convey the world's obscurities, the most accurate representation is indeed obscure writing. Levi riposted in the letter pages of *La stampa*, declaring that obscurity was an end for Manganelli, whereas for him it was a failing.

Another contemporary author Levi disagreed with, despite a common background in industry which should have united them, was Paolo Volponi. His extraordinary novels *Memoriale* (1962) and *Corporale* (1974) trace the distressingly partial adaptation of peasant mentality to industrialization and modernity. *Memoriale* in particular seems on the surface to have much in common with Levi's experience. The protagonist is a traumatized ex-prisoner of war, with physical and mental problems, trying to fit into peacetime factory life. Volponi's description of Albino Saluggia obsessively machining rough castings covers the same ground as Levi's opening to *The Wrench* and the poem 'The Work' (*Collected Poems*, p. 56; OII, 568), yet the effect is sinister, not celebratory. Volponi's masterly studies in alienation and mental decay during the economic miracle were far from Levi's own rationalist ideology, where the workplace is redemptive. Yet Volponi was on the jury of the 1982 Viareggio prize awarded unanimously to Levi for *If Not Now, When?*.

What the two writers disagreed about in a public debate was the role of the author towards the reader (*Voice of Memory*, p. 125). Volponi, as an ideologically committed writer, believed that authors owed it to their public to 'tow' them like a locomotive, educating them and consciously adopting a superior style to which the reader would be drawn. Levi, more modest, and certainly not Marxist, felt that what mattered was internal clarity, not public engagement. Given the very different kind of stance he had taken in arguments with Manganelli, and in his own remarks on private languages, it is easy to see that Levi, though having very interesting things to say about literature, had not developed a coherent ideology.

Though Levi was against show and excess in his own writing, he actually enjoyed it in others. His penchant for Folengo, for Ariosto and for Rabelais means that we should not be surprised to find two extravagant authors amongst contemporaries he admired. One was Roberto Vacca, whose strange fictions composed of unlikely science, genuine informatics, coupled with societal neurosis and dysfunction, certainly prompted admiration, expressed in two essays, both untranslated: 'L'ingegnere-filologo e i suoi sogni proibiti' ('The Engineer-Philologist and His Forbidden Dreams', OI, 1152–4) and 'Primo Levi all'autore' ('Primo Levi, to the Author', OI, 1196–8). That Vacca worked in the telecommunications industry, while writing in his spare time, may well have made the industrial chemist Levi sympathetic. If Levi called himself a 'centaur', he extended the complement to Vacca, by calling him, for the same motives, a 'minotaur', alluding to Vacca's exploration of cybernetics and emotion in *Il robot e il minotauro*

('The Robot and the Minotaur', 1963), which shares common ground with a number of Levi's futuristic short-stories. A common technical background in industry meant that Vacca's informed review of *The Wrench*, with its accurate understanding of Levi's counter-Marxist paean for the 'world of work', was one of the few Levi really appreciated (*Voice of Memory*, p. 129). What Levi liked about Vacca's writing was its ability to absorb material from a variety of sources. It was eclectic, like Levi's own.

The other extravagant author was Stefano D'Arrigo, whose disturbing *Horcynus Orca* finally appeared, after decades of gestation, in 1975, though the author continued to rewrite it obsessively till he died. In a 1987 interview, D'Arrigo is mentioned alongside Laurence Sterne as the kind of digressive writer, full of 'superfluity', which Levi likes *despite* his own conviction that equilibrium and economy are virtues (*Voice of Memory*, p. 171). Levi also included a passage from this huge novel in *The Search for Roots* (pp. 178–87; OII, 1496–503). For Levi, D'Arrigo was the opposite of himself, and that is why he admits he was so attracted (as he was also to Ariosto, Folengo and Rabelais).

Levi likes D'Arrigo for having developed an inimitable language of his own. This accolade, which we have seen lavished on Carlo Porta and Giuseppe Belli, and which also subtended his response to Volponi in their public stand-off, explains Levi's admiration for Mario Rigoni Stern, who became a close personal friend. Levi's sympathy for the stance of Rigoni Stern was a mixture of respect for a memorialist of lives lived uncomplainingly amidst difficulties, a shared mountaineer's enthusiasm for nature, and perhaps also sneaking sympathy for another 'writer not by calling' as Vittorini described him (Rigoni Stern worked in the Land Registry). Their common experiences of imprisonment, of adventurous repatriation, may also have been a factor. Both also shared similar affinities with the writer Nuto Revelli. A passage from Rigoni Stern's *Storia di Tönle* (1978) appears in *The Search for Roots* (pp. 201–6; OII, 1515–18), and Levi's introduction emphasizes the 'close match between the man who lives and the man who writes', a modern rephrasing of Dante's faith in the writer who reproduces what his feeling 'dictates within'.

A full appreciation of Levi's appropriation of Italian authors would need to be integrated with the equally important impact of classical authors. From Latin, Levi shared with Calvino an enthusiasm for the scientific poet Lucretius' *De Rerum Natura*, but the Ovid of the *Metamorphoses* is much more of a creative influence. Some of the picaresque features of Levi's adoption of the centaur motif may well be a mediation from Apuleius' *Golden Ass*. From Greek, the Homer of the *Odyssey* rather than of the *Iliad* subtends much of the *nostos* (difficult homecoming) programme of

The Truce and *If Not Now, When?*. Again, caution is needed when homing in on Levi's classical sources. The Greek sex-change seer Tiresias, a repeated motif in Levi and the subject of an entire chapter in *The Wrench*, can be seen as merely transgender curiosity if looking at Ovid, but as a much more sinister warning if reading Homer.[21]

Work still needs to be done on the perhaps even greater influence of non-Italian authors, particularly English (Coleridge and Conrad, but also English-language science-fiction writers such as Philip K. Dick, Arthur C. Clarke and Philip José Farmer), French (Rabelais and Balzac, but also comic writers such as Marcel Aymé), German (Heine and Kafka), Russian (Dostoevsky)[22] and South American (Borges). And, of course, in Levi's famously eclectic reading library, there were many and varied non-literary works, in several languages, which nevertheless influenced his own practice of literature.

Levi's canon could only be personal, even if many of the names in it were initially imposed by the kind of reading required by the pre-war *liceo*. But Levi revisited these authors systematically, and drew from them nourishment which went far beyond the arid formulas peddled in his literature classes. The real distinction between Levi and other Italian writers is not the usually advanced one, namely that Levi was a scientist whereas the others were in some strange, inexplicable (and non-institutional) way literary, but rather that he was consciously and deliberately out of step with his fellow literary activists. He followed his own, old-fashioned path, eschewing trends and '-isms', and sometimes making his impatience with engaged literature just a little too obvious.

So how did Levi's autodidact literary culture help him? The authors dealt with here were all 'pabulum' for Levi's literary 'Mimer' (cf. 'Some Applications of the Mimer' ('Alcune applicazioni del mimete'), *The Sixth Day*), and, even where the textual debt is at its most conspicuous, verging on plagiarism, Levi *develops* his sources into new stories, often radically different in morals, language and message from the originals. That he was honest enough to leave traces, and humorous enough to enjoy the game of quotations,[23] only adds to his originality and courage. His writing life was indeed the very personal patterned mosaic of material he had absorbed, and the alternative title he gave to *La ricerca delle radici*, the 'different way of saying me' (*Voice of Memory*, p. 99) stands as a courageous affirmation of a truth not every author admits so openly.

NOTES

1. See 'Guide to further reading', section 2, in this volume.
2. Carole Angier, *The Double Bond: Primo Levi, A Biography*, London, Viking, 2002; Myriam Anissimov, *Primo Levi. Tragedy of an Optimist*, London, Aurum Press, 1998; Ian Thomson, *Primo Levi. A Life*, London, Hutchinson, 2002.

3. See JoAnn Cannon, 'Canon-Formation and Reception in Contemporary Italy: The Case of Primo Levi', *Italica*, 69, 1 (Spring 1992), pp. 30–44. On middle-brow or 'institutional literature', see Vittorio Spinazzola, *La modernità letteraria*, Milan, Fondazione Arnoldo e Alberto Mondadori, 2001, p. 60.

4. See pp. 167–8 above for a bibliography of Levi's translations.

5. For information on all the Italian authors mentioned in the following survey, readers are referred to: Peter Hainsworth and David Robey (eds.), *The Oxford Companion to Italian Literature*, Oxford, Oxford University Press, 2002.

6. For instance, in the poem 'Another Monday' (1946; *Collected Poems*; 'Un altro lunedì', *Ad ora incerta*, 1984, p. 12; OII, 528), the author notes the reference to Dante's poem 'Tanto gentile' (in his *Vita nuova* 26), but omits the echo of *Inferno* V, 4 ('Minos stands there horribly, and barks') in the preceding lines.

7. Not in either *Ad ora incerta*, 1984 or *Collected Poems*.

8. See Sara Vandewaetere, 'La forza dell'immagine nella letteratura di testimonianza: "Ekphrasis" dantesche in *Se questo è un uomo* di Primo Levi', *Studi piemontesi*, 34 (2005), pp. 89–96.

9. Angier, *Double Bond*, pp. 101–2.

10. For railway literature, see Remo Ceserani, *Treni di carta: l'immaginario in ferrovia: l'irruzione del treno nella letteratura moderna*, Turin, Bollati Boringhieri, 1993.

11. *Converszioni e interviste*, p. 155 (not in *Voice of Memory*).

12. Angier, *Double Bond*, p. 126.

13. See *Conversazioni e interviste*, p. 158.

14. Farmer's 'Riverworld' were stories first published in magazines in the 1950s, and in book form in 1971, translated into Italian from 1978 onwards. See: http://www.xs4all.nl/~rnuninga/ (accessed 7 March 2006).

15. See, for example, '*Force Majeure*' (*The Mirror Maker*; 'Forza maggiore', *Racconti e saggi*). For Levi's own bibliographies, see *Voice of Memory*, pp. 98–102, and, of course, *The Search for Roots*.

16. Cf. a similar theme in 'Through the Walls' (*The Mirror Maker*; 'Il passa-muri', *Racconti e saggi*), a tragic re-elaboration of Marcel Aymé's comic French short-story 'Le passe-muraille'.

17. Although Thomson, *Primo Levi*, p. 52, disputes the common belief that he ever actually taught Levi.

18. The Buzzati stories mentioned here are taken from the collections *Il crollo della Baliverna*, Milan, Mondadori, 1954, and *Sessanta racconti*, Milan, Mondadori, 1958.

19. See 'Inventing an Animal' (*Other People's Trades*; 'Inventare un animale'), which builds on *El libro de los seres imaginarios*; or 'A Mystery in the *Lager*' (*The Mirror Maker*; 'Un giallo nel *Lager*'), which refers to Borges' short-story 'Funes el memorioso'.

20. See Giuseppe Bertone, 'Italo Calvino e Primo Levi', in *Il castello della scrittura*, Turin, Einaudi, 1994, pp. 177–211.

21. See Muriel Gallot, 'Primo Levi, de Tirésias à la Gorgone', *Littératures*, 33 (1995), pp. 193–206.

22. See Alberto Cavaglion, 'Dostoevskij presso Primo Levi', *Belfagor*, 56, 4 (July 2001), pp. 429–35.

23. See Levi's defence of citation practice and its motivations in the essay 'Sic!' (*The Mirror Maker*).

I. By Primo Levi

A. *Levi's work in Italian*

1. Editions of Collected Works

Opere, vols. I–III, Turin, Einaudi, 1987–9; includes introductory essays by Cesare Cases, Cesare Segre and P. V. Mengaldo

Opere, vols. I–II, ed. Marco Belpoliti, intr. by Daniele Del Giudice, Turin, Einaudi, 1997 (abbreviated OI, OII); includes a substantial apparatus of notes, bibliography and uncollected work

2. Books published in Levi's lifetime

(First editions only are given, except where there are significant variations in later editions.)

Se questo è un uomo, Turin, De Silva, 1947; 2nd edn, Turin, Einaudi, 1958; in a theatrical version, co-authored with Pieralberto Marché, Turin, Einaudi, 1966; with 'Appendice' from 1976 onward

La tregua, Turin, Einaudi, 1963 (published in some editions together with *Se questo è un uomo* starting in 1972)

Storie naturali, Turin, Einaudi, 1966 (until 1979 under the pseudonym Damiano Malabaila)

Vizio di forma, Turin, Einaudi, 1971

L'osteria di Brema, Milan, Scheiwiller, 1975

Il sistema periodico, Turin, Einaudi, 1975

La chiave a stella, Turin, Einaudi, 1978

Lilít e altri racconti, Turin, Einaudi, 1981

La ricerca delle radici, Turin, Einaudi, 1981

Se non ora, quando?, Turin, Einaudi, 1982

Ad ora incerta, Milan, Garzanti, 1984, incorporating *L'osteria di Brema*

L'altrui mestiere, Turin, Einaudi, 1985

I sommersi e i salvati, Turin, Einaudi, 1986

Racconti e saggi, Turin, Edizioni La Stampa, 1986

3. Translations by Levi

A bibliography of Levi's translations is given at the end of chapter 10 (see pp. 167–8).

4. Schools editions

Einaudi published the following annotated schools editions of Levi's books:

Se questo è un uomo, ed. with notes by Primo Levi (1973)
La tregua, ed. with notes by Primo Levi (1965)
Il sistema periodico, ed. Natalia Ginzburg, with notes by Primo Levi (1979)
La chiave a stella, ed. Gian Luigi Beccaria (1983); ed. by Giovanni Tesio (1992)

5. Collections published posthumously

I racconti, ed. Ernesto Ferrero, Turin, Einaudi, 1996; contains *Storie naturali, Vizio di forma, Lilít e altri racconti*
Il fabbricante di specchi, Turin, Edizioni La Stampa, 1997; retitled and expanded edition of *Racconti e saggi* (with additional pieces from *Lilít* and the animal dialogues included in *The Mirror Maker*)
L'ultimo natale di guerra, ed. Marco Belpoliti, Turin, Einaudi, 2000; contains stories written between 1977 and 1987, including those from the original *Racconti e saggi* and six pieces previously uncollected (in Italian)
L'asimmetria e la vita, ed. Marco Belpoliti, Turin, Einaudi, 2002; selection of over fifty pieces from miscellaneous writing in OI and OII (and one previously uncollected piece)
Tutti i racconti, ed. Marco Belpoliti, Turin, Einaudi, 2005; contains *Storie naturali, Vizio di forma, Lilít, Il sistema periodico, L'ultimo natale di guerra*

6. Volumes of interviews

(The fullest available bibliography of Levi's interviews is at OI, cxvii–cxxvi. For interviews in English, see section B below.)

Collections

Gabriella Poli and Giorgio Calcagno, *Echi di una voce perduta. Incontri, interviste e conversazioni con Primo Levi*, Milan, Mursia, 1992 (largely made up of extracts from interviews)
Primo Levi, *Conversazioni e interviste 1963–1987*, ed. Marco Belpoliti, Turin, Einaudi, 1997

Book-length interviews

Ferdinando Camon, *Autoritratto di Primo Levi*, Padua, Nord-Est, 1987; 2nd edn Milan, Garzanti, 1991
Primo Levi and Tullio Regge, *Dialogo*, Milan, Edizioni di comunità, 1984; 2nd edn Turin, Einaudi, 1987
Primo Levi, *Le Devoir de mémoire*, Paris, Mille et une nuits, 1995
Milva Spadi, *Le parole di un uomo. Incontro con Primo Levi*, Rome, Di Renzo, 1997

7. Uncollected or unpublished work

A handful of further items of miscellany not included in OI, OII have emerged since the publication of the latter (two examples are 'Testimonianza per Eichmann', *Il ponte*, 17, 4 (April 1961), pp. 646–50; and 'La comunità di Venezia e il suo antico cimitero' (1985), now in *L'assimetria e la vita*, pp. 248–51; *The Black Hole of Auschwitz*, pp. 178–80). The only major piece of unpublished work is Levi's incomplete epistolary novel about inorganic chemistry, which was to have been entitled either *Chimica per signore* ('Chemistry for Ladies') or *Il doppio legame* ('The Double Bond'): for extracts and discussion, see Carole Angier, *The Double Bond: Primo Levi, A Biography*, London, Viking, 2002, cf. index entry 'Levi, Primo/ "Double Bond, The"', p. 882.

B. Levi's work in English (UK editions)

(For details of UK and US editions, as well as contemporary book reviews of Levi in English, see Cathe Giffuni, 'An English Bibliography of the Writings of Primo Levi', *Bulletin of Bibliography*, 50, 3 (1993), pp. 213–21)

If This is a Man, tr. Stuart Woolf, London, Orion Press, 1959 (first edition does not include preface or epigraph); with 'Afterword' from 1979 onward (*Se questo è un uomo*)

The Truce, tr. Stuart Woolf, London, Bodley Head, 1965 (published in some editions with *If This is a Man* starting in 1979) (*La tregua*)

Shemà, tr. Ruth Feldman and Brian Swann, London, Menard Press, 1976 (*L'osteria di Brema*; also includes first (partial) translation of 'Afterword' to *If This is a Man*)

The Periodic Table, tr. Raymond Rosenthal, London: Michael Joseph, 1985 (*Il sistema periodico*)

Moments of Reprieve, tr. Ruth Feldman, London, Michael Joseph, 1986 (selections from *Lilít e altri racconti*)

If Not Now, When?, tr. William Weaver, London, Michael Joseph, 1986 (*Se non ora, quando?*)

The Wrench, tr. William Weaver, London, Michael Joseph, 1987 (*La chiave a stella*)

Collected Poems, tr. Ruth Feldman and Brian Swann, London, Faber and Faber, 1988 (*Ad ora incerta*)

The Drowned and the Saved, tr. Raymond Rosenthal, London, Michael Joseph, 1988 (*I sommersi e i salvati*)

Other People's Trades, tr. Raymond Rosenthal, London, Michael Joseph, 1989 (from *L'altrui mestiere*)

Conversations, tr. Raymond Rosenthal, London, I. B. Tauris, 1989 (Levi and Regge, *Dialogo*)

The Sixth Day, tr. Raymond Rosenthal, London, Michael Joseph, 1990 (selections from *Storie naturali* and *Vizio di forma*)

The Mirror Maker, tr. Raymond Rosenthal, London, Methuen, 1990 (*Racconti e saggi*)

Conversations with Primo Levi, tr. John Shepley, Marlboro, VT, Marlboro Press, 1992 (Camon, *Autoritratto di Primo Levi*)

Voice of Memory. Interviews 1961–87, ed. Marco Belpoliti and Robert S. C. Gordon, Cambridge, Polity, 2001 (from *Conversazioni e interviste, 1963–1987*)

The Search for Roots, tr. Peter Forbes, Harmondsworth, Allen Lane, 2001 (*La ricerca delle radici*)

The Black Hole of Auschwitz, tr. Sharon Wood, Cambridge, Polity, 2005 (from *L'asimmetria e la vita*)

Auschwitz Report (co-author Leonardo De Benedetti), ed. Robert S. C. Gordon, tr. Judith Woolf, London, Verso, 2006 ('Rapporto sull-organizzazione igienico-sanitaria del campo di concentramento per ebrei di Monowitz (Auschwitz–Alta Silesia)', *Minerva medica*, 35/2, 47, 24 November 1946, pp. 535–44 (OII, 1339–60)

A Tranquil Star, tr. Ann Goldstein and Alessandra Bastagli, London, Penguin, forthcoming 2007

C. *Levi's work between Italian and English*

Allthough every one of the books Levi published during his lifetime has been translated into English in some form, several of these are only partial translations, and, conversely, several include material not in the Italian originals. This shifting ground was the result of Levi works being for the most part collations of short pieces previously published in newspapers and reviews, creating a pool of material from which he was able to choose and then choose again. A systematic study of this rather confusing state of affairs would be worthwhile, if only because in many cases Levi himself partook in this process of reshaping his work for an English-speaking readership; and also because it points to a substantial body of work by Levi not yet available in English. The following list of significant cases of variation between English and Italian volumes may serve as a start (account has not been taken here of the new translation of Levi's stories, *A Tranquil Star*, forthcoming in 2007; see above, p. xi):

Storie naturali and *Vizio di forma* / *The Sixth Day*

The following twelve stories from the two Italian volumes were not included in *The Sixth Day* :

'Censura in Bitnia'
'Il Versificatore'
'"Cladonia rapida"'
'Quaestio de Centauris'
(from *Storie naturali*)

'Protezione'
'I sintetici'
'Vilmy'
'Knall'
'Lavoro creativo'
'Le nostre belle specificazioni'
'Nel Parco'
'In fronte scritto'
(from *Vizio di forma*)

Lilít e altri racconti / Moments of Reprieve

The English volume contains the 'Passato prossimo' (i.e. Holocaust-related) section of *Lilít*, with a new preface, but omits one story, 'La storia di Avrom'. It also contains three pieces not in *Lilít*: 'The Quiet City' and 'Small Causes' ('Auschwitz, città tranquilla' and 'Pipetta da guerra', *Racconti e saggi*, OII, 873–7, 886–9) and 'Last Christmas of War' (at that time published only in a private pamphlet in Italian; see the later volume *L'ultimo natale di guerra* and OII, 1256–63).

The two remaining sections of *Lilít*, 'Futuro anteriore' (i.e. science-fantasy) and 'Presente indicativo' (various), containing twenty-eight pieces, are untranslated.

Ad ora incerta / Collected Poems

The English collection omits, for obvious reasons, the 'Translations' section of Levi's original, as well as 'L'ultima epifania' (in the main section but also a translation) and 'Pio' (a parody of an Italian classic nineteenth-century poem by Giosuè Carducci).

An unpublished Italian poem, 'Agenda', is included in the English volume with the title 'Memorandum'.

L'altrui mestiere / Other People's Trades

In the English edition, there is some change in the ordering of the Italian original and the following twelve pieces from the Italian edition are omitted:

'Aldous Huxley'
'*Tartarin de Tarascon*'
'L'aria congestionata'
'Calze al fumicotone'
' "Leggere la vita" '
'Lo scoiattolo'
'Tradurre e essere tradotti'
'La *Cosmogonia* di Queneau'
'L'ispettore Silhouette'
'I padroni del destino'
'La parole fossili'
'Il linguaggio degli odori'

Four pieces in the English volume – two stories and two essays – are taken from *Racconti e saggi*, not *L'altrui mestiere*. In the order they appear in *Other People's Trades*, they are:

'A Bottle of Sunshine' / 'Una bottiglia di sole'
'Frogs on the Moon' / 'Ranocchi sulla luna'
'Love's Erector Set' / 'Meccano d'amore'
'The Hidden Player' / 'Il giocatore occulto'

Racconti e saggi / The Mirror Maker

The 'Essays' section of *The Mirror Maker* omits two pieces from *Racconti e saggi*:

'Bionda ossigenata'
' "Bella come una fiore" '

The 'Stories' section includes (as one piece entitled 'Five Intimate Interviews') five short dialogues with various living organisms not in the Italian original (they were published in a nature journal called *Airone* in 1987).

The 'Essays' section contains five pieces not in the Italian original:

'Jack London's Buck'
'Adam's Clay'
'The Spider's Secret'
'The Dispute among German Historians'
'Defiance in the Ghetto'

(the latter two were retranslated for *The Black Hole of Auschwitz*).

The English version contains three poems not in the Italian volume (nor in *Collected Poems*) ('To My Friends', 'The Thaw', 'A Valley').

NB: as noted above, a later edition of *Racconti e saggi*, entitled *Il fabbricante di specchi*, added to the first edition the original versions of the 'Five Intimate Interviews' and several stories from *Lilít*.

L'ultimo natale di guerra

Five of the six previously uncollected pieces included here ('Cena in piedi', 'In una notte', 'Anagrafe', 'Le fans di Delta Cep', 'Fra Diavolo sul Po') remain untranslated into English.

Asimmetria e la vita / The Black Hole of Auschwitz

A handful of the pieces in the Italian collection had already appeared in English. The English version substitutes other miscellaneous pieces from OI, OII in these cases.

II. On Primo Levi

The fullest available bibliography of recent work on Levi is: James Tasato Mellone, 'A Bibliography of English and Italian Scholarly Writings on Primo Levi, 1985–2002', in Stanislao Pugliese (ed.), *The Legacy of Primo Levi*, New York, Palgrave, 2005, pp. 233–66. The following offer useful surveys of the critical field:

Marco Belpoliti, *Primo Levi*, Milan, Mondadori, 1998, pp. 194–203
Ernesto Ferrero, 'La fortuna critica', in Ernesto Ferrero (ed.), *Primo Levi: un antologia della critica*, Turin, Einaudi, 1997, pp. 303–84
Jane Nystedt, 'I critici e l'opera letteraria di Primo Levi: panorama cronologico (1947–1990)', *Studia Neophilologica*, 64 (1992), pp. 101–16

In order to make this selection of further reading as focused and as useful as possible for the English-speaking reader, it has been largely restricted to items in English which are wholly or in large part dedicated to Levi. It is subdivided into three sections: A. book-length studies; B. edited collections; and C. a selection of key articles and essays. Italian items are included in the first two sections, for those who wish to follow up major contributions to the field in Levi's own language. (There are many books and essays on Levi in other languages also, French and German especially).

Three items in section A are marked with an asterisk (*), indicating the best places to start further exploration for the student reader.

Of course, for a rounded understanding of Levi's work, much contextual reading, in fields far too vast to be catered for here, is also essential: for example, on the Holocaust, and Holocaust memory and representation; on modern Italian culture, language and literature; and on the history and culture of science. To follow up on these, see the relevant bibliographical material in the notes to chapters 1–11.

A. Books on Levi

Agamben, Giorgio, *Quel che resta di Auschwitz. L'archivio e il testimone*, Turin, Bollati Boringhieri, 1998; translated as *Remnants of Auschwitz: The Witness and the Archive*, New York, Zone Books, 1999

Angier, Carole, *The Double Bond: Primo Levi, A Biography*, London, Viking, 2002

Anissimov, Myriam, *Primo Levi, ou la tragédie d'un optimiste*, Paris, Lattès, 1996, translated and revised as *Primo Levi. Tragedy of an Optimist*, London, Aurum Press, 1998

*Belpoliti, Marco, *Primo Levi*, Milan, Bruno Mondadori, 1998

Benchouiha, Lucie, *Primo Levi. Rewriting the Holocaust*, Leicester, Troubador, 2005

Bianchini, Edoardo, *Invito alla lettura di Primo Levi*, Milan, Mursia, 2000

Borri, Giuseppe, *Le divine impurità. Primo Levi tra scienza e letteratura*, Rimini, Luisé, 1992

Cavalgion, Alberto, *Primo Levi e* Se questo è un uomo, Turin, Loescher, 1993

*Cicioni, Mirna, *Primo Levi. Bridges of Knowledge*, Oxford, Berg, 1995

De Luca, Vania, *Tra Giobbe e i buchi neri. Le radici ebraiche dell'opera di Primo Levi*, Naples, Istituto grafico editoriale italiano, 1991

Dini, Massimo, and Stefano Jesurum, *Primo Levi. Le opere e i giorni*, Milan, Rizzoli, 1992

Gordon, Robert S. C., *Primo Levi's Ordinary Virtues. From Testimony to Ethics*, Oxford, Oxford University Press, 2001

Grassano, Giuseppe, *Primo Levi*, Florence, La Nuova Italia, 1981

Giuliani, Massimo, *A Centaur in Auschwitz: Reflections on Primo Levi's Thinking*, Lanham, Lexington, 2004

Homer, Frederic D., *Primo Levi and the Politics of Survival*, Columbia, University of Missouri Press, 2001

Kelly, Judith, *Primo Levi: Recording and Reconstruction in the Testimonial Literature*, Market Harborough, Troubador, 2000

Lucrezi, Francesco, *La parola di Hurbinek. Morte di Primo Levi*, Florence, La Giuntina, 2005

Mattioda, Enrico, *L'ordine del mondo. Saggio su Primo Levi*, Naples, Liguori, 1998

Moliterni, Fabio, Roberto Ciccarelli and Alesandro Lattanzio, *Primo Levi. L'a-topia letteraria, il pensiero narrativo, la scrittura e l'assurdo*, Naples, Liguori, 2000

Nezri-Dufour, Sophie, *Primo Levi: una memoria ebraica del Novecento*, Florence, La Giuntina, 2002

Nystedt, Jane, *Le opere di Primo Levi viste al computer. Osservazioni stilolinguistiche*, Stockholm, Acta Universitatis Stockholmiensis / Almqvist and Wiksell, 1993

Patruno, Nicholas, *Understanding Primo Levi*, Columbia, University of South Carolina Press., 1995
Poli, Gabriella and Giorgio Calcagno, *Echi di una voce perduta. Incontri, interviste e conversazioni con Primo Levi*, Milan, Mursia, 1992
Rubinacci, Carlo, *Primo Levi. Un'eredità morale per l'educazione e la scuola*, Rome, Anicia, 2002
Rudolf, Anthony, *At an Uncertain Hour. Primo Levi's War Against Oblivion*, London, Menard Press, 1990
Santagostino, Giuseppina, *Primo Levi: metamorfosi letterarie del corpo*, Turin, Centro universitario di ricerche sul viaggio in Italia, 2004
Sodi, Risa, *A Dante of Our Time: Primo Levi and Auschwitz*, New York, Peter Lang, 1990
Thomson, Ian, *Primo Levi. A Life*, London, Hutchinson, 2002
Toscani, Claudio, *Come leggere* Se questo è un uomo *di Primo Levi*, Milan, Mursia, 1990
Varchetta, Giuseppe, *Ascoltando Primo Levi. Organizzazione, narrazione, etica*, Milan, Guerini e Associati, 1991
Vincenti, Fiora, *Invito alla lettura di Primo Levi*, Milan, Mursia, 1987
Volpato, Chiara and Alberta Contarello, *Psicologia sociale e situazioni estreme. Relazioni interpersonali e intergruppi in* Se questo è un uomo *di Primo Levi*, Bologna, Patron Editore, Quaderni di psicologia, 20, 1999
*Woolf, Judith, *The Memory of the Offence. Primo Levi's 'If This is a Man'*, Market Harborough, University Texts / Hull Italian Texts, 1996
Zaccaro, Vanna, *Dire l'indicibile. Primo Levi fra testimonianza e racconto*, Lecce, Pensa, 2002

B. Edited collections of essays on Levi

Belpoliti, Marco (ed.), *Primo Levi* (Riga 13), Milan, Marcos y Marcos, 1997
Cavaglion, Alberto (ed.), *Primo Levi: Il presente del passato*, Milan, Franco Angeli, 1991
Primo Levi per l'ANED. L'ANED per Primo Levi, Milan, Franco Angeli, 1997
Farrell, Joseph (ed.), *Primo Levi: The Austere Humanist*, Oxford, Peter Lang, 2004
Ferrero, Ernesto (ed.), *Primo Levi: un'antologia della critica*, Turin, Einaudi, 1997
Frassica, Piero (ed.), *Primo Levi as Witness*, Florence, Casalini, 1990
Ioli, Giovanna (ed.), *Primo Levi: memoria e invenzione*, San Salvatore Monferrato, Edizione della Biennale 'Piemonte e letteratura', 1995
Kremer, Roberta (ed.), *Memory and Mastery: Primo Levi as Writer and Witness*, Albany, NY, SUNY Press, 2001
Levi Coen, Clara *et al.* (eds.), *Primo Levi: la dignità dell'uomo*, Assisi, Cittadella, 1995
Levi Della Torre, Stefano (ed.), *Scritti in memoria di Primo Levi*, special issue of *Rassegna mensile di Israel*, 55, 2-3, May–December 1989, 191–346
Mattioda, Enrico (ed.), *Al di qua del bene e del male. La visione del mondo di Primo Levi*, Milan, Franco Angeli, 2000
Momigliano Levi, Paolo and Rosanna Gorris (eds.), *Primo Levi testimone e scrittore della storia*, Florence, La Giuntina, 1999
Neiger, Ada (ed.), *Primo Levi: il mestiere di raccontare, il dovere di ricordare*, Fossombre, Metauro, 1998

Pugliese, Stanislao (ed.), *The Legacy of Primo Levi*, London and New York, Palgrave/ Macmillan, 2005

Tarrow, Susan (ed.), *Reason and Light. Essays on Primo Levi*, Ithaca, Center for International Studies, 1990

C. Articles on Levi in English

The following are some of the most significant essays on Levi to have appeared in English, outside the many important contributions made in the collections listed in section B. (Some key contributions in Italian are cited in the notes to chapters 1–11.)

Banner, Gillian, 'Primo Levi', in *Holocaust Literature: Schulz, Levi, Spiegelman and the Memory of the Offence*, Portland, OR, Vallentine Mitchell, 2000, pp. 87–130

Baumgarten, Murray, 'Primo Levi's Periodic Art: *Survival in Auschwitz* and the Meaningfulness of Everyday Life', in R. Rohrlich (ed.), *Resisting the Holocaust*, Oxford and New York, Berg, 1998, pp. 115–32

Benchouiha, Lucie, 'The Perversion of a Fairy Tale: Primo Levi's "La bella addormentata nel frigo"', *Modern Language Review*, 100, 2 (April 2005), pp. 356–66

Cannon, JoAnn, 'Canon-Formation and Reception in Contemporary Italy: The Case of Primo Levi', *Italica*, 69, 1 (Spring 1992), pp. 30–44

'Memory and Testimony in Primo Levi and Giorgio Bassani', in Peter Bondanella and Andrea Cicioni (eds.), *The Cambridge Companion to the Italian Novel*, Cambridge, Cambridge University Press, 2003, pp. 125–35

Cheyette, Bryan, 'The Ethical Unicertainy of Primo Levi', in Bryan Cheyette and Laura Marcus (eds.), *Modernity, Culture and 'the Jew'*, Cambridge, Polity, 1998, pp. 268–81

Chiompi, James, 'Testifying to His Text: Primo Levi and the Concentrationary Sublime', *Romanic Review*, 92, 4 (November 2002), pp. 491–501

Cicioni, Mirna, 'Bridges of Knowledge: Re-reading Primo Levi', *Spunti e ricerche*, 3 (1987), pp. 54–94

Clendinnen, Inga, 'Surviving', in *Reading the Holocaust*, Cambridge, Cambridge University Press, 1999, pp. 34–52

Della Terza, Dante, 'Primo Levi, the Story Teller: Memories, Technology, Invention', *Italiana*, 9 (2000), pp. 258–72

Druker, Jonathan, 'A Rational Humanist Confronts the Holocaust: Teaching Primo Levi's *Survival in Auschwitz*', in Marianne Hirsch and Irene Kacandes (eds.), *Teaching the Representation of the Holocaust*, New York, MLA, 2004, pp. 337–47

'The Shadowed Violence of Culture: Fascism and the Figure of Ulysses in Primo Levi's *Survival in Auschwitz*', *CLIO*, 33, 2 (Winter 2004), pp. 143–61

Eberstadt, Fernanda, 'Reading Primo Levi', *Commentary* (October 1985), pp. 41–7

Emmett, Lucie, '"L'uomo salvato dal proprio mestiere": aspects of *Se questo è un uomo* revisited in *Il sistema periodico*', *Italian Studies*, 56 (2001), pp. 115–28

Epstein, Adam, 'Primo Levi and the Language of Atrocity', *Bulletin for the Society for Italian Studies*, 20 (1987), pp. 31–8

Finter, Helger, 'Primo Levi's Stage Version of *Se questo è un uomo*', in Claude Schumacher (ed.), *Staging the Holocaust*, Cambridge, Cambridge University Press, 1998, pp. 229–53

Gambetta, Diego, 'Primo Levi's Last Moments', *Boston Review* (Summer 1999), pp. 25–9

Gilman, Sander, 'To Quote Primo Levi: "If You Don't Speak Yiddish, You're Not a Jew"', in *Inscribing the Other*, Lincoln, University of Nebraska Press, 1991, pp. 293–316

Gordon, Robert S. C., 'Primo Levi's *If This is a Man* and Responses to the Lager in Italy, 1945–47', *Judaism*, 48, 1 (Winter 1999), pp. 49–57

'How Much Home Does a Person Need? Primo Levi and the Ethics of Home', *Annali d'italianistica*, 19 (2001), pp. 215–34

'Which Holocaust? Primo Levi and the Field of Holocaust Memory in Post-War Italy', *Italian Studies*, 61, 1 (Spring 2006), pp. 85–113

Gunzberg, Lynn, 'Down Among the Dead Men: Levi and Dante in Hell', *Modern Language Studies*, 16 (1986), pp. 10–28

Harrowitz, Nancy, ' "Mon maître, mon monstre": Monstrous Science Primo Levi', in Keala Jewell (ed.), *Literary Monsters*, Detroit, Wayne State University Press, 2001, pp. 51–64

'From Mt. Sinai to the Holocaust. Primo Levi and the Crisis of Science in *The Periodic Table*', in Alan Rosen (ed.), *Celebrating Elie Wiesel*, Notre Dame, University of Notre Dame Press, 1998, pp. 19–39

Jagendorf, Zvi, 'Primo Levi Goes for Soup and Remembers Dante', *Raritan*, 12, 4 (Spring 1993), pp. 31–51

James, Clive, 'Last Will and Testament', *The New Yorker* (23 May 1988), pp. 86–92

Katz, Adam, 'On "Maelstroms Large and Small, Metaphorical and Actual": "Gray Zones" in the Writings of Primo Levi', *Cultural Studies*, 13, 3 (July 1999), pp. 423–47

Kluback, William, 'Primo Levi, a Friend of Empedocles and Rabelais', *Journal of Evolutionary Psychology*, 18, 3–4 (August 1997), pp. 164–73

Langer, Lawrence, 'Legacy in Gray. The Ordeal of Primo Levi', in *Preempting the Holocaust*, New Haven, Yale University Press, 1998, pp. 23–42

Lorenz-Lindeman, Karin, 'Wieviel Heimat braucht der Mensch? Aspects of Jewish Self-Determination in the Works of Jean Améry and Primo Levi', in Hans-Jürgen Schrader *et al.* (eds.), *The Jewish Self-Portrait in European and American Literature*, Tübingen, Niemeyer, 1996, pp. 223–30

Losey, Jay, 'From Savage Elements: Epiphany in Primo Levi's Holocaust Writings', *Journal of European Studies*, 24, 1 (March 1994), pp. 1–21

Lucamante, Stefania, 'The "Indispensable" Legacy of Primo Levi: From Eraldo Affinati to Rosetta Loy Between History and Fiction', *Quaderni d'italianistica*, 24, 2 (2003), pp. 87–104

Martin, Stephen, 'The Quest for the Ultimate Sign: Binaries, Triads and Matter in Primo Levi's *Il sistema periodico*', *RLA*, 8 (1996), pp. 225–31

Matt, Luigi, ' "Scrivere è un trasmettere": note linguistiche sulle poesie di Primo Levi', *Linguistica e letteratura*, 1–2 (2000), pp. 193–217

Motola, Gabriel, 'The Varnish-Maker's Dreams', *The Sewanee Review*, 98, 3 (Summer 1990), pp. 506–14

Ozick, Cynthia, 'Primo Levi's Suicide Note', in *Metaphor and Memory*, New York, Knopf, 1989, pp. 34–48

Pell, Gregory, 'From Document to Fable: The Simulacrum of History in Mihaileanu, Benigni and Primo Levi', *Forum italicum*, 38, 1 (2004), pp. 91–114

Pireddu, Nicoletta, 'Towards a Poet(h)ics of *techne*. Primo Levi and Daniele Del Giudice', *Annali d'Italianistica*, 19 (2001), pp. 189–214

Rudolf, Anthony, 'Pikolo, Three Great Poems and Primo Levi's "The Mensch"', *PN Review*, 19, 6 (July–August 1993), pp. 12–13

Sachs, Dalya, 'The Language of Judgement: Primo Levi's *Se questo è un uomo*', *Modern Language Notes*, 110, 4 (September 1995), pp. 755–84

Sanders, Mark, 'Reparation and Translation: Primo Levi's "Letters from Germans"', in Daniel Terris (ed.), *Literary Responses to Mass Violence*, Waltham, MA, Brandeis University Press, 2004, pp. 75–83

Simborowksi, Nicoletta '"Il ritegno": Writing and Restraint in Primo Levi', *Romance Studies*, 19, 1 (June 2001), pp. 41–57

Sodi, Risa, 'The Memory of Justice: Primo Levi and Auschwitz', *Holocaust and Genocide Studies*, 4, 1 (1989), pp. 89–104

Stuart Hughes, H., 'Two Captives Called Levi', in *Prisoners of Hope. The Silver Age of the Italian Jews 1924–1974*, Cambridge, MA, Harvard University Press, 1983, pp. 55–85

Todorov, Tzvetan, 'Telling, Judging, Understanding,' in *Facing the Extreme*, New York, Holt and Co., 1996, pp. 254–83

Usher, Jonathan, 'Primo Levi's Science Fiction and the Humanoid', *Journal of the Institute of Romance Studies*, 4 (1996), 199–216

White, Hayden, 'Figural Realism in Witness Literature', *Parallax*, 10, 1 (2004), pp. 113–24

Wilson, Jonathan, 'Primo Levi's Hybrid Texts', *Judaism*, 48, 1 (Winter 1999), pp. 67–72

Wood, Nancy, 'The Victim's Resentments', in Bryan Cheyette and Laura Marcus (eds.), *Modernity, Culture and 'the Jew'*, Cambridge, Polity, 1998, pp. 257–67

Woolf, Stuart, 'Primo Levi's Sense of History', *Journal of Modern Italian Studies*, 3, 3 (Fall 1998), pp. 273–92

INDEX OF REFERENCES TO WORKS BY PRIMO LEVI

Page entries in this index are tied to the titles of the published English translations of Levi's works, except where the work in question is not currently available in English or where the reference made within the *Companion* is specific to the Italian title.

GENERAL INDEX

Cambridge Companions to ...

AUTHORS

Edward Albee edited by Stephen J. Bottoms

Margaret Atwood edited by Coral Ann Howells

W. H. Auden edited by Stan Smith

Jane Austen edited by Edward Copeland and Juliet McMaster

Beckett edited by John Pilling

Aphra Behn edited by Derek Hughes and Janet Todd

Walter Benjamin edited by David S. Ferris

William Blake edited by Morris Eaves

Brecht edited by Peter Thomson and Glendyr Sacks (second edition)

The Brontës edited by Heather Glen

Frances Burney edited by Peter Sabor

Byron edited by Drummond Bone

Albert Camus edited by Edward J. Hughes

Willa Cather edited by Marilee Lindemann

Cervantes edited by Anthony J. Cascardi

Chaucer, second edition edited by Piero Boitani and Jill Mann

Chekhov edited by Vera Gottlieb and Paul Allain

Coleridge edited by Lucy Newlyn

Wilkie Collins edited by Jenny Bourne Taylor

Joseph Conrad edited by J. H. Stape

Dante edited by Rachel Jacoff (second edition)

Charles Dickens edited by John O. Jordan

Emily Dickinson edited by Wendy Martin

John Donne edited by Achsah Guibbory

Dostoevskii edited by W. J. Leatherbarrow

Theodore Dreiser edited by Leonard Cassuto and Claire Virginia Eby

John Dryden edited by Steven N. Zwicker

George Eliot edited by George Levine

T. S. Eliot edited by A. David Moody

Ralph Ellison edited by Ross Posnock

Ralph Waldo Emerson edited by Joel Porte and Saundra Morris

William Faulkner edited by Philip M. Weinstein

Henry Fielding edited by Claude Rawson

F. Scott Fitzgerald edited by Ruth Prigozy

Flaubert edited by Timothy Unwin

E. M. Forster edited by David Bradshaw

Brian Friel edited by Anthony Roche

Robert Frost edited by Robert Faggen

Elizabeth Gaskell edited by Jill L. Matus

Goethe edited by Lesley Sharpe

Thomas Hardy edited by Dale Kramer

Nathaniel Hawthorne edited by Richard Millington

Ernest Hemingway edited by Scott Donaldson

Homer edited by Robert Fowler

Ibsen edited by James McFarlane

Henry James edited by Jonathan Freedman

Samuel Johnson edited by Greg Clingham

Ben Jonson edited by Richard Harp and Stanley Stewart

James Joyce edited by Derek Attridge (second edition)

Kafka edited by Julian Preece

Keats edited by Susan J. Wolfson

Lacan edited by Jean-Michel Rabaté

D. H. Lawrence edited by Anne Fernihough

Primo Levi edited by Robert S. C. Gordon

David Mamet edited by Christopher Bigsby

Thomas Mann edited by Ritchie Robertson

Herman Melville edited by Robert S. Levine

Christopher Marlowe edited by Patrick Cheney

Arthur Miller edited by Christopher Bigsby

Milton edited by Dennis Danielson (second edition)

Molière edited by David Bradby and Andrew Calder

Nabokov edited by Julian W. Connolly

Eugene O'Neill edited by Michael Manheim

George Orwell edited by John Rodden

Ovid edited by Philip Hardie

Harold Pinter edited by Peter Raby

Sylvia Plath edited by Jo Gill

Edgar Allan Poe edited by Kevin J. Hayes

Ezra Pound edited by Ira B. Nadel

Proust edited by Richard Bales

Pushkin edited by Andrew Kahn

Philip Roth edited by Timothy Parrish

Shakespeare edited by Margareta de Grazia and Stanley Wells

Shakespeare on Film edited by Russell Jackson (second edition)

Shakespearean Comedy edited by Alexander Leggatt

TOPICS